Praise for *Murder Survivor's H*

Our non-profit agency in Virginia uses Connie Saindon's materials with homicide survivors in support groups and professional trainings. I cannot say enough good things about these materials, [which] center around true survivor stories, emotions, and journeys toward re-capturing hope, while honoring their loved one. The materials are also evidence-based, so you can rest assured that the materials and methods have been researched as a sound best practice. We also utilize Ms. Saindon's expertise to train allied professionals working in the field with survivors. Whether you are a professional in the field or a survivor, you will want to own anything that Ms. Saindon writes. We are grateful to have found her.

—Dina Blythe, Homicide Survivor Support Group Coordinator
Virginia Victim Assistance Network

This handbook is the absolutely perfect tool for survivors of homicide victims and those professionals who work to support them. Through the voices of survivors, the stark realities of learning to live with homicide are clearly exposed. The incredible depth of sorrow, daunting financial impact and the long term challenges that survivors face are effectively presented. The wealth of information contained in this handbook needs to be on the bookshelves of everyone who interacts with survivors of homicide.

—Carol Gaxiola, Mother of Jasmine Gaxiola
Director/Victim Advocate, Homicide Survivors, Inc.

Connie Saindon extends a loving and much-needed helping hand to those who have suffered the loss of a loved one. She provides great helpings of wisdom, compassion and inspiration while showing the way to what will surely be an appreciative readership. Heartfelt and well written, it will serve as a benchmark in the genre for years to come.

—Carlton Stowers, two-time Edgar Award winner for Best Fact Crime

I know this book will be a tremendous help to those unfortunate enough to find themselves in this terrible situation. It is organized in such a way that people can read each section as the need arises. I wish there had been such a helpful resource for my family when we so desperately needed it!

—Joyce Knott, mother of Cara Knott, murder victim

This is exactly the book I would have loved to have had in the beginning so I wouldn't have made so many mistakes with Homicide, and that I would have had some idea how this entire process works. Soon others will not have to try to figure out the craziness of it all; it will be right there in their handbook.

—Dayna Herroz, Survivor/Co-victim Peer Advocate/Violent Loss

This book is wonderful. It will be very helpful not only to my new participants but for myself and my chapter leaders. You covered all the steps that victims will be having to deal with. The chapters are broken down and very easy to read and follow. The resource section after each topic is great. This will help our leaders as a guide working with our participants new and old, and having this book on hand for all. Thank you, this is a one-of-a-kind book much needed!

—Rose Madsen, Director of Families & Friends of Murder Victims, Inc.

This book covers the full spectrum of grief and loss as well as criminal justice system. It is written with a very personal and practical tone that connects the reader to the writers and makes it easy to understanding the legal part. It was a more emotionally difficult read than I anticipated, but, ultimately, so full of hope and comfort.

—Yolanda Boyd, Sister of Willie Jones

I got a tremendous amount out of it, a wealth of information as I head toward the criminal trial. It's unfortunate that a person wouldn't necessarily be inclined to read it before tragedy strikes; if they did, they would be so much better prepared. Survivors will find this of great help when the unthinkable happens.

—Valerie Wagner, Survivor/Co-victim

The stories of loss shared by survivors in this book shed light on the fact that when this type of trauma happens, lives are touched with both tragedy and renewed capacity for resiliency. Every time I hear on the news of someone just murdered, I cry inside for their families and loved ones. This book will be of great benefit to the newly bereaved.

—Celeste Vinzant, Survivor/Co-victim

We know your book will be a tremendous asset to survivors who will suddenly be faced with dealing with the unimaginable and all that follows. It will help them learn the unfamiliar language of violent loss and provide them with the kind of guidance and resources we all wish we had at the beginning our journey, when it is desperately needed.

—Timothy's Family, Survivors/Co-victims

Very thorough. Love the practical suggestions, safety ideas, outlining what you want to say about your loved one to the media, and the resources and online links. There is so much "brain freeze" during the aftermath that these suggestions can help a great deal. The personal stories are very touching. The reader knows they "get it."

—Michelle Iliff, MA, Survivors of Violent Loss Counselor

I am extremely impressed with the content of this book. As a co-victim, I am so proud of the individuals who so bravely have offered to share their experiences so others can have some point of reference if they should ever have to walk this unfortunate path. So many scenarios that can arise are addressed in these pages. Here they will find a roadmap to help navigate their way through this maze of heartache. Most important they will find the tools and a guide to resources that has taken many of us years, even decades, to stumble upon.

—Dee Dee, Survivor/Co-victim

This book is fantastic! It will be so helpful to survivors, professionals and our colleagues working with Homicide Survivors.

—Director, Crime Victims Assitance Unit, District Attorney's Office

The book was truly wonderful! It contained all the info and guidance I know that would truly help someone navigate the legal aftermath as best a book could. I think this fills a much needed gap. Very well written and organized! I look forward to hearing the wonderful feedback from survivors who used it.

—Kerry Essakow, PsyD, MFT, former
Program Director of Survivors of Violent Loss Program

Murder Survivor's Handbook

Real-Life Stories, Tips & Resources

Connie Saindon, MA, MFT

Wigeon Publishing

San Diego

Wigeon Publishing
San Diego, California
www.WigeonPublishing.com

First Edition: September 25, 2014

ISBN-10: 0989691306
ISBN-13: 978-0-9896913-0-7

Library of Congress Control Number: 2014944392

SEL010000: SELF-HELP / Death, Grief, Bereavement
FAM014000: FAMILY & RELATIONSHIPS / Death, Grief, Bereavement
PSY052000: PSYCHOLOGY / Grief & Loss

Edited by Larry M. Edwards

Cover design by Tim Brittain

Cover image courtesy of Nicole Toesca
Back cover image courtesy of Margaret Steven

Printed in the United States of America

The sale of this book supports programs for survivors of violent loss.
To obtain the book, go to:
http://svlp.org/resources/books.html

This book is dedicated first to all the Survivor Writers who brought forth their stories for everyone who may follow in their footsteps. They balanced their pain and passion with a promise to make the world better for those whose lives have been changed forever after murder.

Secondly, this book is dedicated to all the contributors and reviewers who were committed to supporting this work to ensure more resources exist for those who both live and work with the aftermath of murder.

Acknowledgments

In working with this project, I liken myself to a conductor of an orchestra melding the various sections into a harmonious whole. The first six months were committed to doing more research to expand my knowledge. I explored other authors' websites and programs looking for resources and answers to questions I heard survivors ask about. Much of this information has been woven into this book, and I am grateful to the many people who provided it. While there is much more information that could be included, one must decide, as I did, when we had enough clarinets, violins, and the like. The book includes a list of resources and references to take an inquiry further.

The next year I committed to taking this research and existing knowledge and placing it in one of ten chapters. I am deeply appreciative of all the survivors and their families that I have known, and that I have worked with, for their contributions to this work. Their stories, questions, and lessons have emphasized what is important to include in a book of this nature. They balanced their pain and passion with a dedication to make the world better for those whose lives have been changed forever after murder. Many survivors have been important reviewers of this book; many requested anonymity, others include: Celeste Vinzant, Marilyn Chew, and Cassandra Devereaux.

In addition, I thank the leaders in the field that are my colleagues and have added to my sensibilities and knowledge with their own important work. These include Ted Rynearson and Fanny Correa at the parent program of the work I have dedicated myself to at the Separation and Loss Services Program/Homicide Support Program at Seattle, Washington's Virginia Mason Medical Center. I also include my friends and colleagues Bethann Holzhay and Vilma Torres in New York; Alison Salloum in Florida; Carol Gaxiola in Arizona; and Alyssa Rheingold in South Carolina.

Local sources in our community in San Diego have been priceless. First and foremost, contributing many hours to this project has been Dayna Herroz, Peer Advocate. Her commitment has been unwavering and her review deeply valuable. Thanks also to San Diego County Deputy District Attorney Tracy Prior, Deputy District Attorney Per Hellstrom, and District Attorney Investigator Richard Wissemann, as well as San Diego Police Homicide Detective Sergeant Dave Johnson, and Detective Jim Johnson of Crime Stoppers, all of whom have been candid and generous in providing input.

Last but not least are two people who without their contributions this book would not have taken form. First is Carmela Caldera, who both participated in all phases of this work and was the prime underwriter and original visionary for this book. Second is the book's editor, Larry Edwards. His consistent critique and suggestions have been invaluable, especially in Chapter 3, Dealing with the Media.

Contents

Author's Statement

I moved to California in 1970. Besides raising two wonderful children, a daughter and son, I went to school and became a licensed Marriage and Family Therapist and had a successful private practice. After turning 50, I spent time visiting my home state of Maine, going to libraries to learn more about my sister's death, which had been a dormant issue in my life. l discovered microfiche and pulled out all that I could find of newspaper accounts of my sister Tiny's murder. I was then prompted to ask each member of my family, still in Maine, if they would talk with me about what they remembered, what their experiences were, and to tell the story of the effect of this event on their lives. Everyone I asked agreed.

I joined the San Diego Police Department's Intervention Team and worked with them for three years. I was clear that I didn't want to have my own story be the only story that I had experience with. I worked with a well-known trauma specialist, Charlie Nelson, PhD, for six months to strengthen boundaries between my professional work and personal story.

I wrote an article in 1995, which was published in a local newsletter, *The Victim's Voice*, for the Victims Assistance Coordinating Council, of which I was a member.

Recovery for Homicide Survivors

By Connie Saindon, MFT
Victim's Voice, 1995

I skipped Christmas this year. I went to Maine to be with my family on a mission related to the only other time that I remember "Christmas was skipped."

DEAD BLONDE IN GRAVEL PIT, the headline read.

My sister, the third child in a family of eight and nicknamed "Tiny," was murdered December 8, 1961, at the age of 17. As is so true in many families, there was The Rule: "Don't talk about it; it would be too upsetting."—and this goes on for years. What really happened gets distorted, and unresolved grief is traded for avoidance, denial, family feuds, and repressed feelings.

When each of my parents and siblings said they would be willing to talk about what happened, my mission was to put together our family's story, the story of "Tiny" and how her death impacted us all. How are paths taken, our lives changed, our decisions made as a result of this traumatic event?

It Never Ends!

Through my work as a therapist, my research in trauma, and my own personal experience, I have learned that it never ends. The effect of trauma continues to play out in one's life. When I was first in private practice, I had a serious case that I dealt with, with an intensity that I knew was driven by the murder of my sister. This was 13 years after her death. This was also the first time I experienced the emotional grief over her death. When she died, I was

11

in charge of the arrangements, of getting things done. I learned from this that everyone has his or her own timetable for grieving. My oldest brother agreed to help only if it were to help others. This led him into pages of journaling and hours of sobbing for the first time since she died.

The Story

It started out as a cool New England morning. Coats were a must for this time of the year. My brother Bill remembers seeing her walking her usual route to catch her ride to a city 40 miles away. She'd told him earlier that she had a toothache but was not staying home as she was graduating from beauty college that day. Dad passed her on the road that morning. He can still see her smiling and waving at him. He knows she'd still be alive if he had only stopped and given her a ride. Overwhelming guilt continues to plague him.

Instead of Dad giving her a ride, an acquaintance, someone she'd met just a couple of times, offered her a ride that chilly morning in Maine. She was so happy, as was her nature; that day was more special because of the graduation. The driver needed to find a part for his boat, and there was time to look for it at the local dump. Some say she laughed at him because his truck wouldn't start. He stabbed her, and when she went to get out of his truck, he hit her on the head with a brick. She died 10 minutes away from the hospital.

She was pretty, she was shy, and she was so proud of being able to graduate. Her studies were difficult, and she'd worked so hard. Instead, her diploma was buried with her as she lay in her favorite lavender dress that she had worn at my wedding just six days before.

Family Leftovers

Her death was not the only damage done. My entire family got bludgeoned! The damage is so far-reaching. Its tentacles grab systems of belief in the world and tear them apart. Here it is 33 years later, and we are still working to hear and put pieces together of what happened. I found out that after all these years, I remembered that we skipped Christmas the year Tiny died, we actually didn't.

Neighbors made sure there was a tree and gifts for all. I have no memory of this whatsoever. My parents split up and divorced. One brother has had violent reactions to seeing knives. The day one sister was told by a teacher that her sister was dead, she found a closet, to weep alone. She still hides her painful feelings from others. One sister "can't go to funerals." Everyone has protected both of my parents by "not talking about it."

In addition to putting together the pieces of her death, we've been putting together our memories of her life and how she still lives on in all of us. The words we use to describe her are: sweet, good-natured, always with a smile, and wouldn't hurt anyone. My two youngest siblings don't remember her at all. They were 10 and 11 when she was murdered. Tiny's death and life will be remembered by my family and my children. I want you to know her as well and that the damage to families lasts forever. My goal, to share with my family, is to give a voice for the long-term victims of trauma. Judith Herman, in her book, *Trauma and Recovery* (1992), calls such efforts, in the final stage of recovery, a "Survivor's Mission."

At Christmas, I invited my family to participate in a healing ritual, with materials from a company that sells albums with scrapbook, journaling, and memorabilia pocket pages with the best preservation qualities. Each family member is putting together at least one page of old photos and memories of Tiny. The inscription reads: "This album is dedicated to our loving sister and daughter who lives on in all of us."

My story led the way for me to search for better answers for other survivors in the following ways:

Spokesperson: Each of my siblings, if they were to tell this story of the impact on them, would write their own version. This is my version only. I have included voices from other survivors and leaders in this emerging field, as I remain a student of them all.

Death Notification: My mother was driving when she heard on the radio the name of her daughter, who had been murdered. I was with her. She pulled over quickly and when she was more composed continued to drive, as there were no other drivers in the car. I have no memory of how we got home. I do know we drove directly to the police station.

Headlines: "Dead Blonde in Gravel Pit." A hurtful image that I have reacted to again and again. This book will address issues related to the media, including social media.

Isolation: My mother was a zombie for days; she sat in a chair without talking or moving, like a stone. There were no crisis intervention teams, no victim advocates, no legal representation for my family nor funds for counseling services. No one talked with the kids: me or my siblings. There were six of us. One of my sisters was married and living in Florida. This book will discuss issues related to grief, the impact of murder, and incredible strengths that emerge along this journey.

Blame: My brother, aged 11, was told by a friend that his mother said he couldn't play with him anymore. Another brother lived with lifelong guilt, as he had had a fight with Tiny the day before and said he had wished she were dead. He died a premature death after years of neglecting his health. Guilt and blame are some of the dangerous reactions that can cause additional problems.

> *One*
>
> *doesn't*
>
> *recover*
>
> *from*
>
> *this,*
>
> *but*
>
> *one*
>
> *can*
>
> *learn*
>
> *to*
>
> *live*
>
> *with*
>
> *it*
>
> *better.*

Family Costs: The same year I went back home to do a memory album with the family about our sister/daughter's life. I didn't understand the ridicule and reluctance from them after agreeing to participate in it. That same year I purchased a plaque, with my sister's name on it, to be placed on a National Memorial Wall as a gift to my family. Later, I got word that family members were upset with me for doing this as I had not included them in that decision. I was surprised that a gift could be seen as a way of hurting them. Clearly, I had not given any thought to wanting to hurt my family in this way. They had concluded otherwise.

Justice: Although we were fortunate that there was a quick arrest and trial with a guilty verdict, the killer served less than eleven years of a life sentence. My parents were not informed of any hearing to protest this decision. In my work with survivors, justice is rarely the satisfying outcome families hope for. This realization inspired expanding options for survivors in this book.

My Professional Journey continued in dedicated study. Not only did I become certified in trauma work in various organizations, I focused on and was passionate about understanding the aftermath of homicide. What I found was disappointing, as there was so little in the specialization on homicide. It became increasingly clear that I would specialize in this area.

I started accepting new clients who had lost someone to murder in 1995. It is interesting to note that the very first case I had was one whereby the loved one had lost her husband on the same day of my sister's death, albeit many years later. I took that as a sign that I was headed in the right direction. I increasingly experienced a driven-ness, a compulsivity, and realized I could not **not** do this  work. I created the adjacent image to show how unimportant I became and how "Tiny" dominated my world.

My Professional and Personal Viewpoint gave me a unique perspective that few others would have. Not only did I learn about criminal death, but I was also a survivor. It didn't take long for me to realize little was

The "Changed Forever"

As I walk through the shadows of death,
and I now know evil,
I refuse to let the shadow of evil keep me from appreciating life,
the newness and joys available every day.

Whether that be seeing a new mural in a small town
or noticing dried leaves blown into a bouquet by the wind;
seeing the drops of water on an unopened bud,
the smile on the faces I pass.

As I walk through the shadows of death,
and I now know evil,
I refuse to let evil keep me from appreciating life,
the newness and joys available every day.

Smelling the pine-filled breeze in the forest,
tasting a slice of foot-high lemon meringue pie found off the Illinois I-40,
or noticing the strengths in people who also know evil,
as they have lost loved ones to murder.

They too are "the changed forever."
I refuse to let the shadow of evil keep me from seeing their strengths
amid their raw devastation,
or honoring their work, making a difference for
those "changed forever."

As I walk through the shadows of death,
and I now know evil, I am not lost.

—Connie Saindon (2013)

known about the impact on folks after murder. I discovered that there was more knowledge about the murderer who had many systems, studies, and stories in place . . . but not much about those folks who lost someone to murder. This book has been influenced by the many hundreds of survivor families that I have worked and the colleagues I partnered with for the survivors' care.

My next step was to research this subject area. As a faculty member at the university, I had access to many journals. My son, a doctoral student working in the computer lab, did searches for me. One of the most important articles came from a British psychiatric journal. This is where I found Edward "Ted" Rynearson, MD, and his work at Virginia Mason Medical

Center's Homicide Support Project in Seattle, Washington. Everything he said made sense —the most sense of anyone I had found so far, both personally and professionally. Fortunately, he was in Seattle, not England, and was most generous in sending to me many articles about his work. This began a continuing relationship with Dr. Rynearson, the preeminent leader in violent death bereavement and Medical Director of Separation and Loss Services at the Virginia Mason Medical Center.

Changes continued as I moved along this learning journey. A new article, study, or a survivor expanded what I knew. My article above, "Recovery for Homicide Survivors," has a title I can no longer use. The word **recovery** misstates the profound consequence after murder. I now say: "One doesn't recover from this , but one can learn to live with it better."

In addition to my interest in post-homicidal bereavement, the inspiration for this book comes from one of the two groups that we replicated from the work of Dr. Rynearson in our home base in Southern California: the Restorative Retelling Group and the Criminal Death Support Group, the latter of which was a ten-week process of support and education. Participants were folks who were interacting with the legal system as the death of their loved one was prosecuted as a crime. This book grew out of that support-group process.

Foreword

Connie Saindon and I met fifteen years ago when I was organizing a training project, funded by the U.S. Department of Justice, to initiate community-based treatment centers for traumatic grief after violent death across the United States. San Diego was one of the West Coast sites I considered and soon learned Connie was actively involved in providing peer support there after the homicidal death of her sister many years before.

At the outset, Connie taught me a valuable lesson in beginning such a project. Many of the clinicians most likely to maintain themselves in such work over time have lost a beloved friend or family member to a violent death (I include myself in that group), and it is this personal experience that generates and maintains their specific professional commitment. I suppose the work is personally meaningful because the professional activity brings some degree of personal coherence and meaning to the aftermath of violent death which is so despairing and meaningless.

Connie is a refreshingly direct and honest professional about her own personal experience in her clinical interactions. In treating many hundreds of adults with traumatic grief, she has had more clinical experience than almost anyone in this dreary specialty and is wise in recognizing the indications for and limits of short-term interventions, which she is an expert in organizing.

Openly curious about what is not known about traumatic grief after violent death, Connie is a rigorous reader and student of the limited empirical studies and clinical innovations on the topic, much of which is annotated in this book, and recently a contributing author herself. She is also an accomplished teacher of psychiatric residents and interns through the University of California, San Diego, who have trained at her center, as well as conducting workshops for counselors she has organized locally and nationally.

Her writing is also refreshingly direct and honest, including the voices of clients she has treated. *Murder Survivor's Handbook* follows her first book, *The Journey: Adult Survivors Individual Workbook Kit* published in 2008. The earlier book is a very readable and highly recommended workbook to guide survivors of a violent death through written and pictorial exercises to accommodate the traumatic thoughts, feelings, and behaviors that swirl in the aftermath.

The present volume, *Murder Survivor's Handbook*, deals with an earlier phase of adjustment—beginning with notification and the unavoidable interactions with the community agencies of murder (police, media, and the court). Connie and the other survivors present a comprehensive and coherent tapestry of responses to this early phase of adjustment. The many voices add richness and reality to the text. The format of multiple respondents confirms the uniqueness of each individual and dismisses the over-simplified lists of a single author's arbitrary observations.

Connie is to be congratulated on organizing such a relevant and useful text and you, the reader, will be pleased with your choice and enriched by your reading.

—Edward K. Rynearson, MD
Clinical Professor of Psychiatry, University of Washington;
Medical Director, Separation & Loss Services,
Virginia Mason Medical Center,
Seattle, Washington

Introduction

I, along with the contributors, hope this book helps guide the readers on the difficult journey that follows the murder of a loved one, from rebounding after this death, to dealing with the media, to dealing with the criminal justice system, to finding new meaning or a mission to help others, and to understanding their rights as a survivor and co-victim of a criminal death.

In some instances, contributors to this work have not been identified. They requested anonymity; for some, their professions demand it, for others it helps safeguard their lives.

How to get the most out of this book

Go to the chapter that you have questions about first. Get a notebook (optional, but highly recommended) and answer the questions that pertain to your situation. You will find that some events need to happen before you can describe your experiences. You may have a lot to say and having your own notebook will allow you more space to do so and help you keep a record. Recommend a notebook for members of your family and support team. Each of you have your own story and experience.

Scan this book for tips, guides and resources in each chapter. Skip around in this book as it fits for your energy and interest. Useful resources are listed at the end of each chapter and in the References section at the back of this book.

Major influences

A book of this scope requires input from many people and many sources. The three major influences for the content and structure of this book have been:

First, my professional experiences as a violent-death bereavement specialist that began in 1995. I have worked with hundreds of families and professionals and am the founder of Survivors of Violent Loss. Due to the murder of my sister in 1961, which I described in the Author's Statement, I was particularly interested in post-homicidal bereavement. Ninety percent of the work at Survivors of Violent Loss was with folks who had lost someone to murder. The survivors not only needed help in dealing with their loss, they needed practical information on what to expect, and what they could and could not do.

This book has been significantly influenced by the work of Ted Rynearson. He developed the Restorative Retelling model and two, ten-week groups: Restorative Retelling and Criminal Death Support for survivors of violent loss. The latter group suggested content areas for this book. More information on Restorative Retelling has been published in *Death Studies Journal, 2013*. (See References.)

Second, the heartfelt and heart-wrenching submissions of Survivor Writers, who have answered the questions that relate to each chapter. Survivors have lessons important for us all to hear and learn from. Anonymity has been provided to protect writers and increase their ability to be forthcoming.

Third, the work of Susan Herman, author of *Parallel Justice* (2010). Herman has more than 30 years of criminal justice experience, including serving as executive director of the National Center for Victims of Crime. She is an associate professor of criminal justice at Pace University, and in January 2014 was appointed as a Deputy Commissioner of Collaborative Policing by the New York Police Department.

Throughout the writing of this book, I have kept in mind the principles she presented in her book, listed here with permission:

- Justice requires helping victims of crime rebuild their lives.
- All victims deserve justice.
- Victims should be presumed to be credible unless there is reason to believe otherwise.
- Victims' safety is a top priority.
- Victims should experience no further harm.
- Rights should be implemented and enforced.
- Victims should be allowed an opportunity to talk about their experiences and their needs.
- Victims should be told that what happened to them was wrong and that every effort will be made to help them rebuild their lives.
- Decisions about how to address victims' needs should be based on sound information and research.
- Victims' needs should be addressed through a comprehensive, coordinated, communal response.

The sum of these components led to the writing of this book. If you think of ways to make this book even more useful, please contact me with your suggestions: cdsnetwork1@gmail.com.

You may send messages to the Survivor Writers at this email address as well. Although they can't reply to emails, they would love to hear from you.

—Connie Saindon, MA, MFT
San Diego, California

1

First Things First

No one understands the magnitude of this.
You end up a body with no life in it.
—Co-victim of Homicide, 1998

Why This Book?

This is a "Murder 101" book that provides a map to navigate unknown territory when someone has lost a loved one due to murder. I do this by asking important questions and providing answers that come from survivors as well as criminal-justice and violent-death specialists, and authors.

Whom Is This Book for?

This handbook focuses on the Criminal Death Journey and its aftermath. It is written for you and those who work with you. This book will provide some of the information you will likely need when you are thrown into a world you don't know or comprehend. It is designed, as well, to be an aid to peer advocates and professionals who want to provide support and a window into resources and information for co-victims.

To start, we will explore how and why this book came about.

Close to a third of people in the United States report losing a loved one to violent death; i.e., homicide, suicide, or accident (Norris, 1992). **Death by homicide shatters lives and communities** like no other death because it adds many more demands and complexities. One's world and ways of being have been shattered, leaving survivors in a new and painful reality.

Decisions must be made that impact the most vulnerable people—those who are traumatically grieved. The speed of events spawns a whirlwind of activities and emotions from many competing priorities, which in turn produces an onslaught rarely experienced by most families. Results are long-term consequences that survivors describe as their "life sentence."

The questions alone can be overwhelming:

- What happened?
- Who did it?
- Why?
- What to do?
- What are our rights?

- Whom should I talk to?
- What do I say?
- What can I do?
- Is my family safe?

The journey does not always follow exact patterns and time tables. However, there are certain things that are likely to occur, and we want to prepare you as much as possible.

The content contained in this book comes from many sources, and we would be remiss if we did not say that due to the uniqueness of each case and family, we realize we are not able to cover all circumstances.

Nonetheless, because so few maps or manuals on how to manage or what to do exist for survivors, we saw a need for this book. Survivors often take many missteps that add more trauma to the family or thwart the successful prosecution of a criminal case. Those impacted by violent loss are also at risk for significant health problems and life changes.

This book contains information and links to resources as a murder case moves along over time. The book provides a way for readers to document their own stories while reading the words of others who have already walked this path. The book will include wisdom and tips from survivors for those who have become "new members of a club they never wanted to join and are paying the highest of dues."

Stories from Real Survivors

Survivors of murder victims tell us, at first, that they are inconsolable, confused, and they don't know what to do, but they need to do something.

"No one gave us a manual," says Rose. "I don't know how to do this and don't want to make any more mistakes."

In this book, two elements identify the special support and information areas: (a) true stories and tips from Real Survivors in their own words, and (b) professional resources. Questions are provided in each chapter for the readers to document their own journeys as well.

Real Stories from survivors of homicide victims are among the specialists included here. Their names have been changed, but their words are their own words. They answer the same questions asked of you; they offer ideas about how things could have been better and ways to help you.

The survivor writers want you to know: "We are all victims, just like you, volunteering to do this book with other professionals. There is no manual on what you are to do when you are suddenly a victim. We want to add to the knowledge that you will need as you move forward. When traveling the road ahead, you will need courage and patience. Although each of our stories are different, you will not be alone as we travel this journey with you." Everyone who contributed to this book hopes that your journey will be better for going with us on ours.

Safety has been shattered. No longer can you say that bad things happen only to other people. You know this up close and personal. "It will bring you to your knees," said a father after his daughter was killed. (Doka, 1995)

You will be provided with ways to consider increasing your sense of safety.

Definitions

Definitions that may help you:

Murder: The FBI's Uniform Crime Reporting (UCR) Program defines murder and non-negligent manslaughter as the willful killing of one human being by another. Murder includes an unlawful killing of another, a death that occurs during a crime such as a rape or robbery, or a barbaric death, as in warfare. Murder is considered the most serious of crimes and deserving of the most severe punishments. The FBI's Crime Clock (2010) states there is one person murdered in the United States every 35.6 minutes.

Survivor: A person who has lost a family member or close friend to murder or another form of criminal death. Also known as a victim or co-victim. The term **"co-victim"** was created due to the lack of recognition of the needs of survivors (OVC, 1998), who were underserved and, in the case of murder are also victims. These terms will be used interchangeably in this book.

Resiliency: Strengths—what you, your family, your team does that helps you deal with this horrific death. In Chapter Two, this concept will be elaborated on. I assume everyone will not only have distress, but will also have effective ways that they manage what has happened, many times to their own surprise.

Second Wounds: Survivors report unexpected and painful emotional wounds from a variety of sources. I learned about these early on, not only in my own sister's death, but also in setting up a program that provided specialized services for survivors of victims of homicide. Others may wield unnecessary and often unintentional hurts that add to the stress. Watch for them and protect yourself from being thrown off track. Remember who and what is important.

Journey: Although the author is unknown, Ralph Waldo Emerson has been credited with saying, "Life is a journey, not a destination." Journey as it is used here means a trip you never wanted or planned for. It will be the most "expensive" journey in your lifetime, and there are many obstacles along the way. Few road maps or manuals exist for such a journey, which is the rationale for this book.

Your book: This is your book and should be used as your own. Therefore, go ahead and jump to the sections or story that draws you to it at each time of your need. Answer the questions as they fit you, and look up resources that will be helpful.

Survivor Stories: Each chapter asks questions and prompts you to write about your experience. These same questions are answered by the Survivors Writers Group, which formed specifically for this book. Although each story is different and may not cover all the issues you encounter in your own loss, these survivors have gone through the journey you are embarking on and want to help you by presenting their stories. One of the reasons we have included survivors in this book for you is that many survivors tell us they feel so alone; they want you to know you are not alone, and they have tips they want to pass on to you.

Borrowed narratives offer stories of grievers who have faced, survived and sometimes thrived in circumstances similar to or not unlike what clients are experiencing. Paradoxically, the emotional wilderness of one griever becomes . . . an oasis for another.

Many grievers live with unanswerable questions that raid their minds like guerrillas in war. In the telling of our tales, we seek help in finding answers, or at least permission to share burning questions.

—Robert Neimeroff (Smith, 2012)

Survivor Writers

In these pages you will meet the following survivors of homicide victims:

 Connie Saindon, the author, is a mental-health professional and a survivor. Read about her at the beginning and the end of this book. Since 1995 she has focused on studying, researching, and providing treatment and training on violent death and violent loss.

 **Rose**—a mom who lost her only child (a daughter) and a ten-month-old grandson.

 **Marina**—a daughter whose father was beaten and strangled, but the killer spent only one day in jail. She says judicial incompetence resulted in a mistrial. A year later, the case was dismissed for "insufficient evidence."

 Harrier—a son who lives with believing a family member killed his parents.

 **Kaila**—a sibling whose sister was killed by Kaila's boyfriend when he couldn't find Kaila.

 **Yvonne**—a daughter who was ten years old when she and her sister came home from school and found their mother had been raped and stabbed to death.

 Halia—a sibling who waited 30 years to see justice achieved following the brutal death of her older sister.

 **Mary**—a mother whose 25-year-old son died at the hands of a gang of six.

 **JJ**—a father, husband of Mary above, whose son died at the hands of a gang of six.

 Valeria—A mother whose family lost their son and brother when he was held up at gunpoint, robbed, and killed by a parole violator and multiple murder suspect.

 Evelyn—a mother who lost a daughter who was driving home and was pulled over and killed by a highway patrolman.

Follow these stories and read more of the contributions they submitted for you by locating their icons, their symbols for their loved ones. Each reply by the writers was voluntary; each was free to contribute what they wanted. Survivor writers' names have been changed. You may send comments to them at **cdsnetwork1@gmail.com**.

In Chapter Ten, where we discuss remembering loved ones, the writers tell you why they chose their symbols. In your writing, you will be invited to come up with a symbol for your loved one, too. Explore what symbols your family members and friends create. They will help you recall important stories. Collecting these life memories will help cushion the intruding memories of your loved one's death.

First Priority: Safety, for You and Those You Love . . .

Victims' safety is a top priority.
—**Susan Herman** (2010)

The world is not safe. Life may have been different before the murder of your loved one. Now, you no longer say that bad things don't happen. So one of the first tasks is feeling safe, or as safe as you can be.

Here are some things to think about adding to your list of what you can do to help increase your sense of safety:

- ✔ **Form an army of support**, a safety net. Include family, friends, colleagues at work, or classmates. Your army can include law enforcement and social service systems as well. If there has been an arrest, some feel safer while others do not, as retribution may be a worry from suspect's friends or family. Enlist members in your army to take care of items in your list, including these below.
- ✔ **Report threats** or suspicious behavior, direct or indirect, to law enforcement.
- ✔ **Have a security check** done of your home. Ask law enforcement to help.
- ✔ **Family check-in:** set up a system to know where family members are at all times. Extra check-ins are very reassuring.
- ✔ **Check with your Neighborhood Watch** group for safety guidelines.
- ✔ **Have someone in charge of Internet news and messages.** Limit what you say over the Internet and in social media. This is not the place to vent reactions and pain. Keep your own journal instead. Information posted online should be similar to what can be said on a postcard, which anyone can read. Choose carefully what you respond to. Both prosecutors and defense attorneys can use material you post online, and it could harm the prosecution.
- ✔ **Turn off the TV.** Be selective, or have some folks watch and report some news. You are bombarded with what has happened, so when you can, be selective with what you watch. Some of my staff members started "reading the news on the Internet" to protect themselves from feeling the stories as much.
- ✔ **Have a safety kit** comprising emergency phone numbers, cash for expenses, flashlight with fresh batteries, and filled prescriptions.
- ✔ **Give keys to your home** only to people you can trust.

✔ **Cover windows** to prevent viewing; install peepholes for help in identifying someone at your door.

✔ **Put up "Beware of Dog" signs** whether you have a dog or not. While recording your voice-mail message, have a dog bark in the background. (Justice Solutions)

This horrific event is bigger than all of us. Don't do it alone. Let others know. Do you feel safe? What can't you seem to get to that you need done? Who do you need to tell? Make a list for your army and the ways you want things done. Who can do what?

In your personal notebook, on a fresh page, write "My Team" at the top and in the space below write the name of each person on your team and the task(s) assigned to each one:

Name _____ Task(s)_____

Allow yourself enough room to add more team members later on.

Survivor Questions

In your personal notebook, reply to the same questions asked of the Survivor Writers. You can read their replies or wait to do so at another time to keep you from being overwhelmed. Your time table is what is important here.

We know that at different times you may answer the questions differently. For now, just respond with what comes to mind. What has happened is beyond words, so when words don't work, draw, sketch, or cut and paste words, news, or images in your notebook.

Survivor Question: What do you do, specifically, to help you manage what has happened to you and your loved one? What are you able focus on?

At first there may be little here, but as time goes on, you may find moments when you are a bit away from what happened . . . just a bit . . .

Rose
I spend at least a part of every day trying to make some sense out of the senseless, trying to live without them on a day-to-day basis, but mostly trying to continue our relationship albeit on a different level.

I spend a lot of time in my serenity garden that was built after the murders. It is a peaceful place that I can lose myself in and get swept up in nature and the beauty each unique plant has. I like the lavender that Connie always hands out, so I bought myself some this week and planted it in my garden.

I got a dog from the rescue center that was meant to be with our family. The minute she was brought to me to see how we would interact, she jumped into my arms and wouldn't leave. She was nothing like the breed I thought I wanted, but that didn't matter when I looked into her huge gorgeous brown eyes and melted. My heart was opening up and that scared the daylights out of me because my heart was so fragile at this point that I was afraid to allow myself to love anyone or anything new. She did survive and is thriving, and she is nothing but love, so I feel lucky that we found each other.

I also read almost everything I can find on living with a violent loss, spiritual books, and so many self-help books I have lost count.

I write in my journal, sometimes one word, just a sentence, or sometimes I fill up many pages. It all depends on where I am at any given time on this journey.

Marina
I do anything I can to cope. Nothing is too silly or strange. On a purely physical level, **I exercise almost daily**.

Cardio really helps with the corrosive rage and need for revenge. The day after the murder, I was running dirt trails near Dad's house. In my mind's eye, I was pursuing the killer. I felt my heart quicken as I overtook her and smashed her skull with a good-sized rock. I even imagined the noise of bone being crushed. It felt satisfying in a deeply primal way. I would not welcome the burden of taking a life, but I sure enjoyed dreaming about it.

I felt so unequal to the task of avenging my father's murder. I have never in my life felt a greater sense of powerlessness and incompetence. So it was natural to **set up an imaginary scenario wherein I was a clear and competent avenger**. Some might think

it silly, but nothing is too silly when it comes to survival.

I painted porcelain for a long time. Sometimes I did it for the pure pleasure of creating something beautiful or funny.

Sometimes I used it to convey some inchoate emotion. Going macro took me to beautiful places where I had control over the outcome—unlike my larger life.

Self-care became important. I ate well—when I remembered to eat. I reminded myself that, unlike Dad, I was still alive to enjoy the pleasures of life. For example, I could still savor the sensation of chocolate melting in my mouth. I could quench my thirst with a tall glass of sweet water. Dad could no longer could do that. I did not let myself forget it. It was a way to avoid the quicksand of inertia and self-pity.

I was alone when I needed to be alone. **I played music, sang, danced, looked through old pictures**, held Dad's belongings, screamed, keened, laughed— whatever it took. I went to Dog Beach and watched the dogs running in the surf. **I painted my toenails.** I visited friends and let them take care of me when I knew I shouldn't be alone.

I traveled and took myself far away from the teensy-weensy little place

27

on this giant planet where my father was killed. I hiked in the mountains and desert, and used the knowledge of my own impermanence in this world to savor life as much as I could.

I continued my work as a child-abuse case assessor. To this day, the work helps me to step out of my own life momentarily. The children in my cases are helpless. I am not.

Finally, **I stay away from toxic people or situations**. I don't waste my time feeling sorry for folks who won't help themselves. They're on their own.

Harrier

In the days, weeks, months, and years following my parents' deaths, writing in a journal became my greatest release. I silently put on paper the emotions and words that I wanted to scream from the top of the highest tree on the highest mountain. **Writing gave me a great sense of relief** and kept me from doing things I might later regret or even land me in jail.

I engaged (and continue to do so) in activities that helped divert my thoughts and helped me feel better about myself. These activities include playing my fiddle for dances and public performances, and occasionally composing new melodies.

I participate in historical reenactment, which allows me to leave all the travails of modern life behind and forces me to focus on things critical to my survival—building a shelter, starting a fire using flint and steel, cooking over a campfire, and turning acorns into a palatable meal.

Hiking in the mountains or at the beach calms me down and reduces stress and anxiety. Bird watching or playing Free

Cell (a computer game) also reduce stress and anxiety.

I have become an advocate for survivors of violent loss so I can help others travel this often lonely journey of dealing with traumatic grief.

Kaila

After my sister's homicide, I found myself **liking the outdoors, the mountains, desert, beach, going for a long walk, or just being outside. If I must be indoors, I love crafting or getting a hobby finished.** A twisted obsession that brings me comfort is **listening to the voices of Peter Thomas and Bill Curtis from the forensics TV shows**.

Yvonne

As I reflect back, my best coping mechanism in dealing with loss has been time spent outdoors. I was afraid of the loneliness and the silence in our home that day, which continued to haunt me. I'd **sit at the beach on a warm day with the cool breeze of the ocean**, simply listening to seagulls, the crashing of the waves, and breathing fresh air, which provided me so much peace at a very difficult time in my life. It was complicated enough as a teenager and without my mother I was overwhelmed.

Listening to music was my therapy. It gave me the power to reflect on and convey my inner sadness while expressing my feelings of inner pain. Therapy through music proved tremendously healing in my teenage years. Shortly after, I remember **playing "Stairway to Heaven" by Led Zeppelin, repeatedly**. I believed that there was no coincidence that the song had been released soon after her death. The power of music remains as one of the strongest resources I use to cope in an ever-changing world.

Beginning in my teens and to this day I've run countless miles, both short and long distances, thousands of miles. While I've had many days when I questioned why I needed to run, even in pain, there's still a continuous, strong, emotional component to why I run. Running has provided me a sense of empowerment in an otherwise senseless world. It's been an escape for my problems, especially toward the beginning of her murder; running calmed and relaxed my anxiety. I found it easier dealing with the emotional hopelessness that I felt following her loss. My running was and is a valuable tool that provides me both physical and emotional strength.

Growing older, **I found time to quietly reflect** and cope with stress through **gardening**, especially during tumultuous times in my life, dealing with the loss of loved ones. Through the planting of rose bushes and calla lilies I was capable of honoring her lasting memory. Gardening provided an outlet for my frustration in understanding and comprehending death. I continue to use it as a coping mechanism in dealing with the loss of a loved one.

I've discovered the importance of having a pet. In my case, a golden retriever. Words cannot describe the sense of peace I felt just having her by my side. She truly gave me unconditional love and companionship, a living being that I could trust.

I'd create jewelry using beadwork. It proved calming, and provided me a sense of accomplishment.

Once completed, I'd give the piece as a gift to a friend or family member, which made my efforts that much more fulfilling. Recently, I've learned that beadwork has been used as a therapeutic outlet for patients dealing with cancer, and it makes sense to me.

Halia

My sister loved the Beatles, so when I am missing her, **I listen to that music.** I have her pictures around my desk and living space, and I think about her as well as talk to her out loud sometimes. Before my grandmother died, she told me to **look into the sky at night** and she would be the brightest star in the sky watching over me. Now I look up and see the family star where my sister, grandmother, and other relatives have now joined.

Other things that continue to aid in the healing process are **mindful meditations, keeping a journal**, sharing favorite memories about my sister with other people who knew and loved her, as well as logging a gazillion hours of personal and group therapy.

The shadow side is that from the very day she was murdered, any feeling of safety was ripped away from me. Hours after we learned of her death, I had to go to the gas station and store for baby diapers, and I recall to this day looking around everywhere, afraid that someone might be attempting to abduct and murder me as well. I have never felt safe in this world since then. This has led to an abundance of **security precautions** over the years, including the use of a Post Office box, having very few guests over to my home or aware of my address, hyper awareness in parking lots and while entering or exiting my vehicle, home, or shopping centers.

Mary

I take walks on the beach and think and talk to my son. For the first 2 years, I gathered pictures and mementos of him and looked at them often. I talk frequently about him. Not of his death but of his life. I include him in my everyday life. The first year and a half, I had terrible visions of the night he died, or of my loss, and would sob. What helped me get myself together was **a hot cup of tea**. The hot steam in my face and the warmth the hot cup gave me as I held it would soothe me until I was in better control of my emotions.

JJ

Reading. I have read many books that deal with the grieving process and they have provided many different perspectives. Initially I was in search of someone who could describe the process of healing for me so that I could get on with it. I knew I didn't have any answers and didn't want to just let things happen.

Group sessions. I joined two bereavement groups and found a wealth of information and support there. Every story is different and compelling in its own way. It reinforced to me that there is no one right answer and that I had the freedom to take things at my own pace.

Couples counseling. I continued to see the counselor that we had developed a relationship with prior to my son's murder. Although he was not specifically trained in grief counseling, sharing the story with him helped, and he has also helped focus on this process as a long one.

Music. Listening to music often provides an escape, and I have tried to expand my tastes to appreciate some of the music that my son enjoyed. I feel that he often speaks to me in music that I hear.

At the airport the night of his death as we tried to function well enough to board the plane, I went to the gift shop and noticed their background music was the BeeGee's "Staying Alive" and thought it was a cruel joke, so I returned to the terminal only to hear Clapton's "Tears from Heaven." Other performances have also brought me to tears, but it seems to open a connection for me to him.

Survivor Question: What Happened?

Write your answer in your notebook.

Rose

My daughter, Victoria, was going through a paternity battle with the man who we knew was the biological father.

The problem was that they had taken two mail-in paternity tests, and both tests said he wasn't the father. Victoria swore he had to have tampered with the tests, and the strain this was putting on her was too much for her to handle. The weekend before the murders, we had a long discussion about going to court to have it done through the court system. That was the plan; she was on board with it and planned to tell the biological father that evening.

What happened instead was that he had no intention of having dinner or discussing paternity or child support. He had, however, spent the past six weeks leading up to that night looking into how

30

to get away with murder, get out of paying child support, how to fake a court-ordered paternity, how to knock a person in the head to cause the most damage (which he did prior to strangling her), and how to tie knots (for the noose he used to hang my ten-month-old grandson, Louis.)

I will never forget the fact that the police didn't come to me to tell me about the murders. It wasn't until I got a call from Victoria's work that she hadn't arrived and no one was able to reach her. When I reached her best friend, he was under the assumption that the police had already contacted me, so when I asked if he knew where they were, he told me they had been murdered the night before, and it was all over the news.

I don't remember what happened next except to say I was overcome with this nauseating heat wave and collapsed on the floor. When I got back to the phone, her friend was no longer on the other end. I called 911 and asked if they had my babies in the morgue and gave their names; I was asked for my phone number and told someone would call me right back. When the Sergeant called back, he asked for my address, and within seconds it seemed he was at my front door telling me it was true. Life as I knew it was over in a split second. All I knew was they were dead, and I don't know that to this day I can accept what happened. I can acknowledge that they are gone because I feel that loss every minute of every day; but accepting the why and how is something I struggle with.

Marina

More like, what didn't happen?

My dad's murder was a tabloid editor's dream. Dad was a wealthy and successful businessman. His alleged murderer was a grifter who specialized in finding wealthy men to con. She was physically abusive, a fact Dad kept from us during his five-year relationship with her. Dad was a brilliant business-man, but he was deeply insecure and craved external approval. He was also a late-stage alcoholic who had suffered a debilitating stroke. He was a sitting duck for an ostensible "looker" who set about alienating him from friends and family.

Gradually, she took over Dad's life until he was miserable. She wanted him to account for every moment of his time away from her. We found out later that she was picking up men in her "off hours" when she wasn't with my father.

Ultimately, she murdered Dad be-cause he was ending the relationship. He was planning to move into a gated com-munity where she couldn't get at him. By this time, she was stalking him. She would ring his doorbell for hours on end, late at night, while he presumably cowered in-side. Whenever Dad and I went out for dinner, the phone would be ringing when we got home. It was always her, full of counterfeit solicitude and pointed ques-tions—the hallmarks of an abuser.

How quickly life goes from mundane to unbearable! One summer morning I was drinking coffee and reading the newspaper. Seven hours later, I was answering a knock at my paternal aunt's door. It was the sheriff's coroner, bearing the dreaded manila envelope. I pulled out Dad's wristwatch—it reeked of the sweat of mortal terror—I kid you not. The presence of the envelope confirmed the unthinkable.

Dad had been murdered. A strange and profoundly disturbing story followed: EMTs with the fire department had answered a 911 call from Dad's house at 4:30 that morning. His girlfriend answered the door, naked and disoriented, babbling that she'd gone to sleep the night before, only to find Dad lying on the floor of his bedroom the following morning. She suggested that he'd fallen and hit his head on a bedside table. It didn't take long to figure out that her explanation didn't fit the chaotic scene in the bedroom. Death was not accidental. But how did Dad die?

A week later the cause of death came, and it was far worse than I imagined: manual strangulation, with attendant blunt-force trauma. The police said Dad was bludgeoned with a brass lamp and possibly a telephone receiver. He had three traumatic blows to the skull. According to the coroner, any single one of these blows would have rendered him unconscious, or at least incapacitated. He was disabled as the alleged killer worked her hands around his neck, periodically adjusting the hold so as to better choke the life out of him.

The alleged killer spent about five hours dragging his body around, moving furniture, hiding things, washing things, arranging for bail with a friend. Fingernail marks on Dad's neck corresponded with broken fingernails on the defendant's right hand. His lips and tongue were deeply split.

The coroner said it was possible that she kicked him in the mouth and stood on his neck to hasten strangulation. This last bit of information gave me no end of agony.

I assuaged the pain by telling myself that with such an obvious murder, Dad's alleged killer would surely spend the rest of her life in prison. It was not to be, thanks to a spineless judge, an impotent prosecutor, and an appallingly simple-minded jury.

The accused never spent more than a day in jail. Today the alleged killer is free.

Harrier

My parents died aboard their sailboat. The FBI opened a murder investigation after the survivors gave inconsistent accounts as to how the deaths occurred.

The episode split my family into feuding factions as my parents never got the justice they deserved.

Three decades later, the tragedy resurfaced with the publication of an account of the deaths in a true-crime book. The poorly written, fanciful portrayal of my parents and their deaths ripped my tattered family even farther apart.

Kaila

My sister was found in a trash dumpster, naked from the waist down, with a bullet in the back of her head. She was wrapped in a blanket and found by a man looking for aluminum cans.

Yvonne

While it has been many, many years, I can recall that "day" as if it were yesterday. It is engrained in my memory forever. It was a particularly warm summer's day in late September. My younger sister was 8 years old at the time; I was 10. She came running into my classroom at the end of the school day. She was in shock and repeatedly kept saying, "Mommy has cut herself shaving. She is bleeding bad!" I will never forget her sheer terror.

We lived across the street from the elementary school at the time. As we arrived home the front door was wide open and must have been open for hours, as flies hovered in the entry. I am sure that it all happened quickly. Though time seemed to stand still. It was similar to watching a movie, only frame by frame in slow motion. My mother wasn't in the bathroom as I'd thought, cut shaving. I could see that a struggle had taken place in our bedroom. We made our way into the living room; still we didn't see her.

There she lay behind the coffee table and the recliner. I didn't see her and nearly tripped on her. She was contorted in a strange position, her eyes and mouth wide open. She'd struggled hard, I'm sure begging for her life. There was a tremendous amount of darkened blood on her dress. She'd been stabbed numerous times to her heart. There was an eerie sense of quiet, and the look on her face that still haunts me to this day.

In utter shock and terror, we ran to our neighbor's house for help. I am thankful that our father didn't see her; it was hard enough on the two of us.

Later, I learned from a gossipy neighborhood "friend" that my mother also had been raped. I didn't understand what that meant. I believe because we were children, her rape was never mentioned by the adults. The images of those moments would play over and over in my head.

Halia

In 1982, my sister was abducted from her place of work, taken hostage as a passenger in her own vehicle to a remote area where she was sexually assaulted, tortured with knife wounds, and strangled to the point of causing cardiac arrest. After she was murdered,

she was then dragged 26 feet by her hair and thrown into a canal wearing only a pair of socks. Her vehicle was set on fire to destroy evidence. Her body was found the next day.

Mary

My 25-year-old son was walking the tenth of a mile from work to his home. He was a pizza chef and had closed the restaurant, along with a co-worker. As he walked down the street and was about to cross over to his apartment, he was met by six teens (three from behind him and three in front of him). One asked him for a light. As he reached into his pocket, he was attacked and hit by all six teens. He was punched and knocked down. One of the teens had been dared by another that night to use his knife. My son was then stabbed by this teen 6 times.

My son couldn't get to his apartment as these teens were between him and the building, so he made his way back up the street to get help. He stopped at one building, but no one came to the door. As he got to his restaurant parking lot, he realized it was completely closed up and his co-worker had left. He staggered back to the street where he collapsed.

He was found by a passerby who called 911. My son told the man he had been stabbed and couldn't breathe. He was unconscious when the paramedics arrived. He was taken to a local hospital and airlifted to a trauma center. He was taken into surgery, where he died from massive hemorrhaging, in the early morning.

His girlfriend had been waiting for him at the apartment, and when she found out, she called his brother, who lived 45 minutes away. He then called us where we lived on the opposite side of the country.

We called his sister, who lived near him, and told her what had happened. They were at the hospital when he died. My husband and I were booked on the first plane that morning.

 **JJ**
My son was savagely knifed by a group of teenagers that were bored. He bled to death on the operating table a few hours later, after having been left in the street by these unfeeling hoodlums. He was picked at random as the target for a "beatdown" and the group leader had been dared to use a knife for the first time during this attack. My son was attacked within sight of his front door while walking home after closing the restaurant where he worked.

Resources

Books

No Time For Goodbyes: Coping with Sorrow, Anger, and Injustice After a Tragic Death by Janice Harris Lord. Compassion Press, 2006. This popular book has been well received by crime victims and is a source of both comfort and information on the complexity of a violent loss.

Parallel Justice for Victims of Crime, Susan Herman. National Center for Victims of Crime, Washington, DC, 2010. http://www.paralleljustice.org.

Retelling Violent Death, Edward K. Rynearson, MD. Rutledge: Taylor Francis Group, New York, 2001.

What to Do When the Police Leave, William Jenkins. This book has been popular for its practical tips on what to do after a criminal death and is written by a survivor.

Online

Justice Solutions: A website for Crime Victim Professionals by Crime Victim Professionals. This website has helpful sections for crime victims as well. http://www.justicesolutions.org.

New Mexico Homicide Survivors, Inc. This website has examples of memorials of loved ones, with a tagline that says: Gone but not forgotten. http://www.nmsoh.org/scripts/memorial.asp.

Safety Tips: Justice Solutions: A website for crime victim professionals by crime victim professionals. http://www.justicesolutions.org/art_pub_home_security_for_victims.pdf.

* Some Web addresses may have changed since publication.

2

Grief and Resiliency

At first I was in a daze. I'd walk around and wouldn't know what I was doing. I was confused. I couldn't even think straight. Nothing made sense. (Bucholz, 2002)

Initial Impact

No one is prepared for the worst event in their lives. The pain of loss may be very intense after a murder. There can be a roller coaster of feelings and confusion that results in waves of activity and paralysis. Marina described it this way:

You know how oatmeal looks and feels when it's been sitting for some time? I imagined that was what my brain looked like on murder.

The overwhelming pain one feels is normal in the aftermath of this abnormal event. We are not prepared, no matter how concerned we had been for our loved one(s) before the death. Unless there have been previous losses by murder, there is no experience we can draw on.

There was nothing normal or expected when it came to the murders of my daughter and grandson. This was sudden, this was violent, and this was intentional. Someone was actually planning these murders as I was blissfully thinking our lives were now perfect, with our family coming full circle, and a new grandson too! (Rose)

35

> *I was ravenously hungry. I think my metabolism was cranked up, and I ate well. Eating was something I could orchestrate in a world where so much was out of my control. I drank water by the gallons. I was thirsty all the time.* (Marina)

Death by homicide is different in many ways from natural death or even accidental death. One's view of the world has been deeply shaken; it changes survivors' lives forever. In her book, *Shattered Assumptions* (1992), author Ronnie Janoff-Bulman identifies three basic beliefs that change after a traumatic event:

- **The world is safe**—survivors know that the world is no longer safe; they now know evil occurs.
- **Life has meaning**—one's purpose, life value, and plans are up for change.
- **One has worth**—one's ability to protect a loved one(s) and feel competent is fragile.

> *The murder of a loved one, and its aftermath, is incomprehensible. Those who have grieved this kind of loss know firsthand that there is evil in the world. It is not abstract. We have been pulled to the edge of darkness, our world upended, our beliefs broken, and our trust shattered.* (Valeria)

Violent death increases vulnerability and exposes a world that is no longer a safe place where one is protected from violence. This fragility is increased if the community blames the victim/family, or when there is pressure from the judicial institutions to focus on seeking justice. (Currier, 2008)

What Is Normal?

Survivors wonder "What is normal?" They keep expecting this loss to be like other losses. Grief ideas include believing that the more they talk about it, the faster they will get over it. This doesn't work, and they find that they do not get over this kind of death, that instead they learn to live with what has happened.

Am I Crazy?

> *I saw my sister everywhere I went, I followed her, I would stare at her, only to discover that it wasn't her.* (Kaila)

Three major reactions that many find they have difficulty with are rage, sleep, and thinking.

> *Initially, I experienced intense rage, terror, and anguish. Insomnia became a constant companion. I lost my sense of competency in the world.* (Marina)

The resources you have or have used before may not help you as much as you had hoped. **Until you have acquired new strategies, be protective of yourself.**

- Say no to "incoming" distractions.
- Be selective to keep your strength up.
- EAT food (an apple, yogurt, raisins, carrot sticks, banana, V8 juice) three times a day and limit alcohol.
- Pull yourself back into quiet spaces.
- Focus on your own five senses, one at a time: see, hear, touch, smell, and taste.
- Take notice of any times that you are not absorbed with what has happened. Even if it is brief. See what you can do to lengthen that time to help you as you move in and out of the compelling reality of your loss.
- Breathe slow, deep breaths intermittently.

Consult with professionals, folks who are trained in this kind of loss. Be careful of well-meaning advisors who have just the cure for you. Lean toward those who have had a similar experience or are trained in this kind of loss. In addition, many who have had a murder in their lives may have suggestions that do not fit you, as each person, case, and, therefore, strategy may or may not fit you and your loved ones. **You will remain the primary expert on your situation.**

> *Murder was a catastrophic meteor that gouged out a massive hole in my life on a peaceful summer morning. Dad was gone, just like that. Ripped away. I had no time to prepare for his death, no opportunity to say good-bye.* (Marina)

One does not "get over it" any more than one gets over losing a limb. One adapts and adjusts to it but never gets over it. Deborah Spungen, the mother of a murder victim and founder of the Antiviolence Partnership in Philadelphia, demonstrates this when training others. She has her participants crinkle a new piece of paper, then attempt to smooth it out. They cannot smooth the paper sufficiently to get rid of all the scars on the paper.

You now have an opportunity to answer the questions our survivors have replied to. Each of their stories is true according to their experiences, but none of them are your story. Each loss is as unique as each person, family, and community. You can write your responses in your notebook to help you keep track of your journey.

There are no right or wrong answers here. Whatever did not go well is an opportunity to write about a possible solution. Take the opportunity to write about what you wish had happened and hope it will be corrective for others.

You may find ways you will connect or relate to the writers and of course have tips of your own that you want to pass on to others. You do not have to do it now. Know that you may come back at anytime to edit or add to this information.

Survivor Question: How long has it been since your loss?

In your notebook, write down your answer.

Rose
It will be 8 years since the murders of my daughter and grandson.

Marina
It has been 15 years since my father's murder.

Harrier
My parents died more than 35 years ago.

Kaila
It's been 15 years since my sister was murdered.

Yvonne
In our case, my mother's murder took place in the early seventies.

Halia
It has been 30 years since my sister was murdered.

Mary & JJ
We are in year three of our loss.

Survivor Questions: What did you experience initially? What today?

In your notebook, write down your answers.

Rose
Initially, I would have to say shock took over.

I was in such denial that I thought once I got to see their bodies I would prove them all wrong and it wouldn't be them. It took 5 days before the bodies were released, and I couldn't get to the funeral home fast enough because I still had hope that they were alive and this was all one big misunderstanding. I will never forget when they opened the door and there on the metal slab was my daughter with my grandson lying on her chest (as they would be buried together).

There could be no more denial or so I thought after seeing them like that.

I know that initially I experienced every one of those grief responses from disbelief to bitterness; although once the shock wore off I never had that response again. They came in waves that swept me up and tossed me into the bottom of the ocean of grief only to come out bloody and raw. I didn't know it was physically possible to cry as much as I was crying and not run out of tears. They came whenever and wherever, and I realized along with losing my daughter and grandson, I had lost any control I thought I had over my life.

Sometimes I was able to go some place in my head where everything stopped; it was quiet and I wished I could stay there forever.

Everything I knew and loved was gone in an instant and the world around me was completely different in every way. It no longer had color, meaning, or light. It was a dark place that was so cold; horrific things happen here. No one is sacred, no life is immune. Time stands still on so many levels and moves forward on others. There was no balance, no reason that I would ever accept. This was going to be forever and I had no idea at the time how long forever truly is.

Today I run the full spectrum of those grief responses; not often with the same intensity, but I still find myself in the midst of one or more at random times throughout the minutes, days, months, and years. I also have acquired some new "tools" that often lessen the length and the pain of many of these responses.

I read somewhere that we have a tendency to fight against the waves of grief when they come because we don't think we can go through this another

*time. However, **if we could learn to lean into the waves and roll with them, and all the emotions that go along with it, we would have an easier path through these times.** I have found for me that every time I try to fight these emotions, and try to go around the grief, I have gotten stuck. When I face it head on and walk through the fire again and again, surprisingly I emerge again, different but still standing.*

Marina

I fell into a pattern of not sleeping well for days. I lost my sense of competency in the world. My brain wouldn't work the way I wanted it to work. I couldn't concentrate. I could not absorb any information—unless it was about the murder.

I still had to function in my daily life, but that was difficult. I couldn't process information very well. This affected my work. I couldn't say how many times I "woke up" to find myself staring at a file page I'd been trying to read for an hour.

Insomnia became a way of life. I got into a pattern of not sleeping well for days. Finally, sheer exhaustion would take over. Sleep was fitful. This continued for years.

My digestive processes became quite dodgy. I ate a lot of antacids just to calm things down. My heart felt very delicate and fragile. I was quite convinced that I would have a heart attack at any moment. Terminal illness was a concern, too.

My startle reflex kicked into high gear. Any unexpected noise or movement set my heart to pounding. For that reason, driving was difficult. Every honk of a horn signaled imminent peril. Several times, I drove in the opposite direction on a one-

way street. Want excitement? Dodge on-coming headlights at 10 P.M. on your way home from trauma therapy—that will wake you up!

I drank water by the gallons. I was thirsty all the time.

I tripped a lot, hit my head on things, cut myself. It was hard to do the simplest things, like bathing, dressing, or cleaning. I would just drift off, only to find myself holding a pen, a book, or a bottle of detergent, wondering what the hell I was supposed to do with it.

I found myself looking for Dad. I went to all of the places where we used to eat or shop. Such yearning! Oh, how I wished I could go back in time and find him sitting across the table from me. Even as I was thinking of Dad as he was in life, I found myself going into the room where he was murdered. I sat on the spot where they found his body and imagined the murder scene. Compulsion was definitely a part of it, but I had a conscious desire to face what I feared the most and desensitize myself.

At the same time, doing these things helped me to feel more connected to a father who no longer walked the earth.

***I also felt a drive to talk to people about what happened.** Sometimes I chose strangers, and sometimes I spoke with friends. Thankfully my friends didn't shut me down. Strangers were pretty wonderful about it, too. **I don't generally recommend talking to strangers**, but I'm pretty sociable. **It helped me. It helped them to help someone**, too. Symbiosis, I guess.*

There was an overwhelming need to fix things, to set things right, to see justice done. This created no end of pain and suffering, because things don't happen in real life the way they do on "CSI" or "Law

and Order." I twisted myself into knots trying to think of ways to resolve the murder. It was the worst thing I could do, given my comparative powerlessness, yet I could do nothing else.

Harrier

At first it left me numb; I couldn't come to grips with the fact that they were dead. But the story unfolded over several days, and each day the account of their deaths changed. At first, I thought they'd died in an tragic accident. Then I was told by my brother and sister that my father had died as the result of a fall and my mother had shot herself the following day. When I attempted to claim the bodies, I found out that there were no bodies—my brother had dumped them over the side of the boat in the middle of the ocean.

Then the FBI opened an investigation and said my sister—who'd been injured but survived—did not get hurt in an accidental fall as I'd been led to believe. Rather, she'd been clubbed over the head with a wrench or a gun butt and suffered a fractured skull. The FBI suspected that my brother had done it, and that he also killed our parents. I became a detective investigating the possibility that my own brother had murdered our parents after assaulting our sister.

Kaila

Initially, I experienced disbelief, indescribable mental pain, pain I couldn't feel physically. I cried all the time, even when I experienced happiness. I didn't want to eat, but I slept well. I just didn't like waking up. Today, I've accepted my reality and have allowed myself to move on. I've had more losses since, and I know what the feelings are going to be. Today I have noticed how people grieve, and secretly I know what they are going to go through.

Yvonne

*While the emotional pain subsided with time, our grief process in losing our mother to murder was far more pro-longed. I felt completely iso-lated and sensed that it was also a very uncomfortable situation for adults that knew us. They didn't know what to say. Any form of comfort came mostly from close friends. Our next door neighbors became instrumental during those early days and years to follow. They offered us the only source of trust and comfort we could count on. Unfortunately, any close family rela-tives lived outside the country. **Trying to receive the proper help we needed from long-distance relatives could not be expected for any length of time.***

I remember so many added issues to contend with: how could someone ever take the place of our mother? How could we return to school and pretend it never happened? How could we ever escape being known as "the girls whose mother was murdered across the street from the elementary school?"

We continued to suffer grief and de-pression. We were forced to assimilate as quickly as possible as though it never happened. There were no traumatic grief counselors or services. My grade school teacher, Mrs. D, took it upon herself that I got the support I needed away from the classroom. She made every effort to protect me, and to make sure that I wouldn't fall too far behind in class.

While our initial experience hap-pened so long ago and though many years

have passed since her murder, my view of the world remains the same: one retiled with anxiety. It's a sense that the world is unsafe and that at any time my life could unravel suddenly.

Halia

Initially, I was in shock and disbelief; yet I had a small child of my own and adopted two of my sister's children, so I became very busy. It took four years before I truly stopped long enough to let the grief sink in and start moving through it.

As an Amer-Asian family, emotions were not openly expressed. I recall shed-ding tears at the kitchen table the evening after the viewing and before the funeral, scheduled for the next day. I was prompt-ly told by my mother to cut that out or go to the bedroom.

*Because ours was a cold case that took 28 years to get an arrest, there were many years **we honored my sister's memory by sharing stories and pictures**. However, over the last two years, with an arrest, multiple hearings, and a plea bargain leading to a conviction, there has been a resurgence of emotions for the family and friends of my sister.*

For me personally, losing my sister was worse than losing my own limbs or life itself. If I could have traded my life for hers I would have, in a heartbeat. For the record, this type of pain, grief, and loss, if thirty years bears any predictive factor, is not something one is able to be done and over with.

It pains me to hear others, par-ticularly those in the therapeutic pro-fession, say "how long ago was that" with a tone that implies I should be past my grief, according to their timetable. It takes as long as it takes, and **I have learned to honor the healing processes as part of the journey**. I turned some significant corners in dealing with my grief through the support of the Survivors of Violent Loss Program of San Diego, for which I am eternally grateful.

JJ

My initial experience was mostly characterized by shock, despair, and a long list of things I should do, without the energy to do any of them. Having continued in the bereavement groups, I have seen parents coming to their first meeting, many times just a few weeks after their loss.

Although I find it hard to measure the distance I have covered in my grief journey, it is very clear that I am not in the same place as I was in those early months. Today I still feel a pervasive sadness, a despair for the direction that our world is heading, and a larger presence of evil.

The groups have also highlighted the varied spectrum of grief journeys and coping methods. By way of contrast, my surviving son has declined to participate in groups, saying that he doesn't want to listen to other people's problems. The challenge for me is to understand and accept his position and not tell him what he should do, while continuing to hope for something better for him.

Grief and Resiliency

This section covers two areas that are important for your journey: grief and resiliency. The balance between these two is important. Although we tend to look at symptoms, it is the careful attention to what we are doing—to ensure that we stand up, take another step, breathe, and so on—that is vital on this extremely difficult path.

We begin with some definitions to help clarify both the grief experience and the signs of resiliency you may see in yourself or those around you. We will follow with tips that you can consider to help you manage the best you can under the circumstances.

Definitions:

Grief—one's personal experience of loss; it includes physical symptoms as well as emotional and spiritual reactions to the loss. Grief is a process that can take months or years to work through.

Mourning—the public rituals or symbols of bereavement, such as holding funeral services, wearing black clothing, closing a place of business temporarily, or lowering a flag to half mast. Public expressions of mourning are usually time-limited.

Bereavement—the period of mourning and grief following the death of a beloved person.

Trauma—the feelings of terror, helplessness, and devastation that follow a potentially intolerable "event."

Second Wounds—unexpected and painful wounds that come from a variety of sources; these are often unintentional hurts from others, with ignorance being a key factor. Individuals inflicting such wounds do not know your loved one as well as you do, and they don't understand what loss by murder is like for family and friends of the deceased. Here are a couple of examples:

> "The hardest part is still to come, where there are no rituals, no road map," an uncle of one of the children killed at Sandy Hook, Connecticut, told the news media. He was upset to find that someone had used his nephew's name to solicit for donations that didn't come to the family. Instead of being able to be with his grieving family, he had to work to protect his family against abuse. (CNN, 2013)

> Jackie Kennedy had to dismiss her domestic staff four days after her husband was killed and had to leave the White House in two weeks (Smith, 2012).

My dad said: "She (my sister) would be alive today if I had stopped and picked her up."

Rage—Episodes of free-floating rage may be directed at the killer, or misdirected at any agency, family, or friend.

> *I couldn't eat and survived on Jamba Juice for at least 3 months. The rage I felt was so intense that it vibrated off of me, and it was hard for others to stand in that fire with me, and yet they did. (Rose)*

Delayed reactions—I was one of those who saw everyone in my family falling apart, so I got busy and took care of the necessary tasks, such as picking out the dress my sister was buried in. When you read the survivors' accounts, you will see that Harrier and others had delayed reactions as well. There is no formula nor a set of stages one goes through.

Sue's 17-year-old daughter was shot to death, along with a boyfriend: "I cried everyday for a year. My husband still has trouble, as he left it all up to me. He hasn't dealt with the whole thing. He just keeps it locked away." (Bucholz, 2002)

Survivors Guilt—feelings of guilt for not having protected the victim.

> My dad said: "She (my sister) would be alive today if I had stopped and picked her up."

Marina's example of guilt for her dad's death:

> *The guilt was crushing, too. Surely I could have saved Dad, or prevented his death, but how, when I didn't even know he would be killed? It was an awful dilemma.*

Potential problems—Parents of Murdered Children, Inc.®, has a list of possible problems that may occur for individuals, couples, families, and the community following a murder. Go to their online website for a full list. Here are a couple of them:

- **The strain on marriages (frequently resulting in divorce) and the strain on family relationships.**

  The energy for trying to find out "who did it" can be played out in families when they start blaming themselves or each other. When the suspect is among them, it can add to the already intense confusion. The question of who is safe, who can one talk to, becomes paramount.

  Big events, and this is one of the biggest, are shown to bring families together or splinter them.

  Wendy, who told her story at a Candlelight Vigil, described how no one talked with her and her brother about what happened to their mother. People may have been trying to protect them because they were young children. However, children do need truthful information about what happened, and it needs to be explained to them in a way that fits their age.

- **Effects on other family members, children, friends, co-workers, and others.**

  Here we find job loss and employers, who think they are helping, expecting workers to get back to the job.

Adult children of victims of homicide report again and again that no one talked with them. No one brought "it" up again when they were around.

There are about 10 to 12 people who are significantly impacted after a murder. Adult children of victims of homicide report again and again that no one talked with them. No one brought "it" up again when they were around. Their world changed, and they were left with a void that haunted them until they became adults and began to work on how their lives were altered and often stunted. Hyper-vigilence is one price that children pay. (Salloum, 1998)

Grief

I can still hear my husband's screams in my head, but I can't hear mine because I felt like I was under water and the room was spinning. (Rose)

Ted Rynearson (2001), the leading professional in violent-death bereavement, identifies three ways that the loss by homicide is different from the natural loss of a loved one:

It is **violent**.
It is a **violation**.
It is **volitional**.

The volitional aspect that someone, on purpose, killed our loved one(s) can be the most difficult to reconcile.

The incomprehensible loss can also be **voyeuristic** with the involvement of the news media. One's private life becomes public, whether the personal details have anything to do with the death or not.

Carol Ellis, director of the training center at Victims of Crime Center (VOC), uses the term "homicide differential" when she describes the unique impact of homicide on victims, which include:

- **Stigma**—that is, blaming the murder victim for his or her own death.
- **Isolation**—which can be self-imposed, or others may find it hard to be with them, as they are at a loss as to what to say or do.
- **Traumatic grief**—after a homicide, this is distinctive because homicide is sudden, unexplainable, unjust, and involves violence.

Signs of grief and trauma may include: crying, wailing, anger, confusion, nightmares, sadness, a startle response, and going through the motions of life in a detached manner. Survivors ask when they will stop hurting so much and wonder if they will ever feel better. They try to equate what is happening with the familiar grief experience from accident, age, or disease. Everyone's circumstances are different so a timeline cannot be answered realistically.

It is most important to remember that what you are going through is normal.

Some lose their ability to function on the job, at home, or in school. My mother froze and didn't function for several days; she just sat in a chair without moving, just staring.

The author of *The Ride* (Macquarrie, 2009) describes how the mother, heavy with medication, is not able to shake the nagging questions about her son's last minutes and wonders if he called out for her, while the father becomes busy with both the search and investigative efforts.

One of the mistakes made in responding after a murder is focusing concern on one person at the expense of others: family members, including children, and friends. The dozen or so additional people significantly impacted by one death become less visible. Make it a point to check in with others who may not show their distress outwardly.

> *. . . people often forget about the father's grief and*
> *focus on the mother's as if his grief isn't as intense*
> *or that he being a man and all, he didn't need the*
> *support as much. Nothing could have been farther*
> *from the truth; he was broken, too.* (Rose)

Many people who want to offer support don't know what to say or do after the news that a loved one has been murdered. One's support system may change and the people you would normally rely on may no longer be helpful.

> *I was in the room but I wasn't present and that*
> *worried people who, thinking they were being*

*helpful, would shake me back to reality, which
was like pouring gasoline on my burning soul. It
may have made them feel more at ease but it did
nothing for me that was positive.* (Rose)

Nicholas Wolterstorff, in his book *Lament for a Son* (1987), asks supporters to "just come sit with me on my mourning bench." Being a quiet presence can be powerful when a survivor's ability to listen is limited amid the many decisions, questions, and information they may be bombarded with.

Survivors look to traditional grief stages to get past, only to find that this kind of loss is one that they doesn't fit well into stages. Survivors may unduly berate themselves for being inadequate when a stage repeats itself. It may be more helpful to think in terms of a *state* one is in, which repeats itself over the course of one's experience, not something one accomplishes and is done with. Over time, survivors report, the space between episodes of pain may increase and the rebound is faster.

Ten Tips to Helping Your Children

When a loved one has been murdered, you will have your grief, and you will want to help your children as well. You can't protect them from pain, but you can help them express their feelings, comfort them, and help them feel safer.

1. Tell them the news as clearly and simply as you can. Too much news can be overwhelming. It is better to hear it from you than from a news report or a friend.
2. Reassure them that they can come back to you whenever they have questions or hear something that is upsetting. Tell them the facts. Don't tell them what you don't know.
3. It is okay to cry. Let them know crying is okay. Seeing your tears will help give them permission to cry, too. It is normal to cry when this happens.
4. Reassure them that they didn't do anything wrong. It is not your fault nor their fault.
5. Give them tools to express themselves: paper, pencils, and crayons. Encourage them to express what they want in words or pictures: memories, questions, worries.
6. Give them tools to quiet themselves down. Stuffed animals, bubbles, and so on.
7. Tell them what is in place to keep them safe, as they will worry that the same thing will happen to them or you.
8. Let them know how you and others are available as well.
9. Keep their activities in place as best you can, as they will feel more secure with a familiar routine.
10. Do activities to memorialize the loved one. Talk about ways they will live on by sharing stories, planting a tree, or releasing balloons.

Therese Rando, a well-known trauma therapist and author, describes what happens as Sudden Temporary Upsurges of Grief, or STUGS, which are brief periods of acute grief (Rando, In Press). In my work, I simplified this abbreviation to SUGS—Sudden Upsurges of Grief.

Triggers can come from media coverage, memories, a smell, a food, touch, sound, or sight. Types of SUG reactions also occur due to trigger events, such as the anniversary of the murder, a birthday, or a holiday.

Survivors often report the SUGS they had during the week. This helps them have a language to describe it, along with helping them to normalize it, too.

> *I had a SUG when I went to the beach yesterday. I teared up remembering how she used to love doing this.*

Because survivors are rarely present when their loved one is murdered, they do what most humans do: they imagine what happened. Some survivors say they replay grotesque images or thoughts over and over, such as how the death occurred, or they can't stop seeing their loved one at the morgue, or they wonder how much their loved one suffered. The many scenarios they imagine are often much worse than when the facts are known.

What You Can Do

These reactions, although painful, are part of a normal process. There is not a lot anyone can do to make you not experience these reactions, but there are things you can do to handle these moments of feeling powerless. This life event, the most devastating one you have ever had, does require you to change, to live your life differently. **By focusing on what you can do, what you can change, you will keep your energy at the best it can be under the circumstances.**

- Move your body, such as leisurely walking in a safe place. Many people walk in a shopping center when inclement weather may cause safety concerns.
- Breathe slow, deep breaths in between normal breathing.
- Structure your time, while being flexible. Many a survivor has committed to do something but just couldn't go and canceled. This is normal. Please tell yourself this as well as others who count on you.
- Don't label yourself as crazy; you are normal and having normal reactions.
- Express what has happened to you. For some, it is talking to other people, others take on projects. Find a safe way for you to express what is going on.

> *If you go nuclear, don't leave missiles in your silo.*
> —*The Good Wife*

- If you drink, have only one. Alcohol will increase whatever feelings you are having and, with the right trigger, will change a mood quickly. This advice holds for all mind-altering substances.

- Eat at least three times a day. Don't let your "not hungry" guide you. Your judgment is off and your body does need food. Don't forget to eat. Grab some nuts, a banana, yogurt. This is within your power and important for your emotional, thinking, and physical strengths. Most fast food places have healthy choices, too.
- Keep your life as normal as possible. You have a very good reason to cancel many things to reserve time for yourself and those who are most important. Remember: you are on the top of this list.
- Give yourself permission to feel terrible, safely.
- Keep a journal, draw or write your way through those sleepless hours. Recall what you love and how you may want to keep that alive and growing.
- Retain as much of your routine as you can. (This is especially helpful for kids.)
- Limit news, blogs, and social media.
- Remind yourself that "We're all a little bit stronger than we think we are," says Good Morning America's Robin Roberts in a November 20, 2012, interview while recovering from a bone-marrow transplant.
- Form an army . . . and handout guidelines on how others can help.
- Say no to people and things you no longer have the energy for.

A soldier, who knew he was on the edge of killing himself, told me he finally settled down after he gave up drinking, fighting, and speeding on his motorcycle. He just stopped, stayed home, and turned everything off. No more "incoming"; just quiet.

Survivors can be at risk for both medical and psychological problems after the murder of a loved one. After a murder occurs, the focus is on criminal justice. Working with health professionals may prevent more serious complications for you and your family.

Resilience

Trauma and resilience are important factors in one's well being and ability to function. They are in a constant balancing act. In his leading work on violent death, Dr. Ted Rynearson (2001) says, "The emotions associated with trauma rise to the surface, and resilience 'buffers' them by capping them within tolerable limits. This keeps one from disintegrating by maintaining a sense of 'mastery'—of safety, autonomy, and hope."

He also says that one's innate abilities work in the following ways:

- **The ability to self-soothe or calm oneself down**
  Sometimes I was able to go some place in my head where everything stopped; it was quiet and I wished I could stay there forever. (Rose)
- **The ability to separate**
  Babies begin this process when they realize that they and their mom are two separate beings. Survivors do this when they are not merged with their loved one as if they died, too.
- **The ability for optimism and hope**
  An internal knowledge that life will get better and be more meaningful. One mother said it this way: "I will get better, they will not kill me, too." Another said:

"Optimism is a like a muscle and it gets stronger with use.

My colleague, Vilma Torres, who does similar work in New York at the Safe Horizons program associated with the Bronx Criminal Court, tells this story:

> *An unforgettable experience from the weeks after September 11: I was working at the pier and met a mother whose son had been killed. After we were done, I left her to have some dinner. I was walking away to assist another family. I suddenly was startled to hear someone screaming my name, "Vilma! Vilma!" I turned and the client was motioning me back. I was wondering what did I forget to do for her? The mother said, "I forgot something." I asked, "What?" Her reply: "I forgot to give you a hug." That mother's compassion and warmth always comes back to me. It reminds me of a quote from Emily Dickinson: "We never know how high we are till we are called to rise." I remain in awe by this mother's **resilience** and courage ten years later.*

I have elaborated on resiliencies even more to help you identify them in yourself and the people around you, even if they occur minimally or sporadically right now. I haven't seen anyone who did not have something that was helping them during this most difficult time. Because our tendency is to focus on symptoms and what pain folks are in, I want to point out how to look for what you are all doing as you move along this most difficult path. I continue to be amazed at what people do when they are faced with the worst. I hope this will give survivors some permission to feel proud as well by noticing and acknowledging abilities.

Wolin and Wolin, in their book *The Resilient Self* (1993), define resiliency as "having the ability to bounce back. To face adversity and rebound, like a rubber band." The Wolin and Wolin Project Resilience uses the word "resiliencies" to describe "clusters of strengths that are mobilized in the struggle with hardship." Their vocabulary of resiliencies includes:

- **Insight**—being able to ask tough questions and give honest answers to decrease confusion.

  > *I couldn't make any plans. The legal system was in control of my life, or so I felt. Why make plans anyway, when I could be the next to die? Danger and death were everywhere, even in the most peaceful of settings.* (Marina)

- **Independence**—distancing oneself from the sources of trouble in one's life and acting independently.

  > *I did okay at work as long as everyone left me alone. I could focus and block out what had happened, but when I went home I fell apart.*

- **Relationships**—making fulfilling connections to other people for security and to ward off alienation. This can be seen in the ability to form your "army" of support.

  > *Our next door neighbors were absolutely instrumental during those early days. Because we had an established relationship with the family, they truly offered us the only sense of trust and help we could count on.* (Yvonne)

- **Initiative**—taking charge of problems. Changing powerlessness and despair into optimism, effectiveness, and mastery.

   I became immersed in the investigation and witnessed an extensive FBI interrogation. I didn't have time to grieve. (Harrier)

- **Creativity**—using imagination and expressing oneself in art forms. Taking ugliness and pain and turning it into beauty.

   I painted porcelain for a long time. Sometimes I did it for the pure pleasure of creating something beautiful or funny. (Marina)

The murder of a loved one is beyond words. Art finds a way to help when words won't do. Survivors who had described themselves as having no creativity or as being shy, have written beautiful poems and created incredible artwork. They have also been fearless and passionate in making powerful speeches—things they never had done before.

One mom expressed it this way:

QUESTIONS ABOUT 9/11?
01/05/02

An old adage reads: "No Reason nor Rhyme."
But tell me God: "Was that his time?"
Why that meeting, that morning,
That room
Of all the buildings in Washington
To meet his doom
At the Pentagon
Consulting with three-star General Maud
Proposing a plan they now applaud?
Why couldn't he have finished
And begun walking away
To his car, far, far from
The horror of that
Cruel end?
When, when will I ever mend?

Others created these works of art: A: Emotional Prison; **B:** Ten stripes with one missing in my family of ten; **C:** Art created to honor loved ones.

A.

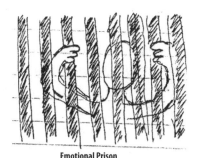

Emotional Prison

B.

C.

• **Humor**—finding the comic in the tragic.

To experience humor is indeed a resiliency, as it does counterbalance the horrific memories one will live with. Humor can relieve stress and is often related to an uplifting memory of the deceased, such as a prideful event, or a trick they played, a costume they adorned, or a happy moment. However, humor may cause co-victims to stop mid-stream or feel guilt after a spontaneous outburst of smiles, laughter, or giggles. It may be safest to express humor to inside groups, such as family or support group members.

As you will learn, **it is very important to remember your loved one's life separate from their death. They may want to be remembered this way as well.**

My girlfriends attended the arraignment with me. It was at once fascinating and difficult to see the murderer in the flesh for the first time. In order to soften the blow, we had a pizza party that night. The parrots were right on the dinner table with us, chowing down. Everybody was talking and laughing at once. (Marina)

• **Morality**—having the clarity of right and pursing actions for goodness and justice.

The online newsletter CAH, Citizens Against Homicide (2012), is a strong advocate for seeking justice.

Survivor Questions: Did you notice differences in how people around you experienced grief? Is the experience of this loss different than other losses you have had and, if so, how?

In your notebook, write down your answers.

Rose

When it came to others and their shared grief, I noticed that no one really knew how to grieve; it isn't something you are taught and prepared for. We were lucky here because of the fact that no one knew what to do except to wrap their arms around us, and they held on to us for dear life. That was exactly what we needed at that moment.

Everyone who was directly involved in the lives of my daughter and grandson was as devastated and confused as we were. We gathered together in our grief because we were the only ones who truly "got it." I can't tell you how frowned upon that was to our homicide team. But they didn't understand; we needed each other because **this was too big to carry alone**.

Our friends and family picked us up when we fell; they were there when we were lonely; they shared stories of their relationship to my daughter and grandson. **We were broken together**, *and after much time we have found some healing together.*

Not everyone showed their grief for fear it would intensify ours, and they couldn't stand to see us in any more pain than we were already experiencing. Some tried to be cheerful, which infuriated me and confused me at the same time. Some stopped saying the names of my daughter and grandson as if I heard them I would remember they were dead! **Some sat quietly on my grief bench and just let me be broken. That probably helped the most.**

I have been blessed to have a husband, father, and grandfather to my daughter and grandson that has walked this journey with me. His grief in many ways has mirrored mine, but there are many differences as well. We went into this with the promise that that monster wasn't going to take anything else from us; he already took more than we were willing to give. Our marriage is stronger now than it has ever been, and not many people are lucky enough to say that.

Three people stand out most because of the different ways they experienced grief:

1. My mother, who, although she rushed to my side the minute she heard, ended up being the last person on earth that I needed. Everything I did was wrong, from the obituary to how I reacted, and so on. At around the 3 month mark since the murders, she said I needed "to get over it." I was "just milking it!" She then spent the next 3 months talking behind my back about how crazy I was, and how I needed to shut up about it already. That ended our relationship for 7 years. In my heart of hearts, I don't think she ever experienced any grief over the loss of her granddaughter & great grandson. I don't think she knew how.

2. My father, who was by my side from the planning of the funeral to the day he passed, nearly 5 years later. My father was devastated; he was enraged; his heart was broken. His health suffered terribly; he had several strokes from the time of the murders until the time of the arrests. He didn't sleep well. This is not how he should have had to spend his last years of life, and I said that to him many times. Every time he responded, "Where else would I be but by your side; you're my daughter and I love you. I can't change any of this for you; all I can do is love and support you and that will never change." It never did.

3. My oldest sister, who has called me every day for the past 5+ years, and she was a lifeline I could not have

things, most of all how proud I was of her. I never got to say good-bye . . .

Marina

Dad's older sister was devastated. She promptly set about making Dad into some sort of saint who never did anything wrong. I got sick of it, but I managed to keep my mouth shut, for the most part. She told the same stories about him over and over again. Thirteen years later, she

---

Some sat quietly on my grief bench and just let me be broken. That probably helped the most. (Rose)

---

survived without. She allowed me to vent and to say she heard things come out of my mouth that weren't very pretty is putting it mildly, and yet she never failed to listen to me, really listen to me. She was my voice of reason, she was my mother figure, she was my sister, she was my best friend & confidant, and she loved me in spite of my brokenness. She is one of the main reasons I am standing today.

The loss of my daughter and grandson is completely different from any other loss I have ever had for so many reasons. The fact that this was all intentional. There was no time to say good-bye.

All the other losses in my life either came from a relative who died after a long and healthy life, to a friend whose death was expected as she had cancer. I had the luxury of spending quality time with her and was able to tell her all the things I wanted to say before she passed. I feel robbed and angry that I was never given the chance to tell Victoria so many

still does, but not as often. I understand. The stories are all she has left of Dad. It's poignant.

My paternal uncle just went into hibernation. He never was the same. He went to his grave after living his last fourteen years in a state of rage, confusion, and misery.

My sister and I had infrequent contact in the aftermath. She went to the funeral, then insisted upon dividing up Dad's belongings the next day. She largely avoided going back after that.

She didn't get involved with the police or the DA. No one did. It was all on me. That was hard. She was critical of Dr. Rynearson's model of therapy, and dismissed it outright. I'm sure she talked to close friends and her therapist about the murder, but I was the one who had to tell my brother-in-law's relatives how Dad died—many months after the fact. Apparently she had some sort of "gag order" in place. I assume this was her way of grappling with the unthinkable.

> *Dad was gone,*
>
> *just like that.*
>
> *Ripped away.*
>
> *I had no time*
>
> *to prepare*
>
> *for his death,*
>
> *no opportunity*
>
> *to say*
>
> *good-bye.*
>
> (Marina)

My parents were divorced in 1971, so my mom wasn't as devastated. If fact, a surprising thing happened: She actually became more charitable in her outlook towards Dad. Before the murder, and for most of my life, she knocked him. After the murder, her attention turned to my mentally retarded younger brother.

Differences in experiencing grief: The list is endless.

I am well into middle age, so I have experienced loss from natural death. My grandparents died of various chronic ailments, so there was plenty of time to come to grips of their passing. My maternal aunt died of breast cancer, but I was not close to her at the time of her death. I did visit her several times during her illness, and it was awful to see the agony and devastation wrought by the disease. But her death was still in the realm of a world I already knew.

Another relative committed suicide after an extended struggle with a terminal illness. This was when I realized that the unthinkable could happen. It was a shock, but I was not a member of the immediate family, so it did not affect me as it did them. Surely there was no involvement with law enforcement or the court system. The grief and the loss, however horrific, could at least be processed in private.

Dad was gone, just like that. Ripped away. I had no time to prepare for his death, no opportunity to say good-bye. Worse, he was dead because someone wanted him that way, and that someone was alive and kicking and out of jail on bail. I was terrified and enraged at the same time. I wanted both comfort and revenge. I was compelled to think about the nature of Dad's murder, over and over again. What happened? How was he killed? Was his death painful? Was he aware of what was happening? Did he struggle, or give up? What did the "murder room" look like? Did the killer have any help, or did she do it alone? How long did it take for Dad to die? Thoughts and images were strung together in no apparent order, and they just kept coming.

Within hours of learning of the murder, I realized there would be a trial. I have worked for years in a courthouse, so I had some sense of what was involved. But the difference was that it involved ME. It involved Dad's private life, ripped open to be picked apart and slavered over by an unknown number of strangers. It was open-ended, with no guarantees, and no time frame. I would have to see the murderer in the flesh, in public, and somehow find a way to control myself.

I found myself incarcerated in a cell fashioned by the volitional act of another human being. No one seemed to hold the key that would unlock the door to my prison. Perhaps no key had ever been made. **I was doomed to a life sentence for a crime I did not commit.**

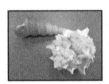

Harrier

I witnessed the full spectrum of grief, from the uncontrolled sobbing of a female friend of my parents to rigid stoicism from male counterparts. A sister, to this day, maintains a fantasy that our parents are merely on an extended trip and will one day return. One of my mother's brothers, refuses to discuss it. He, too, treats it as if they were still alive, living in a faraway place.

I have experienced many losses over the years, but the sudden, violent nature of my parents' deaths has had a much greater impact on me than those resulting from natural death.

I only came to grips with it three decades later when an incident triggered the emotions I thought I had buried forever. Anger and rage consumed me. I could not work without alienating others; I lost my job; I contemplated suicide. I sought professional counseling and was diagnosed with PTSD. Only through counseling with therapists trained in working with violent loss did I

come to grips with and control the emotions that took over my life.

Kaila

I have experienced people dying due to age, illness, and suicide. And although tragic, I've been able to cope much easier.

Halia

I was extremely close to my sister. We grew up together, endured some very difficult childhood experiences together, and were just beginning to navigate the waters of adult life when she was torn from our lives. There still remains a gaping hole there that nothing or no one will ever begin to be able to fill. This kind of loss and pain, it never goes away. **The emotional landscape of it shifts like the sands of time when shaken up in an egg timer.**

I learned that my 35-year-old son had experienced nightmares from the time my sister was murdered; he was four at the time. He wrote to the Judge saying that he did not want to attend the sentencing because, for the first time in his life knowing the perpetrator was behind bars, he no longer dreamt that the killer was coming after him as well.

There were others in the circle of my sister's life who simply could not attend the hearing because they held too much emotion to be in the same courthouse with the killer.

In 2002, my brother was found shot to death. They labeled it a suicide. To this day I believe it was murder. After a month of haggling with in-laws, he was finally buried.

After that **I felt betrayed by any society that would take two of my siblings. I disengaged and withdrew from societal structure, lived in my vehicle for five months**.

In 2003, my Grandmother died. She had raised my sister and me, so losing her was like losing a part of my sister all over again. **When they lowered the casket, I wanted to jump in with her**, and I had to be physically escorted away from her graveside because I could not leave on my own.

JJ
By way of contrast, my surviving son has declined to participate in groups, saying that he doesn't want to listen to other people's problems. The challenge for me is to understand and accept his position and not tell him what he should do, while continuing to hope for something better for him.

The death of grandparents and parents seem to fit with my old worldview. Even the loss of my sister to cancer could be assimilated. My son's death at 25 is tragic to everyone else, but it has disrupted my entire view of things in a profound way. Bad things happened before, but to other people. Now there is evil around every corner, and **I view my own life in a much more temporary sense than I ever thought possible**.

Survivor Questions: What was your experience with counseling and peer support services? What helped in those early days? What helps now? Do you have any tips for others?

Write down your answers in your notebook.

Rose
Trust your own instincts. If someone isn't the right therapist for you, find the one who is. Ask them if they specialize in violent death and how many clients they have worked with who have experienced a violent death. In other words, interview them. They are going to play a crucial part in your journey, and you have to feel confident and trusting when it comes to this person.

Same goes for a psychiatrist and a support group. If something doesn't feel right for you, look for something that does. **Ask other people that have experienced this sort of loss what they did, where did they find help**, what groups did they go to, and what were their experiences on this journey.

Since I had zero "tools" to guide me through this, **I read everything I could get my hands on** that had to do with surviving the VIOLENT loss of a child, grandchild (not much out there on this), and any other type of grief book I could find.

I wrote in a journal all the time because I couldn't keep my thoughts straight and having something in writing to refer back to was very important in the beginning. I didn't sleep often so I spent a lot of time on the computer trying to stop the blogs &

forums from writing about my daughter and grandson.

Fortunately, I also had a support team like no other. From the moment the news broke about the murders, I was surrounded by a network of friends and family, and my daughter's friends as well.

Our support system incorporated us into their lives. They held us up when we couldn't stand on our own; they listened without judgment (for the most part); they helped plan and attended every event at the cemetery that celebrated some milestone for my daughter and grandson. When the trial started, we were never alone; the court room was always full of our supporters.

Fast forward, and I no longer spend my time trying to find answers on the computer, or the blogs, or anywhere else for that matter. *I still have a lot of the same support system all these years later, and many new ones that I can turn to at a moment's notice.*

I see color again *and find peace in my garden. I couldn't appreciate it before, but now I see life blooming right in front of me.*

I got a dog*, and although I was afraid to be responsible for its life when mine was such a mess, I have found that I had nothing to worry about here.*

I also work in the community*, now trying to help others who have found themselves in these shoes. I take great pride in this type of work, and I know it's where I have found my purpose. There is something to be said about getting out of yourself and helping others. For me I get back so much more than I could ever give.*

Marina

My only advice is to find help! *Do not put it off. I know that I would have found a modicum of healing and resolution without the specialized therapy. Doubtless my recovery would not have been as rich or as profound. I use the word "recovery" with some caution, because one never really recovers from murder. One learns how to manage it. Therapy gave me the tools for this lifelong occupation.*

Nowadays I don't even think of the murder for long periods of time. *When I remember how bad things were fifteen years ago, and look at how satisfying and fulfilling my life is now, I know I have undergone recovery from what I consider a potentially fatal illness.*

I went into group and individual therapy within two months of Dad's murder.

Therapy lent structure and meaning to my grieving process. *I was compelled to talk about the murder with anyone who would listen, and it helped. But it was far more fruitful to discuss it with a therapist who understood the exact nature of traumatic loss. A therapist without extensive training and experience in violent death could have made matters far, far worse.*

My work as a volunteer child-abuse case assessor for a local non-profit helped. *It was incredibly difficult, but it bolstered my sense of self-worth.* ***There is no better way to help yourself than to help others.***

After the arraignment, my girl-friends and I went to my Dad's house. I brought my Amazon parrots along, as they were quite familiar with the house. Their apparent indifference restored a sense of normalcy.

Dad's house was on a golf course, and when we heard the sprinklers go on later that night, we ran through them and got soaking wet. It was fun! It confirmed **that it is vital to find a way to laugh and play, even in the midst of profound trauma.**

Back home, **I went to a local dog beach just to watch the canines play.** *I admired their ability to go from one thing to the next uninhibitedly. I took up porcelain painting because I found it relaxing. It was nice to have a tangible product of that relaxation.*

Harrier

I did not seek counseling or peer support other than meeting with family members. I was tough. I could handle it—provided I had plenty of alcohol on hand. Only 30 years later did I learn that I suffered from post-traumatic stress and that it tainted my everyday life and relationships; I felt angry much of the time and did not understand how others could just shrug off things that left me outraged.

I recommend that everyone who suffers a violent loss, and especially a

---

I have pictures of them in happy moments, and I look at those pictures when I'm feeling depressed.

Being alone was great when I wanted to cry, though. I screamed, moaned, wailed, and sobbed. **I allowed myself to collapse on the floor, or curl up in a ball and rock back and forth if it felt right.**

I danced a lot, *mostly alone. I had done this for years. I played really frenetic music and leaped about to the point of exhaustion.*

Exercise was vital. I worked out every day. *Once in a while it didn't help at all, but most of the time it did. Experience had already taught me that poor nutrition and a lack of exercise could result in depression and low self-worth. Murder is a battle—war, if you will. I figured this soldier was going to go into it fit and well fed, if nothing else.*

Self-care was important, too. I went to the drug store and bought facials in little foil packets. **I painted my toenails with crazy colors.** *Things like this put me in the moment and slowed me down.*

criminal death, to **get professional counseling from therapists trained specifically in this field.**

I talked a lot with one of my sisters, and we both drank a lot. She did get some counseling, and she said it helped, but when we got together, we cried a lot and we both got drunk.

Through the Survivors of Violent Loss Program, **I learned to visualize positive images of my parents, of them smiling and enjoying life, rather than reimagining their deaths.** *I have pictures of them in happy moments, and I look at those pictures periodically, particularly when I'm feeling depressed.*

I no longer attend funeral services *unless it's for a family member or a very close friend. The services bring up too much emotion related to my parents.*

When emotions threaten to overwhelm me, I use relaxation techniques, breathing exercises, **take walks, or lose myself in a simple computer game.**

Kaila

Meeting the Survivors of Violent Loss Program was the best thing that could have happened to me. The counseling was hard every time, but I left the group with a sense of "I am not the only one this has happened to," and it felt good knowing that I could relate to other people that also thought they were crazy.

What helped in those earlier days was counseling and having one other person that saw everything I went through and supported me through it all. Today I understand human behavior, which allows me to enjoy life a lot better.

Yvonne

The first hours following homicide are critical, lifelong memories are forever be embedded in one's mind at this time. In the first few hours following our discovery, we were brought into the Police Headquarters for questioning. We were two terrified children disbelieved, shocked, and confused.

Not only did we not have our father, any family, or friends present, but we sat among complete strangers attempting to console us, which was far from comforting.

Had we been offered some sort of comfort, a female detective or authority present, we'd have fared much better in the investigation. How were we to be trustful of strangers, men expecting us to answer personal questions about our parents' relationship?

If we had had something as simple as a therapy dog or a female figure there, I believe it would have brought some sense of calm to two terrified children. Juvenile traumatic grief counseling or support was not offered that I was aware of. I'm convinced that some of our longstanding issues could have been easily dealt with had we received the proper support. It may be that longstanding issues with episodic PTSD, depression, and alcohol as a means of escape could have been somewhat curtailed. It is for this reason that I believe the presence of a crisis counselor is essential following the loss of a family member to homicide.

Not only did our experience with the justice system go terribly wrong, early in our loss our father had approached the local parish our mother had attended on a regular basis, believing that with their help we'd receive emotional support to get us through the crisis. As I recall, we were offered little to no help. In turn, I lost faith in the church. This lack of support left a lasting impression on my ability to trust the church for guidance and counseling.

Overwhelmed with two young children, my father didn't know where to go for help. I never knew if, consumed by pride, he convinced himself that he didn't need counseling. My father's support system came from his close friends. I couldn't blame him if it was pure distrust of an unjust Justice System. He was on a journey of complete distrust and isolation in an unimaginable hell he didn't deserve, left with two children to raise on his own.

Halia

Over the last 30 years, I have been through counseling off and on a number of times. I have gone through Cognitive Therapy, DBT for Depression, Individual, and Group. While they have all been helpful in one way or another, what has been extremely beneficial and dialed in specifically to the issues is the 10-week Restorative Retelling Group at the Survivor's of Violent Loss Program in San Diego.

The group I was in was a particularly small group, and it allowed for the building of trust, bonding, doing some very intensive work, and the making of a lifelong friend. **I have a much higher level of resiliency from the individual and group therapy I did at SVLP.**

appreciate the changes I am experiencing. My wife and I were lucky enough to have an established relationship with this counselor before our son's murder. If you are searching for a counselor, I would recommend you not be afraid to try several to see where there is a good match.

The peer support services have been a lifeline for me, not only because of the meetings, but also the resource net that I have become aware of as a result.

Reading helped because I could get information without having to

---

I find that there are activities that successfully distract me now. (JJ)

What helped in the early days was staying busy, getting sober, going to therapy, and the kind and gentle voice of others who would share their experiences of loss with just enough detail and hope so that I, too, knew that others both knew my pain and had survived it as well.

What helps now is giving back to others, staying sober, self-care, self-care, self-care, therapy, SVLP support group meetings, prayer, meditation, walks on the beach, and recognizing that the duality exists—some people make choices that end lives that affect others and cause grave emotional and mental pain that is survivable one day, hour, minute, and nano-second at a time.

 **JJ**
My experience with counseling and peer support groups has been very positive. Even though I have brought my counselor to tears on numerous occasions, it has been a shared experience and he has helped me recognize feelings and better

be with people, and yet there were other times when crying in the group was a blessing. **Hearing about my son through his peers was wonderfully uplifting**, although not all of the stories would have qualified him for sainthood. Spending a Thanksgiving holiday knowing that the murderers were still at large, potentially sitting down at a table with their families, while our son was gone forever, hurt deeply. When they were apprehended, there was a sense of relief.

I still read frequently, some grief-centered works and some other works. I find that there are activities that successfully distract me now. **I also have reached the point where I do not judge my emotions. They are what they are and I need to acknowledge them rather than judging them.** They will appear unexpectedly and often for no reason. I also find music soothing and uplifting; it can change my mood dramatically.

Resources

Books

And I Don't Want to Live This Life, Deborah Spungen. Ballantine Books, 1996. The true story of a mother and her experience with the loss of her daughter. This story leads her into a life mission of advocacy for other murder victims whom she found in her community.

Children Mourning, Mourning Children, edited by Kenneth J. Doka. A practical book with tips on how to help children of different ages, with additional tips for the school.

The Healing Journey Through Grief, Phil Rich. Wiley, 1999. Recommended by one of our Survivor Writers who found it helpful, as it has places to write your experience as you go. She found it very helpful to look back and see how far she had come.

Coping With the Sudden Death of Your Loved One: A Self-Help Handbook for Traumatic Bereavement, Therese A. Rando, Dog Ear Publishing (in press).

I Remember You, a grief journal, Laynee Wild. L O a Pubns, 2000. A book of empty pages with words of inspiration for you to write your experiences in. This book was recommended by one of my survivor clients in hopes that it would help others as it helped her.

The Journey: An Adult Self-Help Workbook Kit, Ten Steps to Learning to Live With Violent Death, Connie Saindon. C. Saindon, 2008. http://www.svlp.org.

Lament for a Son, Nicholas Wolterstorff. Eerdmans Publishing Company, 1987.

Point of Fracture: Voices of Heinous-Crime Survivors, Amy Zuckerman, Karen Nystedt. A. Zuckerman, 1998.

Reactions: A Workbook To Help Young People Who Are Experiencing Trauma and Grief, Alison Salloum, whose work has been a leader in helping children. Compassion Books. http://www.compassionbooks.com.

The Resilient Self: How Survivors of Troubled Families Rise Above Adversity, Steven and Sybil Wolin. Villard, 1993.

Retelling Violent Death, Edward Rynearson, MD. Brunner/Routledge, 2001.

When Families Grieve, a Sesame Street Kit. In Spanish and English, a well-done instructional guide that includes a DVD and booklet to guide discussion with younger children, narrated by Katie Couric. http://www.sesameworkshop.org/grief.

Online

Citizens Against Homicide online newsletter
 http://www.citizensagainsthomicide.org.

Parents of Murdered Children, Inc.®; http://www.pomc.org.

* Some Web addresses may have changed since publication.

3

Dealing With the News Media, Social Media and Public Stories

We can't choose to not have this horrible thing happen to us. . . . But we can choose how we react to it. Please respect our need to be alone and . . . have that personal time to continue on our journey of grief in the way that serves us.
—First Selectman Pat Llodra
Newtown, Connecticut, Dec. 9, 2013

So far, you have been asked what happened, how you are managing, and ways your resilience is shown. Now the focus is on helping you interact with others, especially the news media. Most people, reporters in particular, want information about what happened and "who did it?" We want you to be able to tell them who your loved one was, not only as a murder victim, but as a living, breathing person.

This demand for information occurs when you may be engulfed in the hailstorm of grief and confusion, with many other competing and compelling demands. People will say the darnedest things, including unnecessary yet hurtful remarks.

As with other topics we cover, this area can become overwhelming. Keep in mind what you identified in the previous chapter: your resiliencies, what you rely on to help you. You may be surprised when new strengths emerge as well.

Where to Begin

It would be a mistake to not guide you in describing your loved one. In preparation for talking to others, it is important to identify who your loved one was and what you want others to know about them. Remind people of their name and what was important to them. We know that recalling your loved one is a double-edged sword, as this is coupled with recalling what happened. However, who they were will help buffer what you can't stop thinking and seeing in your minds about their death.

The public is learning about what happened to your loved one. It is important that you have some say about how they are described.

Survivor Question: Who was your loved one?

In your notebook, write down who they were: at home, at school or work, and in the community. What did they do for fun? What was important to them?

Many of our survivors tell us that no one asked this question before. The focus has been on what happened, who did it, and what is the update on the crime.

This question is vital when it comes to dealing with the news media, social media, and others. It may be very hard to talk about your loved one's life as their death absorbs your focus and attention. The public is learning about what happened to them. It is important that you have some say about how they are described.

It may be useful to have conversations with other people who knew them, such as family members, friends, neighbors, peers. Ask people to write down what they remember. We provide many tips and ideas from a variety of sources for you and your family to use as a guide in dealing with the news and social media later in this chapter.

What Words Describe Your Loved One?

If you are having difficulty trying to think of what to say, that's understandable. Here are some prompts to help you. You are not limited to these words:

funny, loving, curious, adorable, honest, leader, well-liked

Write down some things you would like others to know about your loved one as it relates to their . . .

- Role in family
- Favorite story
- Activities (play, school, work)
- Hobbies/activities
- Dreams and aspirations
- Accomplishments

Accomplishment examples from our Survivor Writers:

- hard worker
- angel on earth
- sold a company he founded to a large corporation
- built his own house and sailboat
- volunteered for many nonprofit organizations
- a people person
- committed to being a perfect Mom
- fished for squid for food
- finished beauty school

Rose

I have often thought that my daughter, Victoria, was born an adult; I guess the term would be an old soul. When she was a little girl, she loved to read most of all. She also loved to play dress-up and wear those plastic high-heel shoes that had just come out for girls. **Her favorite game to play was "store,"** and she would put prices on her belongings, and I would come in with fake money and buy stuff from her. She loved the cash register and making change; she loved playing with money. She said when she grew up she was going to be a cashier. The funny thing is that for a brief time she was a cashier at a grocery store.

Simply put, our grandson, **Louis, was "an Angel on Earth."** He was so beautiful; his eyes sparkled and his smile melted your heart. He was the missing link in our family that we didn't even know we were missing until he arrived. He took forever to learn how to crawl; **his head was heavier than his body so he crawled backward for a time**, dragging his head on the carpet. When he couldn't get somewhere fast enough, he would just roll over to where he wanted to be.

Victoria's love of reading continued till the day she died. She didn't like educational books; she liked romance novels or mysteries. We had some of our best times lying in bed, before she was pregnant and while she was pregnant, reading a book and exchanging them with each other so after we had both read the same book, we could have our own personal book review.

There was no rhyme or reason to how she chose her friends. She didn't like cliques in school; she didn't run with the popular crowd, or the so-called nerds. She was not a loner, either. If you were the new kid, she was one of the first people to introduce herself and show you around.

Victoria was a hard worker and more than once a boss of hers would say she had the strongest work ethic they had seen in such a young person. Clothes didn't have to be designer labels, but she loved shopping. It was my least favorite thing to do, but I would go to any mall at any time just to be with her and Louis and watch her eyes light up when she found a cute pair of jeans or a darling outfit for him.

My daughter never drank, she never did a drug, she didn't go to bars, she had never been in a club, and she didn't hang out with the wrong crowd. She was a single mother who loved her son, and she was struggling financially. **She took responsibility for Louis and the fact that she chose to have him. She didn't have a mean bone in her body;** she didn't want to hurt anybody. I think one of the hardest things she ever had to do was swallow her pride and ask for child support. However, having child support would afford her the ability to feed him, diaper him, clothe him, provide day care while she worked. She had dreams that were attainable. Murder was not one of them.

Marina

Dad was a "larger than life" personality. His charisma, warmth, and intelligence were hard to miss. When he walked into a room, the energy level rose perceptibly. People loved being in his presence and sought him out for advice, or just the latest shaggy dog story. He adored the latter.

Dad was born to parents who fled the Mexican Revolution in the early decades of the twentieth century. The family was desperately poor. My paternal grand-

father was an extremely handsome ne'er do well who couldn't be bothered to support his wife and children. As the oldest male child, Dad was expected to pitch in, and he did. By the age of eight he was hawking newspapers to longshoremen. It must have been a rough and tumble existence, but Dad liked the money, and he liked selling.

He longed to get out of the barrio, and dreamed of becoming an airplane mechanic. At the age of 15, he lied about his age in an attempt to enlist in the Army. He was found out and kicked out, but he managed

roni-and-cheese days" and "Di-Gel nights." At the beginning, he made cold calls in the Pentagon by walking through endless corridors in search of an open door or a friendly smile. I cannot imagine the humiliations and setbacks he must have endured. Yet he persisted.

Fourteen years later, he sold out to a large corporation. *I thought he would become a world traveler, spending his days on golf courses and his nights in the finest restaurants. But he couldn't stop. He was always chasing the dream. I wish he hadn't.*

I cannot imagine the humiliations and setbacks he must have endured. Yet he persisted. (Marina)

---

to enlist when he came of age. **He went into the Army Corps of Engineers, where he made Officer Candidate School.** *He became a Second Lieutenant, which was an endless source of pride.*

Dad was a "can-do" sort of guy. After the Korean War, he used the GI Bill to attend community college. He picked up enough engineering know-how to find a job in the nascent aerospace industry. He loved it at first, but in time he became bored. He slowly realized that he enjoyed marketing and sales more. His conversancy with engineering was a huge help in closing deals with various private and government entities. But that wasn't enough, either. He knew he was smarter than his bosses, and it stung him to hit the glass ceiling and find he could rise no further as long as he worked for someone else.

Against my mother's wishes, **he scraped together enough money to start a high-tech electronics firm**. *He specialized in defense contracting. It wasn't easy.* **He struggled through "maca-**

He became an "angel investor," looking for start-up companies to grow and sell for a profit. *He did really well with some investments, but heavy drinking, insecurity, and pride extracted a price. People took advantage of his generosity, and he started to lose enormous amounts of money. We tried two separate interventions, but they didn't take.*

After the stroke, he became more despondent. He went from being energetic and optimistic to being paranoid and intolerant. Any attempt at honest conversation was cut short.

In the end, a predator smelled blood and took over his life, slowly cutting him off from all he held dear. I could not understand how a man who walked with presidents and generals could come to such an ignominious end.

In the intervening years, the memories have trickled back. Dad was such a bright flame. When I was a child, he was just plain fun. The kids in the neighborhood flocked to him because he loved

66

to organize games and instigate mischief. He was an unrepentant practical joker and an excellent storyteller. He loved to dance, and he did it well. He instilled in me a love of people and a never-ending fascination with their foibles.

He gave me experiences more than he gave me things. **He taught me to be a competent and independent person,** though he sure didn't like it when I used my confidence to defy or disagree with him!

One morning not long after the murder, I looked into the mirror. To my surprise, I saw him looking back. There was his smile, and his optimism. The intelligence was irrepressible, as was the keen grasp of human nature. I have never lost the fascination for the world and its cultures that he instilled in me. And he loved to laugh! To this day, when I hear a good joke, I imagine how hard Dad would laugh if he could hear it.

Harrier

My parents loved and lived life. My father built houses, including the house where I grew up, situated on nearly 2 acres of land and surrounded by woods, where I spent many delightful hours as boy. **He built a 53-foot sailboat** to take the family on an extended cruise to the South Pacific. He was generous to a fault, always willing to lend a hand to those in need. He joined the Elks Club and helped to integrate the previously all-white organization in the mid-1960s.

My mother grew up on a small farm and yearned for a more adventuresome life. She ended up a housewife caring for five children, but she made time for adult athletics and volunteered with the American Red Cross, Cystic Fibrosis Foundation, and the Children's Hospital Ortho-

pedic Guild.

Every summer, under her supervision, we canned fruit and made jam; she baked wonderful pies, cakes, and cookies. One of my fondest memories is of canning peaches in the backyard; we used wood-fired stoves because Dad had only just begun building the house. I'm sure Mom hated it, but as an eight-year-old, it thought it was good fun.

My parents took us swimming and waterskiing in the summer and at one point **my father built a vacation cabin near a small lake, where we spent many a weekend and summer days.**

These are the memories I choose to recall.

Kaila

My sister was a free spirit. She loved to travel and was a people person—where ever she went, **she made friends who treated her like family.**

Yvonne

Over many years, what remains in my memory are disturbing, frozen images of our mother and the last time I saw her. These prevailing images and memories of how we lost our mother erased almost all of my childhood memories.

Any remaining pictures were hidden away or destroyed in an attempt to protect us. Maybe it was for the best, because I cannot see pictures of her to this day; the disturbing images of what we'd seen that day remain. It's almost like a cruel joke that the smiles and joy of her in any remaining photographs are completely replaced in my mind by the look of terror on her face. What remains are

> *Funny, it's the imperfections that I remember most and love about her.*
>
> *She'd poke fun at herself, and her moments of laughter are the happy memories that remain and I cherish.*
>
> (Yvonne)

recurring images that I cannot change despite any images of happier times.

My mother did everything in her power to take good care of us. It saddens me that she always put our needs before hers. Her children were her pride; she loved us deeply. Funny, it's the imperfections that I remember most and love about her. She'd poke fun at herself, and her moments of laughter are the happy memories that remain and I cherish. I remember the comfort food she'd prepare, the sense of home.

While she'd do anything for us, it broke my heart to see her so unhappy; she worried constantly. She was frustrated and desperate to return to her hometown and country. We were the only reason she remained here; it was evident that she was unhappy in her marriage. Here her life became one of isolation, with the exception of a few friends.

When she visited her home town, she'd transform into a completely different person. She'd smile and laugh with her sister, family, and friends. I wanted to see her happy forever and was willing to return with her. Less than a month after our last visit to her home, she was gone. She deserved that dream, but never had the opportunity.

Halia

D. was 24 years old when she was murdered. She was a mother, daughter, sister, and friend to many. **She was the type of person who would go out of her way to help others** and make personal sacrifices to do so. **She loved to fish** off the Huntington Beach pier often catching Squid fish and preparing many Asian dishes. Her favorite color was blue.

To know D. was to also know that she had a tougher side and could at times be found in biker bars playing darts, getting into an occasional brawl—usually landing on her feet.

At the time of her death she was in an abusive relationship and had an escape plan in place. However, before she was able to follow through with it, her life was cut short.

Dealing with the News Media

The news media may be one of the most challenging obstacles family members have to deal with following a criminal death. Sadly, an unwritten rule of thumb in the news business, especially with television, is "If it bleeds, it leads." A microphone is instantly shoved in the face of the most distraughtly bereaved. Homicide takes a family from being ordinary citizens to being household names. As disgusting as this sounds, it is a fact of life you cannot change. You have a right not to talk to the news media (see Victim's Media Rights), but weigh that decision carefully.

If you don't talk to reporters, you lose control of your message.

Talking to the media is not easy when you are grieving the traumatic death of a loved one. You have no clue whom to trust or what to say. You may just want to be left alone. However, if you or a family spokesperson do not speak, then the reporters will talk to others. They may interview a disgruntled neighbor, co-worker, or even the as-yet unidentified killer.

She died the subject of ridicule and scorn. The press called her Nauseating Nancy. Their story made it seem like she had "asked for it." They make it seem like she got what she deserved. In life, the media had made my daughter into a distasteful celebrity; in death, they made her a freak.
—Deborah Spungen, author
And I Don't Want to Live This Life

What to do? Turn the tables and take advantage of it.

Make the media your ally rather than your enemy.

Use the opportunity to tell the story you want to be told about your loved one. It could result in a tastefully written obituary that portrays your loved one's life in a positive light and does not dwell on the tragic death.

In addition, this is your chance to correct errors, misstatements, and misrepresentations that have been published or broadcast in relation to your loved one's death.

The important thing is controlling the message. This requires someone from the family, or someone who represents the family, to be pro-active and take charge of the interviews. Ask the investigation team if they have any guidelines for you when talking with the media. Each situation is different and you don't want to hinder the attempt by law enforcement to do their job. Consulting an attorney may be helpful and can be wise in special situations, such as when a family member is also a suspect in the case.

> *The family was amazed at how easy it was for the Press to get unlisted phone numbers and other info. They and the police were all over the neighborhood interviewing folks.* (Porch, 1997)

As the first anniversary of the mass murder of 26 students and teachers at Sandy Hook Elementary School in Newtown, Connecticut, approached, the town asked the news media "for privacy and a restrained media presence."

In a statement to the press, First Selectman Pat Llodra said, "We can't choose to not have this horrible thing happen to us. It happened. We cannot make it un-happen. But we can choose how we react to it. Please respect our need to be alone and to be quiet and to have that personal time to continue on our journey of grief in the way that serves us."

For the most part, the news media honored that request. Had the survivors and the community as a whole not taken this pre-emptive action, in all likelihood the town would have been overrun with TV trucks and camera crews trying to capitalize on this horrific tragedy.

True-Crime Writers

Murder is mostly played out in newspapers or newscasts, but also in books and magazines. This is because the public's interest in murder is strong: In 2013, Amazon.com listed 86,771 references to murder in books and 12,216 in TV and movies. It is less common for these references to include the lives of real families and what they must live with.

Some authors have exploited these horrific events by writing accounts without interviewing anyone in the family; unfortunately, they have the legal right to do so.

They also have an obligation to the get facts right. The death and loss is difficult enough for families to bear, but they may be additionally traumatized by inaccuracies and the liberties taken in published accounts of a loved one's death.

If your loved one's death has sensational aspects to it, it's quite possible that someone will write a "true-crime" account of it, either as a lengthy magazine article, a full-length book, or a TV show. True-crime writers are often news reporters or former news reporters, and they have a legal right to write about events that occurred. They can do it without your permission or cooperation.

Some writers and producers are more respectful and tasteful than others. You may not have any choice over who writes the story, unless you take the initiative and seek out a writer and/or publisher, or TV producer.

There are advantages and disadvantages to having a true-crime account written/produced about your family's tragedy. The advantage is that you will have the opportunity to talk about your loved one in your own words, and it may give you some control over what gets published or shown on TV. It could become a living legacy for your loved one. The disadvantage is that if you prefer to keep the matter private, you may not have any input and you may not like what's been written or produced.

Generally, a writer or producer will approach the family and request interviews. This may occur before the criminal proceedings are concluded. I recommend that you at least meet with the writer or producer and listen to the proposal.

Ask questions: What are your credentials? Have you written previous books? Who is the publisher? Who is the editor? Have you produced similar TV shows? What TV show or network are you with? Then do some research to verify what you've been told and get more information on the background and reputation of the writer or producer.

Do not expect to get paid. True crime writers and TV producers see themselves as journalists and will not pay their sources. You may request that a portion of the proceeds be donated to a charitable organization, but even that's a long shot.

True-crime writers have a legal right to write about events that occurred. They can do it without your permission or cooperation.

Some family members have written their own books, and you may consider this. But unless you have the skills to do so, seriously consider working with a professional writer, editor, and publisher.

Whatever you do, think about it carefully and do not make a hasty or ill-advised decision. In one case, where two teenage girls were raped and murdered by a serial rapist, one of the families refused to cooperate with the writer. The murdered girl's mother wanted to write her own book and refused to be interviewed. The girl's father demanded payment for his contributions, and when the writer refused to pay him, he refused to cooperate. Ultimately, they had no direct input to the book, and the writer relied on statements made to the news media and other, perhaps less reliable, sources.

After the book was published, the parents protested and disrupted book signing events, creating a public spectacle. The net result: Their daughter's death, and life, were overshadowed by her parents' antics, which in turn shined a brighter spotlight on the book.

In another instance, a family member, who also happened to be the prime suspect in the FBI's murder investigation into his parents' deaths, signed a contract with a movie production company without telling his brother or sisters. When the siblings found about the movie deal, they had little choice but to sign contracts as well. Otherwise, they would have had no input into the story being told about their dead parents and family. This led to a further disintegration of the family in the aftermath of violent loss.

In his book ***Dare I Call It Murder: A Memoir of Violent Loss*** (2013), Larry Edwards describes how he learned of a true-crime book that contained an account of his parents' deaths:

> I answered the phone and [my sister] Aileen barely let me say hello. "There's a book . . . about Mom and Dad," she said between sobs. "You have to do something."

I'd heard of people who said their skin crawled in reaction to a sudden fear. At that moment, I knew what they meant. My skin crawled; my gut Gordian knotted; I could barely breathe. . . .

Why now, after all these years?

Written by Ann Rule, the book *But I Trusted You and Other True Cases* comprised a collection of stories about Pacific Northwest murders. The second story—"Death in Paradise: The Haunting Voyage of the Spellbound"—featured our parents. No one in our family had been interviewed or forewarned of the book by the Seattle-based author. It had come out of the blue, from left field, fallen from the sky. Pick your cliché. We'd been blindsided. . . .

Not long after our parents died, the rumor mill posited that a true-crime writer had a book in the pipeline, but we never heard any more about it. Until that night. Aileen had purchased the book after being alerted by a childhood friend.

"It's filled with mistakes, especially about Mom," she said. "From her car accident to how she met Dad to how she died."

"What else?"

I heard her flip through the pages. "It says no one had heard from them for almost ten days."

"That sounds more like Gilligan's Island." . . .

Aileen read more passages to me, her words boozy and broken by frequent sobs. Some of the errors niggled but were inconsequential. However, the descriptions of how and why our parents died perpetuated the inaccuracies published in news accounts thirty-one years earlier.

Ann Rule said Dad had been struck on the head by the boat's out-of-control boom and died almost instantly. Never mind that Gary had changed his story when talking to the FBI, and I never heard Gary or Kerry say that Dad had died instantly. Rule described the wound over Kerry's right eye, omitting the more serious of the two wounds—the wound doctors said could not have been caused by an accident.

"That's not journalism; it's a joke," I said.

In another instance, an unauthorized movie was made about the death of Deborah Spungen's daughter. Later, in a "60 Minutes" interview (winter 1997) about her well-known program, the Antiviolence Partnership in Philadelphia, she said that some people congratulate her while others accuse her of selling her story. She says that neither she nor anyone in her family had anything to do with the movie, and she refuses to ever see it. She says she has her own horrible memories, and she doesn't need to add to them someone else's fictitious account of what happened.

Know Your Rights

You have rights, and you should insist that the news media respect these rights. Below are your rights in dealing with the news media, as well as tips and strategies.

You are entitled to:

- Be treated with dignity, courtesy and respect.
- Grieve in private.
- Refuse to provide an interview.
- Refuse to answer inappropriate questions.
- Exclude children from interviews.
- Appoint a spokesperson who will speak on your behalf.
- Issue your own statement to the press.
- Conduct on-television interview using a silhouette or give a newspaper interview without having a photograph taken.
- Request specific reporters or decline to speak to specific reporters.
- Ask to review a story before it appears, if there is time.
- Ask the news media to use restraint in revealing the identity of child victims or witnesses, especially in sensitive cases.
- Request that offensive visuals be omitted from a story.
- File a complaint with a reporter's employer, victim service providers or the police if you feel harassed by reporters.
- Seek a correction if a report contains inaccurate information.

Social Media

Social media—Facebook, Pinterest, Twitter, texting, blogging, and so on—is increasingly a major forum for social contact. Anyone can view your profile. This means anyone, people you like and don't like and people you know and don't know. You can and should change this by making changes in the privacy settings on these websites. Word gets out quickly and can have a force of its own whether the information is true or not.

What you do have control over is what you send out or submit to a blog or discussion forum, such as Facebook. As suggested above, people can respond by saying many things, and there is little you can do about it. We talk later about the implications and risks when a case goes to trial. Here it is important that you see your social media communications as public information that can go anywhere and to anyone, with little control on your part.

As a word of caution, never disclose private information such as birthdates, marital status, and personal photographs. It is also not a place to rant and vent, although it may be very tempting to do so. The cost to you may be much more than your need to talk about your loved one right now.

Tips and Strategies

You have the right NOT to talk to the media; however, it's probably better if you do. You set the time and place—and be prepared. These guidelines will help you organize your thoughts and decide what to say:

- **Choose a photo** or two of your loved one and make it available as a print and an electronic image file.
- **Appoint a spokesperson.** If you are too emotional, this can be a trusted family member, close friend, attorney, representative of your faith, or public relations professional.
- **Write a statement** from the family and provide biographical information of your loved one to hand out to reporters; make it available as an electronic file that can be sent by email.
- **Write "talking points"** for quick reference when being interviewed, but limit this to three to five key points that can be easily and quickly stated.
- **Talk in "sound bites,"** which are short sentences that quickly make your point and allow ease in quoting.
- **Do not agree to be recorded or videotaped unless you are prepared. If you get "ambushed"** by a reporter, try not to be defensive; take charge. If you are not prepared to talk, politely decline and offer to schedule an interview at a more convenient time and in a more appropriate setting.

Definitions

Talking points: brief statements that summarize the most important information you want an audience to know, written simply and clearly. For example:

- My sister, Tiny, was murdered by a monster this week.
- She was a sweet, innocent girl.
- She was well known for her good deeds.
- Tiny was to graduate that day from Beauty School.

Media/news release: a written statement directed at the larger audience of the media source, such as TV, radio, newspapers, or the Web. (See **Resources** at the end of the chapter to find more guidelines and examples).

Sound bites: short, clear sentences with a pause between them. Practice saying these in advance in the comfort and privacy of your home. For example:

December 8, 1961, Topsham, Maine: My sister, Tiny, was murdered by a monster this week. She was a sweet, innocent girl. Tiny was well known for her good deeds. She was to graduate that day from Beauty School. Find her killer so other girls will feel safe. Call the police right now if you can help them.

What to Say . . .

In your notebook, write up a few "talking points"—the topics that are most important to you and your family. This will help you stay focused.

Examples:

- This is a tragedy; [name(s)]_____ did not deserve to die.
- He/She/They was/were . . . fulfilling their dream, just finished school, adorable, loved by many . . . [List the positive traits and accomplishments of your loved one.]
- We want to see justice served.
- We are cooperating with the police/law enforcement in every way possible.
- If you know something, please tell the police . . .
- Please correct the errors or misrepresentations [if any] in prior news coverage.
- Please respect our privacy.
- We're not able to talk with you right now. Let's set up a better time.

Survivor Question: What has been your experience with the news media regarding your story?

In your notebook, write down your experiences with the news media, good and bad.

Rose

For us, the media was a double-edged sword, and we, of course, were ill prepared. We were lucky that the media stayed away from us in the beginning, but the media coverage of the murders was on every TV channel, from the night of the murders when I didn't know it was my daughter and grandson, through the next day, only by that afternoon, they had names to go along with the details.

On day three, I heard a reporter say that my grandson had been hung in his crib. The wind was knocked right out of me, and I screamed, "Noooo!" I called my Sergeant and asked him to tell me it wasn't true. He said he couldn't, that it was true.

To this day I recall that newscaster and what he said, and I am still haunted by that. I am sure he didn't know that we hadn't been given that detail, and the homicide department was very unhappy with that fact getting out. From there on out there seemed to be a media blackout on the murders.

We gave one interview to the newspaper a few weeks later. On the one hand, I was grateful that Victoria and Louis were going to be remembered, and I thanked them for the article and keeping them in the forefront when no one else would.

That said, as far as the article went, it was filled with nonsense that the reporter dug up about Victoria that had nothing to do with her murder. As her mother, I knew it gave such a tainted portrait of my daughter, but I also knew that she wouldn't care what anyone said about her anyway, so long as they fought for justice for Louis.

There was nothing negative that anyone could ever say about Louis; he was an innocent ten-month-old baby, and that is where the outrage in the community came from.

Again, silence. Every reporter that offered to help get the story out hit the same brick wall as we did. Tens of thousands of letters went to every news organization in the country—nothing. I didn't know where the brick wall was coming from, but I assumed it came from the homicide department, since I was quite familiar with that wall myself.

I felt like the case was being swept under the carpet because of who the murderer's family was. Knowing what I know now, it was not in the media often

tried to get someone to say who my grandson's biological father was. I got panicked emails and calls from those who had been contacted. I knew it was going to come out sooner or later, and I was going to be the one to say his name publicly for the first time.

A breaking news story aired two days before Christmas, with me naming the biological father and, "in my opinion," the person responsible for the murders. His face was all over the news, and for the first time he could no longer hide and walk amongst us like he was human. His family's social status was so important to

---

Talking to the media did hurt the relationship I had with my homicide team for many months to come. I should have gotten their permission. (Rose)

---

because the police didn't want "to jeopardize the integrity of the case." However, I didn't know that then, and the silence was deafening.

As months passed, an unconventional sort of media (now known as social media) was in full force discussing the murders of my daughter and grandson. At one time there were six blogs or forums going on and on about my babies and none of the bloggers had even met them. At first I was outraged and wanted them shut down, and I thought that as my daughter and grandson's next of kin I could stop it, but there is this little thing called "Freedom of Speech." It turned out that the bloggers were the only voices out there keeping Victoria and Louis from being forgotten. They were a very strong force of support for us, even though we didn't know any of them.

In December, five months after the murders, a producer from a local station

all of them, and it began to crumble. I couldn't think of a more appropriate Christmas gift for those people!

I felt for sure this would get the case moving. Imagine my shock when I was visited by my Lieutenant and Sergeant. They were not happy to say the least. It did hurt the relationship I had with my homicide team for many months to come. I should have gotten their permission, but if they had said no, I would still have done it.

Again silence. I learned that it is next to impossible to bring back a story unless there is something new to report, so it was a long seven months to the one-year mark of the murders, where we came out in full force again.

We held a press conference in front of the police department, begging for anyone with any information to come forward. We went to the murder scene, to her high school for a candlelight vigil, and *to the cemetery, and the media were right there with us. I have to say they were so kind, non-intrusive, and some of them couldn't hide their tears. I felt like they got it in some way.*

More silence. It would be another six months before the arrest. The call came and I heard the words "We got them; the two of them were just arrested." This turned up the media attention within minutes.

I agreed to do one interview after the arrests. When the reporter was leaving, there stood numerous other reporters and cameramen with lights and questions.

How ironic. I wanted to be left alone to just absorb the fact that one step of this journey was over—the killers were under arrest—and I could take a breather for a minute. That was not meant to be.

After the initial hearing, I made a short statement with an entire support system behind me. We had already decided that all interviews were going to go through me, because one wrong

by friends, family, homicide team, and, of course the media.

We gave interviews after that, and in many ways I felt like they had walked through hell with us; I trusted them to respect Victoria and Louis in their reporting. After all, they had had a front-row seat into my daughter and grandson's lives and deaths, and couldn't help but be affected by what had happened.

Marina

I did not experience the media intrusion most survivors face. For one thing, Dad lived in a desert resort town many miles away from my home. By the time I arrived in town, the local news affiliate had already done a piece on the murder. Using Dad's house as a backdrop, they filmed the coroner's deputy trundling Dad's poor, shrouded body out the front door and down the sidewalk. MY FATHER'S BODY!!!

I had tried so hard to keep media attention on the murders, and now that I had it, I didn't know how to handle it. (Rose)

---

statement at that time could be disastrous. From then on, every time we went into the court room, there were the media. They always wanted a statement, but if I didn't feel like giving one at the time, they respected that fact and left us alone.

As the trial got underway, we got to know the media quite well and in many ways I felt sorry for them having to see and listen to the horrors in the court room. At the same time, I think it is because they were in there they showed us great respect by leaving us alone. When the verdict was read, we were surrounded

Five minutes before the footage was shown that night on the news, I shut off the television. I was already overloaded. My sister later said that the sight of Dad's body on the evening news helped her to accept the fact of his death. I knew instinctively that it wouldn't be quite that easy for me, and I didn't need a one-minute television spot to remind me of just how hard it was going to be. I had had enough trauma for one day. I didn't regret my decision, as it was made in the spirit of self-preservation.

During the first year after the murder, coverage was minimal. There were no lurid stories. Neither relatives nor friends were interviewed. During the second year, token mention was made of the various court dates leading to trial. Around that time, I tried to put an In Memoriam in the local classifieds. I was very careful with my wording, but the classifieds editor still asked me to delete some phrases. The powers-that-be at the paper were terrified of a libel lawsuit on the part of the murderer. I've seen far worse in "big city" papers than what I wrote, but this publisher was small-

There was no recourse whatsoever. It was just over, just like that.

It burned me when the headline after the trial stated that Dad's girlfriend had been acquitted of murder. The Jury was forced to acquit on Murder One and Two, though they were visibly at odds with one another and clearly unable to reach a consensus. The prosecutor didn't even bother to come that day, and the young man who came in his stead had no idea what was going on. When the jury deadlocked yet again on Voluntary Man-

---

I don't recommend going it alone, but it was the only thing I knew to do at the time. (Marina)

---

town, small-time, and not terribly sophisticated.

I can say that the female reporter who was assigned to the case was extremely respectful of the family's privacy. She didn't force anything. I spoke with her during and after the trial. I sensed that she was giving her own editorial opinion in a very subtle way via her writing. She managed to do it without crossing any professional boundaries.

I did wish my family were more involved. They tell you to appoint a family member to deal with the media. I was the sole family member who was willing to deal with any of it—the police, the DA, the media, etc. So there was little point in "choosing" a spokesperson—I was it. Those of you who have family who are willing and able to be involved can count yourselves lucky. I was a "lone ranger" and it nearly killed me.

That sham court didn't protect the case. They bobbled it and squandered it. Then they threw our family—and by extension, Dad—on the garbage heap.

slaughter, the judge sensed he was losing control of the courtroom and abruptly declared a mistrial.

A year later, the case was dismissed for "insufficient evidence" and the local paper ran a headline stating the accused had been acquitted. Newspapers know readers want a neatly packaged little gift with a pretty bow on top. Judging from the coroner's testimony and autopsy photos, Dad's body was the antithesis of a neatly wrapped little package.

Just before Thanksgiving, more salt was rubbed in the wound. The accused ran a self-serving ad in the classifieds, thanking the community for supporting her in her "time of need." She even had the nerve to say she walked with Jesus as she thanked members of her church for praying for her. I never detested organized religion as much as I did in that moment. I couldn't blame the newspaper; it merely displayed an ad it was paid to run. But the knowledge did nothing to alleviate the pain of an extremely deep secondary wound.

Harrier

This is an especially important topic to me in that I not only had to deal with inaccurate news reports at the time of the deaths, but again three decades later when two inaccurate and error-riddled accounts of my parents—their deaths as well as their lives—were published. One in a true-crime book, the other by a family member with a mother (my sister) who had an ax to grind.

I have been on both sides of it, having also worked as newspaper reporter after my parents died. In retrospect, I understand the mindset of the news business. However, at the time of the deaths, I shunned the news media, in part because the FBI asked me to, but also because I naively believed that if I didn't talk to them, they didn't have anything to write about.

Wrong!

Not only were facts misinterpreted and at times reported inaccurately, but the reporters talked to other people and published those statements, even though the information may have been inaccurate. In my case, a newspaper published an absurd account of how my mother died, which then gave the suspect and his defenders an opportunity to cast reasonable doubt on his guilt.

Kaila

My experience with the media was frustrating because they made an effort to contact me and hear my story, but in the paper it was not quite what I had said to them. Some things where not true and others were left out, and when I tried contacting them back, they didn't return my calls.

Yvonne

On a positive note, if you could call it one, we were protected from media attention because we were children. And after decades I have found it in my best interest not to obtain old news articles. Tragically, in our case, it was my father who was so negatively impacted by false accusations and his reputation marred because the initial blame was directed to him as the prime suspect. So-called friends, co-workers and neighbors were quick to pass judgment. This would further drive my father into a downward spiral of depression. It's difficult to repair the unwarrantable damage done by the media. The headline news comes and is gone quickly; the family is left picking up the pieces in their shattered world.

In the past, social media was so much simpler. For the most part, coverage came from the local television broadcast stations, which consisted of ABC, CBS, and NBC. My heart goes out to anyone affected by the social media attention today. Headline news is obtained in seconds and at the tip of your fingertips; it would be nearly impossible to escape completely.

Halia

At the time of arrest, there were a dozen or so Internet articles regarding the cold case being solved. Other than that, there was no other media involvement during the hearings, and our case was plea bargained to second-degree murder. Therefore, we did not have a trial, which also deterred media involvement.

Mary

The local newspaper and television first reported on our son's murder. They showed a candlelight vigil on the night of the day he died. The television teams followed us through the initial events and on through the Court proceedings. They were always respectful of us, his family.

The newspaper had a reporter who wrote during the month following his murder. She was respectful of us also and asked for interviews but never invaded our privacy. After the murderers were

interview them in some cold office, but in a calm and comforting setting in a park.

Her writing was so right on. She captured who they are, and how these two deaths have affected them. The newspaper itself published not only the reporter's articles but also commentaries put out by other writers. It reported on different events over the last 2 ½ years where our son's murder by 6 teenagers affected the entire community, and what the town was doing to try to change because of it.

I have a box full of clippings from this one local newspaper. I have

---

Tip: Newspapers are made to disintegrate. You can buy acid-free paper and make copies of articles for longer term saving.

---

caught (a month after the murder), there was a special court reporter used by the newspaper. She wrote every detail of what happened and was with us until the final court proceedings, when all 6 of my son's murderers were put in prison. We developed a great rapport with her.

There were several over-the-telephone interviews as well as in-person interviews. She also interviewed our son's older brother and his wife, just this past year. On New Year's Day the article was posted in the paper about how both had lost a sibling to murder (Her sister had been murdered by her husband in a domestic dispute a year before our son's murder).

This same brother doesn't usually talk about what happened and finds it difficult to deal with the crushing blow of his brother's death; the reporter was very sensitive in her interview. **She didn't**

nothing but good things to say about the media and how they handled our son's death and how they treated his family.

JJ

The local media treated us very well. At our first contact, the reporter introduced herself and asked if she could do an interview and run a picture. We agreed, and she ushered my wife and me into the photographer's studio. He set us up for a shot together, and we did what we have done since childhood, smiled for the camera. What an embarrassment would have resulted if he had quit then, just wanting to just get the job done. He took some more pictures after making some gentle suggestions, and we finally understood what he was looking for.

The same reporter followed the case from start to finish. She kept things off the *record that we asked her to and kept interviews short. The media served as a valuable recap of events, keeping the story fresh and updated as time went on. The TV news was equally cooperative, providing us with a copy of the video footage on request. At a time when we were very vulnerable, we were protected and yet information was provided to the community.*

One early report from the police prior to our arrival improperly characterized the murder as drug related and that there was no hazard to public safety. This politically motivated article was very hurtful and bordered on slander, but my wife and I stayed with no comment, and later editorials cleared the air and rebuked the author of the statement.

Survivor Question: What do you wish you had known? What do you wish to pass on to other Survivors?

Write your responses in your notebook.

Rose

I have learned that the media is always going to be a double-edged sword. The problem is that they aren't there when there is nothing new to report, and that is when we really need them; we need the media focus to stay on those cases and keep them in the public eye. That isn't how it works. They are a business; they are there to get a story, true, but they are there for ratings and who breaks the story first. Sometimes facts don't matter so long as they break the story.

Boundaries were set in the beginning, and that turned out to be extremely important as we moved through the criminal justice system.

In my opinion, only one person should be responsible for dealing with the media so there is some control of what goes out. I don't know who that person should be, but for us it had to be me; no one else could speak for Victoria and Louis without my permission. Whomever you choose should know their rights with the media and go from there.

I have always treated the media with respect, and for the most part they did the

same with me, especially since this was a high-profile case. It could have been so much worse.

Be prepared for the media to be in attendance and for them to want a statement after a hearing. Be cautious with what you say; now isn't the time to go off on a tangent (although you really want to). I believe I made my statement not only to the murderer but to his family as well when I said, "Welcome to hell; this is where you belong, not us."

Marina

I don't recommend going it alone, but it was the only thing I knew to do at the time. It comforts me to know that I was the only one who had the courage to do what had to be done, in spite of my fear.

Looking back, I wish that more information on the murder had come out. But that is a double-edged sword. If more information had been disseminated, there probably would have been aspects discussed which would have been embarrassing to or unfavorable for our side.

When a loved one is murdered, the first thing the police and

the DA tell you is to keep your mouth shut in order to "protect" the case. *I kept my mouth shut. I was a "good girl."* **Looking back, I definitely would have said more to the media.** *I wouldn't have spilled my guts, but I would have said a whole hell of a lot more.*

Harrier
In hindsight, I made a big mistake, *and I advise others to be pro-active and deal with the "legitimate" news media. Hire a media-relations professional, if you can afford it. I refused to speak the news media, but because the suspected killer (my brother) did talk to the news media; he had sole possession of the public forum and manipulated it to his advantage.*

Were I to do it over, I would prepare a news release and hold a news conference to ensure that the things I believed to be true were included in the published accounts *of my parents' deaths.*

Kaila
I wish I had known that I didn't have to speak to the media at all. *Survivors need to know that the media can be helpful in some ways, depending on the nature of the crime. Not every detail gets printed.*

Yvonne
By nature, children are curious beings and the long-term effect of discovering any news about the death of their parent can be detrimental in

overcoming loss. In the past, and especially now, great measures would need to be taken to protect children from any outside influences; that would present a major challenge.

Sadly, a child today would need to be so closely monitored that the child would need to become nearly isolated for their best interest. This breaks my heart because this only serves to further isolate a child who is scared and distrustful of the world around him, especially at this time.

Therapy, such as pet therapy, could be tremendously beneficial at this point in a child's life. *I am convinced that it would have provided my sister and me comfort through various stages early on.*

Mary
The only thing I can think of to say to other families is that **the media wants to get it right in what and how they report events.** *Try to be as calm as you can (in view of the emotional turmoil that you are going through), and do be careful of what and how you say things. If you aren't careful, you could say something you really don't want printed in the paper, and if you don't say "this is off the record," it can be recorded.*

Sometimes it is about timing and when is best to speak. **If you are really upset or angry, it might be best to wait until you are more in control to speak.** *If you are honest and just tell the reporter why this is not a good time to speak, they will be respectful of you (at least this was the experience that our family had).*

JJ
*My recommendation would be that like many things in those first few weeks, **rely on people you trust to provide advice and do not make hasty decisions.** I wish I had developed a closer relationship with the victim advocate's office earlier. They proved to be a tremendous resource.*

Resources

Books

And I Don't Want to Live this Life, Deborah Spungen. Ballantine Books, 1996.

Dare I Call It Murder?: A Memoir of Violent Loss, Larry M. Edwards. Wigeon Publishing, 2013. http://www.dareicallitmurder.com.

Online

A Guide for Victims of Crime
http://crime.about.com/od/victims/qt/victim_guide.htm.

A Victim's Guide to Speaking with the Media
http://media.wix.com/ugd/11784d_80c49ecf0ca0639389be0a1ffe55a343.pdf.

If the Media Calls: A Guide for Crime Victims & Survivors (Canada)
http://crcvc.ca/publications/if-the-media-calls/.

News Media Guide for Victim Service Providers (September 2009), 137 pages, NCJ 236256. Prepared by the Office for Victims of Crime, a component of the Office of Justice Programs, U.S. Department of Justice. http://www.victimprovidersmediaguide.com/.

Press releases:

- Press Release guidelines and sample format
  http://www.victimprovidersmediaguide.com/press.html#b.

- Social media press release template
  http://www.shiftcomm.com/downloads/smprtemplate.pdf.

- PR Web Press Release Grader, free online resource; http://service.prweb.com/learning/article/press-release-grader/news release grader.

Time's Up! A collection of bloggers who are champions for victims of crime. http://timesupblog.blogspot.com.

* Some Web addresses may have changed since publication.

Page intentionally left blank. Use it for jotting notes or your thoughts, if you wish.

4

The Early Response

One of the hardest jobs is to tell someone they lost a loved one. (Hendricks, 2006)

In this section we will cover Death Notification, along with those I refer to as First and Second Responders. Early on it will be important for you to start understanding what your rights are as a survivor of a murder victim, as a co-victim. You may want to refer back to your Key Contacts off and on, and periodically check with the people you encounter where it is applicable for your situation. As in other chapters, the Survivor Writers add information for you about their experiences and wisdom.

There is nothing in life that prepares you for the news that someone has, on purpose, killed someone you know and love. How you get the news can have a long-term impact. The news you have received is followed by a flood of new people in your world adding layers to the confusion and devastation. Murder is personal. How one finds out can be one of the first of unforgettable memories that repeat in one's head again and again.

> *I called my daughter's best friend when I couldn't get her. He took my call immediately and when I asked if he knew where my daughter and grandson were, his response was: "Haven't the police called you?" When I responded, "Why would the police call me?" he said. "They were murdered last night; they are dead. It was all over the news."* (Rose)

> *I was riding in the car and Mother was driving when the radio announced the name of my sister as the murder victim mentioned earlier that morning. My mother, the only licensed driver in the car, stopped immediately, then drove to the police station in a daze.* (Connie)

I learned of the death of my sister from my mother. I asked if they had found her, and my mother's voice cracked in a way I had never heard before. "Yes, she is in the morgue." (Halia)

Initially, co-victims are fluctuating with intense pain and periods of numbness. Co-victims ask, who are all these people? What do they do and why are they in my world? At a time when privacy and time to grieve may be sought after, the nature of this loss prevents control of the direction of one's life. There is an urgency to respond, to take care of all the tasks involved, adding to the burden of family, friends, and acquaintances of the murder victim.

Our family was notified of my father's murder by the alleged murderer herself. (Marina)

My cousin phoned me at work to tell me my father had been killed aboard his sailboat. (Harrier)

"I'm sorry to tell you he expired."
"Expired? What does that mean expired?
Milk expires, food expires, people don't expire.
They don't have a date stamped on their foreheads.
"What do you mean he expired?"

(Bucholz, 2002)

Death Notification

The job of informing families of the death of a loved one usually falls in the hands of the Homicide Detective or the Medical Examiner. Most agencies work with the policy that the names of the victims are not released until the next of kin have been notified. However, sometimes news coverage reveals identifying information before reporting agencies can do their jobs of letting the family know.

Coroner/Medical Examiner

Family members of a murder victim may need and have a right to contact the coroner or medical examiner. If you don't have contact information, check with the investigating officer or your victim advocate. Here's what you should know:

Coroner: investigates sudden, violent, untimely, and unexpected deaths, or, when the cause of death is unknown, to determine cause of death. A coroner is often an elected official and does not necessarily have to be a medical doctor or forensic pathologist. A coroner does not perform autopsies, but will either work with or appoint a medical examiner or forensic pathologist who performs autopsies.

Medical Examiner: a medical doctor with expertise (forensic pathology) in investigating suspicious or unattended deaths, and performs autopsies. If the jurisdiction has a coroner, the medical examiner/pathologist will work with the coroner to determine the cause of death.

> *Autopsies are the voice of the dead; medical examiners have a moral and ethical responsibility to listen to those voices.* (Hendricks, 2006)

Reasons for contacting the Medical Examiner:

1. **Release of your loved one** to the next of kin or to a mortuary or crematorium.

> *They didn't release the body for three years.*
> (Zuckerman, 1998)

2. **Autopsy reports:** Many people do not want this report. It is a personal choice. The report contains details, in medical language, of what happened. You may want to have a medical professional review the document with you, if you do get one.

3. **Death certificates** are issued by this office as well. Agencies will ask you for copies for several reasons, including access to your loved one's personal information at banks and property sites, and when an estate is to be settled. Some Medical Examiner's offices have websites that provide information, forms, and death announcements.

The examination of a victim's body falls to someone in your community. Remember to check with your community to learn how things are done where you live and for any differences in their definitions. If you are stumped by a legal term, check out *Black's Law Dictionary: The Free Online Law Dictionary* (see Resources at the end of the chapter).

Survivor Question: How did you hear about the death of your love one(s)? What worked, what didn't work?

Write your answers in your personal notebook.

Rose

I did not hear about the death the way one would think or as seen on TV. I received a call at 6 A.M. that my daughter hadn't shown up for work, and that in itself was strange because my daughter had an excellent work ethic and never missed a day without calling.

My first call was to my daughter's cell phone, leaving her a message that she had to get to work, and to call me back and let me know she was okay. The second call was to her best friend and the person who usually took my grandson to daycare each morning.

He didn't answer his cell phone either, so I called his home phone. He took my call immediately, and when I asked if he knew where my daughter and grandson were, his response was: "Haven't the police called you?" When I responded, "Why would the police call me?" he said, "Victoria and Louis were murdered last night; they are dead. It was all over the news."

I don't remember anything because a wave of heat engulfed me from my feet to my head and I fell to the ground. When I picked the phone back up, her friend was no longer on the line. I called my husband in Puerto Rico, where he was working and told him. He said that was impossible, to call 911, and call him right back.

I called 911 and asked if they had my babies in the morgue. They asked me who I was talking about and I gave them the names, and she asked me for my phone number & name and said someone would call me right back. I have no concept of time, but it seemed like the phone rang as soon as I had hung up. The caller was a Sergeant, and he asked me for my address and said he would be right over.

*When the **Sergeant of the Homicide team** assigned to the murders entered my home, he confirmed that it was indeed my daughter and grandson who had been murdered the night before. I started showing him photos of them so he could say, "Oh, we made a mistake."*

But he didn't say that. Before he left my home, he said, "I can't promise you that we will get an arrest; but I promise you we will never stop until we do." There was something in the way that he said it, and the look in his eyes, that made me believe he wasn't just saying it to make me feel better; he not only said it, he promised it. I held on to those words like they were gospel.

*My husband's two daughters arrived. I had one of the daughters start taking notes because I couldn't comprehend a word they were saying. Then a **Victim's Advocate** arrived from the DA's office, and she came with information about funeral arrangements, the Victims Assistance program, something about the investigation, and then it was going to the DA's office.*

Marina

Our family was notified of my father's murder by the alleged murderer herself.

Early in the morning, she called my sister's house. My brother-in-law answered the phone. Breathlessly, she informed him that she had awoken to the sight of Dad lying on the floor of the master bedroom. There was a lot of blood, so she thought that perhaps he had taken a fall and hit his head on a glass nightstand. My brother-in law asked her if she'd called 911. No, she had not.

He asked her if she was crazy, and forcefully told her to call 911. She said she would. We learned later that by the time she contacted the family, the authorities had already been in the house for hours. But we didn't know that then.

notion that it was all just a misunderstanding. The next six hours are a blur. I packed and waited for my boyfriend to come and pick me up. I was calm, but **I knew I was too confused and agitated to be a safe driver.** When we got to Dad's town, we drove straight to my aunt's. We waited for my sister and brother-in-law to arrive.

The three of us were together when that awful knock came. I knew who it was and got up to answer the door. I was in a

---

My aunt was made to stand in the street and watch as a covered body on a stretcher was loaded into an ambulance. No one would tell her a thing . . . (Marina)

My brother-in-law next called a paternal aunt who lived near my father, and asked her to run over to Dad's to check on the situation. When my aunt arrived, she immediately saw that something was wrong. The street was full of fire department vehicles and police cars.

Alarmed, she tried to enter the house but was stopped by a sheriff's deputy, who told her Dad was dead. He added that Dad's girlfriend was in the house. My aunt was made to stand in the street and watch as a covered body on a stretcher was loaded into an ambulance. No one would tell her a thing, so she went back home and called my brother-in-law to give him the news.

At about 7 A.M., I got a call from my sister. I knew it had to be something bad, because my sister is not an early riser. She told me that Dad was dead. This came as no surprise. I had visited Dad only days before, and he didn't look good at all. But then I heard the words "police" and "coroner." Dad's girlfriend was there, and she was not being allowed to leave. This was bad, very bad, but I clung to the

dreamlike, detached state at this point. The deputy sheriff, a stocky, dark-haired man with a bushy mustache, was obviously uncomfortable with the task at hand. He handed me a manila envelope, and I knew what was in it—my father's personal effects. The poignancy of it nearly made my legs buckle, but I forced myself to remain still so that I could extract as much information from the deputy as possible.

Yes, it was murder. Yes, it was a very obvious murder. Yes, there was ample evidence of a murder, so much evidence that **it was a prosecutor's dream case.** In answer to my final question, he assured me that there was "no way" that Dad's girlfriend would "get away with it."

I cordially thanked him for his kindness. He was very kind and respectful, but he couldn't get out of there fast enough.

He was the only first responder with whom I dealt. . . . I had no further contact with the authorities until I was compelled to track them down myself, some two months later.

Harrier

My cousin phoned me at work to tell me my father had been killed in an accident aboard his sailboat.

The news stunned me, but after a moment I asked what had happened. My cousin said my father had been hit by the boat's boom, and my sister lay unconscious. The others on the boat were all OK. My cousin said she'd call me back when she knew more, but communications were difficult since the boat was at sea and they could only communicate by shortwave radio.

My boss sent me home, and I went sailing, alone. As I slipped the boat's mooring, I yearned for a blustery day, to be pummeled with wind, pelted with rain; the boat heeled hard, and I wrenched the tiller as I struggled for control of my craft, seeking proof that I was still alive. Instead, I suffered the insolence of a balmy afternoon.

The next morning, I learned that my mother had also died but got no explanation. Then my brother said he was lost at sea.

I immediately became enmeshed in a criminal investigation. The police did not believe what the survivors had said. Instead, they suggested there had been a melee aboard the boat, that my brother had killed our parents and assaulted our sister.

The lack of clear communication frustrated me, and my brother's reports from the boat troubled me. His explanation didn't make sense. So I did the only thing I could do—try to get answers for myself. But **when the police began accusing my brother, I got defensive**, refusing to believe he could have done anything so horrific. **There had to be a better explanation.**

As a survivor, tend to your grief, your emotions. I did not. I became a detective.

Kaila

I heard about the death of my sister when a detective called me over the phone and proceeded to tell me that they found a body of what they believed was my sister. The detective wanted me to come down to their office so they could speak to me. My sister had her ID and pager with her when they found her body.

Halia

I learned of the death of my sister from my mother during one of the numerous calls to check on her. I asked if they had found her, and my mother's voice cracked in a way I had never heard before as she stated, "Yes, she is in the morgue."

I screamed at her, telling her that it was not at all funny, and the stoic woman she is began to cry, repeating the same statement. At that point I attempted to calm her and assured her I'd be there shortly.

I attempted to hang up the payphone, crossed the room toward my husband who was still in a meeting at the Hotel we were in, and I went hysterical right there in the Hotel lobby.

Apparently the shrills were loud enough that my mother heard them on the dangling payphone as well as raising concerns for the Hotel manager. I was in complete shock at that point. The ladies in our business meeting were of great support as well as my then-husband.

Somehow I managed to call the family minister and asked him to meet us

Tend to Your Grief

Harrier says it well: *"Tend to your grief."* One of the mistakes that survivors make is to miss this important task. It is understandable in terms of what you are facing. Your needs seem so much less important than this huge and consuming event. You can support, cooperate, and help some, but it is important for you to do your job, which is tough enough, and let law enforcement do theirs.

Provide police officers with what you know, what theories you may have, but stay out of their lane. It may seem like they are not doing their job . . . and they may not be some of the time. But until you know they are not doing their job, help them where you can, then stay out of their way.

Let the police know you want to hear from them. This is a very frequent request by co-victims. Investigators can do more to keep the family informed and supported by assuring family members that the case is moving forward.

If you can afford it, hire an attorney and let the attorney look out for your interests. While you are passionate and want progress to be made, you do not have objectivity. Yes, politics do get involved, people do make mistakes. You should keep track of your concerns and let others in your "army" know.

Displaced anger and rage is understandable. Blaming family members, law enforcement, and yourself is common. While understandable, it doesn't help. **You need safe places and people to express this hurt to. Displaced anger and judgments can interfere with progress.**

We all want to pin the cause somewhere. Everyone is on the same side. The only person responsible for this crime is the person who committed it or helped in some way. Everyone is a suspect, and the police will work to cut this list. Their objectivity and inclusivity is important here. It will help them get the job done.

at my mother's house for prayer and support.

What might have been helpful was to instruct me to have someone with me and/or to call her when I was in a private room, not in a public *place. That way I could have had some privacy to contain the reaction a bit better and have support in the environment. The thing about shocking news, though, is everyone reacts differently, and it takes time for it to really sink in at different levels.*

For the most part, as Edmund Burke phrased it, "All that is necessary for evil to triumph is for good men to do nothing."

For the most part, the job gets done right and well, but Gene Cervantes writes in the Citizens Against Homicide Newsletter in May 2012 that:

*Police and medical examiners believed the death of a 49-year-old male, we shall call him Henry, to be **natural causes**. Henry's body was already* *embalmed in preparation for burial when someone at the funeral home noticed something suspicious. The funeral home returned the body to the county medical examiner's office after discovering three bullet holes in Henry's head.*

Mr. Cervantes suggests:

- All violent deaths should be treated as homicides.
- Demand a complete and thorough investigation, no matter how many hours it may take.
- Ask for a second or third professional opinion.

Most survivors remember how and when they got the news, and who notified them. If handled poorly, it becomes a painful part of the traumatic experience that is talked about and relived over and over again, as is the death of their loved one.

> *There's this hope that this nightmare will pass. Son Jeffrey was kidnapped by gang wannabees. They put a gun to his head, pulled the trigger, and then set his body on fire. The officer's gentle manner helped me the most. Brent Frogley, Detective, Boise Police Department, Idaho, says he tries to think how he would like to be told to help guide him.* (NSADJ, 2008)

Captain Terese R. Dioquino, Pinellas County Sheriff's Office in Florida (NSADJ, 2008), in a training DVD for First Responders, advises attendees to be respectful: "You're the one that is going to give them the worst news they'll ever hear, and how you leave that residence is how you'll be remembered."

First and Second Responders

You see people with that "thousand-mile stare." (NSADJ, 2008)

The bombardment in the aftermath of the notification that a loved one is no longer alive can result in confusion, paralysis, or frantic activity. One's life has been assaulted. Survivors don't know what to do, when to do it, or whom to turn to. Survivors are impacted by a flood of people from many different agencies.

Life becomes instantly complicated, with waves of the most intense pain and chaos. It is as if nothing else matters: not eating, not taking medicine, not picking up children or not feeding the dog. Everyday maintenance becomes secondary to the focus on this still shocking news. First responders are there to attend some of the initial activities. Friends, neighbors, and extended family may be needed to take care of forgotten tasks.

The bereaved as well as responders bring their prior lives and beliefs to this initial scene. When the past has been adversarial or suspicious, it can add additional distress and complication. Only the family knows of many of the special circumstances that pertain to their loved one(s). Only the responding team members know what their experience and training tells them. Hold off on making judgments and quick appraisals. The accused are not found guilty until a fair trial has been conducted. At this early juncture, don't jump to conclusions; be open to all of the possibilities.

First Responders: It is common knowledge that no two calls for response are the same. There can be many different agencies involved at the death scene and soon after, including law enforcement, medical examiners, forensic teams, paramedics, firefighters, crisis interventionists, clergy, clean-up teams, and so on. This can result in much chaos and confusion for survivors. These teams are often times brief and their jobs clearly defined. You may see them first on the scene and again when there is a trial. Many of them you will never see again. They will come in and do their jobs and be gone. Special circumstances may call in additional types of specialists as well. This can be a hurricane of activity. **Form a relationship with a key member of the investigation team.**

Second Responders: These are folks who may not be on the scene at first, but you will encounter them soon after. They include Victim Advocates and financial services, such as banks, insurance, and trust or estate contacts, and trauma counselors. Later on you may want to work with Crime Stoppers as well. Second responders may be a group that you will be involved with for a longer period of time.

Survivor *Valeria* elaborates on role of the office of Victim Advocates in her community:

> *Sometime soon after your loss, you should receive contact by mail or phone from someone in the Victim's Advocate Division. You will be notified by this office of the "State Victim's Compensation Program" which is a capped reimbursement amount that varies from state to state. It is a dollar amount that can be claimed by you to cover your loved-one's funeral expenses and ongoing mental health counseling for you and your family members. You will be given a claim I.D. number, and put in touch with a person from this office who will process your claims. You will also be assigned a Victim Advocate—someone whose job it is to answer any questions, inform you, assist you through the legal process, and be a liaison between you and the Prosecutor throughout the case.*

In your notebook, list your contacts. What agency are they from? How can you reach them?

Name	Agency	Contact Info
_____	_____	_____
_____	_____	_____
_____	_____	_____
_____	_____	_____
_____	_____	_____
_____	_____	_____

Have a friend help you collect business cards or have the contacts sign in your notebook. It is normal for survivors to say they never heard from an agency, even though the agency had a representative there.

Survivor Question: Who did you first have contact with? What did you understand were their roles? What did you learn about what/who was helpful? Do you have any tips for others?

Write your answers in your notebook.

Rose

*I first had contact with the Sergeant of the homicide team assigned to my daughter's and grandson's murders. If I had any questions, I was to direct them to him. There were 5 other officers assigned to our case, and although I met 4 of them, they were assigned to different friends and family members who they needed to question/interview, one being my husband. **I didn't understand why my husband had some other detective to answer to than I did**, but I didn't understand anything that was happening anyway.*

*I learned that while each of us had different detectives, sometimes their roles intertwined with another detective on the case, so I would see more than one at a time. I also learned that while **I was begging for answers as the investigation went on, and my Sergeant was giving me nothing**, some of the other detectives shared more of what was going on with the ones they were working with, and I had to get my information second hand from friends.*

*I was none too happy about this, but that didn't really matter to my Sergeant. Instead he tried to contain all information regarding the case to stay in-house and not to share anything with any of us. **That didn't stop some of the others from telling me things,** and I found that I would just keep my displeasure to myself so I could keep getting my information/updates one way or the other.*

*I learned that **some detectives may be great investigators, but they have no business interacting with a grieving family because they don't know how to talk to us in a dignified manner.** We become more or less a bother to them, and they would prefer not to have to even see us.*

I went once to find out what personal items they had of my daughter and grandson, something I had been asking about for over six months. One detective came in while I was sitting with the Sergeant and a friend of Victoria's, and he slammed a binder down on the table and said my grandson "was wearing shorts when he was found hung in his crib. As for your daughter's things, it was impossible to know what belonged to whom because those girls (my daughter & the two roommates) all lived like pigs!"

I went ballistic on him for his callousness, and he left the room. I was so stunned and angry that I told the Sergeant not to ever let him speak to a family member again and I left.

You know what I learned here: They played good cop/bad cop with me, and in the end I left without the information I had come for, which is what they had wanted me to do.

Harrier

Not knowing whom to contact regarding my parents' deaths, I went straight to the hospital to see my sister and a family friend who was aboard the boat at the

94

time. Luckily, I got there at 6:30 A.M. and found only a janitor on duty. Otherwise, I might not have been able to see them.

Shortly after I got there, the police arrived and ordered me out of the room. They said I could not visit or talk to my sister, and they posted a policeman at the door.

That afternoon, I went to the police station and sat in on the interrogation of the family friend. The police lieutenant shouted and banged his fist when the friend's answers did not satisfy him. I

contradicted himself at times. My brother became the FBI's primary suspect in a murder investigation.

After that, I viewed the FBI and the police as my allies, and I helped them with the investigation as much as I could. But I couldn't offer them much, since my brother refused to talk to me about what had happened.

What I learned: Not to make a quick judgment and jump to conclusions. I distrusted law enforcement; I

I came to realize that my brother and sister probably weren't telling the truth. (Harrier)

---

objected to his behavior, and he ordered me from the room.

Two days later, I learned that the FBI had opened an investigation and agents were on their way.

At the time, I wanted to believe that our parents had died in an unfortunate tragedy. I viewed the police and FBI as adversaries. I just wanted them to let us be so we could take care of the matters at hand. The FBI entering the frame stalled things for a full week.

But as the FBI investigation progressed, I began to see the incident in a new light. Although the agents did not tell me much, they said my sister's skull fracture was not an accident. They also said they did not believe my brother's explanation for what had happened, and he would probably have to testify before a grand jury.

The FBI let me observe one of its interviews with my brother. The things my brother told them and had said to the news media didn't add up. There were inconsistencies in what he said, and he

wanted to believe that my brother and sister were telling me the truth. But in the days and weeks following the deaths, I came to realize that my brother and sister probably weren't telling the truth. **I realized that I'd be most helpful to the FBI by answering their questions honestly and staying out of their way.**

 **Kaila**
I had contact with the homicide detectives. **They asked a lot of questions but would not answer mine.** I understood that they were doing their job and were just trying to help find my sister's killer.

 **Halia**
Initially, we had contact with the detectives and police department. This went on for a few years with no results as to who was responsible for my sister's death. It became a cold case until twenty-eight years later, when an

arrest was made. A serial rapist had abducted her from her place of work, rendered her unconscious, taken her to a remote site in her own vehicle, and then raped her. At some point she suffered a cardiac arrest and was then dragged by her hair 26 feet and dumped into a canal. He went home and had a party that night.

She was "discovered" the next day by relatives of the person who killed her, and he was at the crime scene as well. The detectives questioned him and set him free. However, we were fortunate enough to have a relentless Detective S. on our case who picked up clues and, with current DNA and forensic technology, pursued the case until an arrest was made.

Crime Victim Rights

[Victim] Rights should be implemented and enforced. (Herman, 2010)

The United States Congress enacted the **Crime Victims' Rights Act** in October 2004 as part of the National Justice for All Act. Many states have adopted these rights for crime victims and added more, such as California's Marcy's Law. (See Resources.)

Be patient in finding your state's Victims' Rights List. Two of the most important resources are the Office of Victims of Crime (OVC) and your state Attorney General's (AG) office. These agencies or their websites should get you to your state's victims' rights. If not, go to website called Victim Law, which has a map to help you find victims' rights state by state.

Survivor Question: Crime Victims Rights

Thanks to the efforts of many, there are increased rights for crime victims. Document what happened in your case. Some survivors have important questions regarding protections that seem to exist for criminals but not for survivors of murdered family members. It may be premature for you to do this now. You may want to answer these questions later. When you do, please review the lists below and write what you experienced.

1. What was the date of your loved one's death?
2. When was the conclusion of the case?
3. What was that outcome?

Two of our Survivor Writers comment on their experience regarding Crime Victims' Rights:

Rose:
1. What was the date of your loved one's death? ***Summer 2006.***
2. When was the conclusion of the case? ***Our last day in court was late 2009.***
3. What was that outcome? ***Guilty of 2 counts of 1st degree murder; 2 life sentences without the possibility of parole; 1 count of obstruction of justice. An additional 3 years per victim equaling an additional 6 years.***

Marina:
1. What was the date of your loved one's death? ***Summer 1999.***
2. When was conclusion of the case? ***October 2002.***
3. What was that outcome? ***Case dismissed for insufficient evidence a year and a half after a mistrial was declared in the first trial.***

Survivor Writers comment on the statutes contained in the Justice for All Act of 2004 (18 U.S.C. § 3771), which provides Crime Victims with the following rights:

1. The right to be reasonably protected from the accused.

Rose: Not for us. We had our car broken into twice, and I made police reports both times, but nobody really cared. Our computer was hacked and a flyer with the suspect's photo on it—a flyer we had never printed out—had been placed on the passenger's seat of my car. We were followed on an almost daily basis when leaving the cemetery; everyone that went with me noticed; I made complaints but they went unanswered.

Marina: The accused called a friend and arranged for her own bail as Dad lay dead or dying. Within 24 hours, she was out on the street on $250,000 bail. It was devastating to realize that Dad's life was valued at $25,000 —approximately ten percent of the bail amount. Less than two days after beating and strangling Dad, she was free to kill again. Within three weeks she was arrested for public lewdness after propositioning a number of male patrons at a local nightclub. She was found performing a lewd act upon a man in a car outside the building. What if the idiot had taken her home? I felt sorriest for my elderly aunt, who lived in the same town. Every day she had to contemplate the possibility of running into the alleged murderer anywhere, anytime.

2. The right to reasonable, accurate, and timely notice of any public court proceeding, or any parole proceeding, involving the crime or of any release or escape of the accused.

Rose: Yes, we were always notified for court proceedings (other than the secret Grand Jury) for the murderer. We were informed of the appeal being denied so he will never have a parole hearing or be released. As for the other person charged with "obstruction of justice," we were informed of his court hearings as well, but not when he was released on parole. He violated his parole, and we were again notified of a new hearing where he was sentenced to a year, but again we were not notified of his release.

Marina: We were only notified of the accused's release after the fact, and then only because my brother-in-law called the local police station the morning after the arrest. By the time we learned that she was once more roaming the streets, she'd been out for hours. When the case was dismissed, we were not notified of the hearing beforehand, so she got the last word in the local newspaper.

3. **The right not to be excluded from any such public court proceeding, unless the court, after receiving clear and convincing evidence, determined that testimony by the victim would be materially altered if the victim heard other testimony at that proceeding.**

Rose: The defense had me on their witness list so the defense attorney asked the court to keep me out of the trial; however, that request was denied because I had been in every previous hearing, from arraignment through the preliminary hearing. There was a stipulation, however, that if I could be in the court room throughout the trial so could the killer's parents. His fiancée could not be present until after she testified.

Marina: The alleged killer's lawyer wrote false subpoenas on scraps of notepaper summoning any person on our side of the courtroom who looked halfway sympathetic, intelligent, or respectable. I was barred as a potential witness—but was never called to testify. My older sister was subpoenaed, even though she had no use as a material witness, so that her obvious grief and anger would not be observed by any juror. She was forced to leave the courtroom and was never allowed to return.

4. **The right to be reasonably heard at any public proceeding in the district court involving release, plea, sentencing, or any parole proceeding.**

Rose: None of this pertained to us except for the sentencing, which was automatic two life sentences, but we still were allowed to give our Victim's Impact Statements.

Marina: Immediate family members were not notified or allowed to play a part in the hearing involving the accused's release.

5. **The reasonable right to confer with the attorney for the Government in the case.**

Rose: If the attorney for the Government is the prosecutor, then yes, we were able to speak with him. We met him a few months before the arrest and established a very good relationship. He was always available to us, including during the trial where we would ask him things we didn't understand about the proceedings of that day. In fact, we still talk with him every few months.

Marina: The first DA in the case was dismissed after being accused of sexually harassing a female witness in an unrelated case. The second DA made it abundantly clear that he didn't "like" the case and didn't want it. He did answer my queries and returned my phone calls, but I always had in my mind a picture of his reluctant, resentful countenance at our first meeting and anytime I spoke with him. It was very demoralizing at a time when I already felt emotionally battered. After the trial I wrote a letter to the Assistant DA, which was critical of "our" DA's shoddy work. I was also critical of the judge, who was so intimidated by the defense attorney that he allowed him to take total control of the trial. Afterward, the DA did not call to inform us of further proceedings. We only heard of the dismissal because my aunt saw an article in the local newspaper. Now I'm glad I let those incompetents know that I thought them cowards, and their court a sham.

6. The right to full and timely restitution as provided in law.

Rose: *Not true in our case. It is being looked at now as to what is happening as far as this goes.*

Marina: *Are you kidding? How about restitution to my severely retarded brother, who adored my Dad and was forever deprived of his company?*

7. The right to proceedings free from unreasonable delay.

Rose: *The case took two years to come to court. Any time frame seems like an eternity to someone who has lost a loved one to murder.*

Marina: *There were delays that the defense was responsible for, but I don't think they would be categorized as unreasonable. A year and a half passed before we heard about the dismissal. Those cowards at the DA's office were hoping we'd cool off before they "kicked" the case. Real tough guys. I have no respect for their Court of Last Resort. We were mistreated and cheated in the end.*

8. The right to be treated with fairness and with respect for the victim's dignity and privacy.

Rose: *I believe all parties involved protected my daughter's dignity as much as it could be, due to the circumstances of paternity.*

Marina: *I do believe this to be true in our case. Given the outcome, it is irrelevant.*

Victims' Bill of Rights Act of 2008: "Marsy's Law"

California Constitution, Article I, Section 28(B)

Here is an example of a state's (California) addition to the National Victims' Rights Act. Both of the Survivor Writers were from this state, so we provide Marsy's Law as an example.

In order to preserve and protect a victim's rights to justice and due process, a victim shall be entitled to the following rights:

1. **To be treated with fairness and respect for his or her privacy and dignity, and to be free from intimidation, harassment, and abuse, throughout the criminal or juvenile justice process.**

   Rose: Due to the fact that the victims were murdered, I would answer this as the co-victim. No, we were not protected from intimidation or harassment.

   Marina: The defendant strutted back and forth repeatedly right in front of members of our family who were seated outside the courtroom. She had to go out of her way in order to do this. When my aunt and uncle were provoked into making negative remarks aimed at her, they were told by the DA not to come inside the courthouse any more. I had already been banned from the courthouse for doing horrible things like: wearing a crime victim's ribbon, giving my boyfriend a peck on the lips, and making a sour face back at the killer's mother after I tired of her glaring at me with open hatred and contempt. I'm sure the criminal attorney instructed the killer and her family to provoke us—and it worked. You'd have to be a marble statue not to react under such circumstances.

2. **To be reasonably protected from the defendant and persons acting on behalf of the defendant.**

   Rose: No, we were not protected.

   Marina: The defendant intentially provoked us but was not reprimanded.

3. **To have the safety of the victim and the victim's family considered in fixing the amount of bail and release conditions for the defendant.**

   Rose: Bail was denied and there will be no release.

   Marina: Well, that one flew right out the window less than two days after the murder. Protecting the innocent? Dream on!

4. **To prevent the disclosure of confidential information or records to the defendant, the defendant's attorney, or any other person acting on**

behalf of the defendant, which could be used to locate or harass the victim or the victim's family or which disclose confidential communication made in the course of medical or counseling treatment, or which are otherwise privileged or confidential by law.

Rose: *This came up during the restitution and was the reason I didn't want to pursue restitution. I didn't want my medical history shared with the defendant nor any counseling or psychiatric information to be public. In the end, the prosecutor simply stated restitution for medical expenses and loss of wages.*

Marina: *The defendant already had been to all of our houses, so she knew where we all lived.*

5. **To refuse an interview, disposition, or discovery request by the defendant, the defendant's attorney, or any other person acting on behalf of the defendant, and to set reasonable conditions on the conduct of any such interview to which the victim consents.**

Rose: *When I was contacted by the defense, I refused any involvement with them whatsoever.*

6. **To reasonable notice of and to reasonably confer with the prosecuting agency, upon request, regarding the arrest of the defendant if known by the prosecutor, the charges filed, the determination whether to extradite the defendant, and, upon request, to be notified of and informed before any pretrial disposition of the case.**

Rose: *Yes to all of the above. We even had a meeting with the District Attorney prior to the trial and discussed what charges the killer would face. This was a death-penalty case until we sat with the District Attorney and explained why we didn't want the death penalty. I did not want the murderer to have access to countless appeals; I already had a sentence of life without my loved ones, and I didn't want to be attending hearings for the person responsible for that. I asked the District Attorney if she would put the needle in my arm and put me out of my pain and misery, to which of course she said she couldn't do that. I responded: then please don't do it for him.*
We also had many letters sent in asking the District Attorney to please abide by the family's wishes and charge him with 2 life sentences without the possibility of parole. That is what he got!

7. **To reasonable notice of all public proceedings, including delinquency proceedings, upon request, at which the defendant and the prosecutor are entitled to be present and of all parole or other post-conviction release proceedings, and to be present at all such proceedings.**

Rose: *Yes, we were notified.*

8. To be heard, upon request, at any proceeding, including any proceeding, involving a post-arrest release decision, plea, sentencing, post-conviction release decision, or any proceeding in which a right of the victim is at issue.

Marina: The defendant was released some hours before we were informed—and we were within a few miles of her at the time. Considering that my father was brutally beaten with a lamp base, fists, and feet before being manually strangled, her release invoked no small amount of terror and apprehension in all of us.

National Organizations with Information for Survivors

(Contact information for each resource is at the end of this chapter.)

Office of Victims of Crime (OVC) is a resource for crime victim service professionals. Look for the tab called: **Help for Crime Victims**. There you will find lists of crime victim advocates in your location—see the **CONNECT** directory. Each location defines the scope of services, which can include: crisis intervention, applications for victim compensation, liaison with police and prosecution teams, criminal justice process information, court accompaniment. Look at their **GET HELP BULLETINS** for topics on the impact of crime, victim rights, resources for victims for families and friends. There is also a link to the **NATIONAL CRIME VICTIMS' BAR ASSOCIATON** for Civil Litigation.

Crime Stoppers USA is a national organization with local offices comprising strong partnerships with the community citizens, the media, and law enforcement. They help by setting up a fund with a base of $1000 reward for anonymous tips. This award can be increased by the family. Some locations are active in helping create posters for families to post, write and send out **press releases** for the media, and vigils in honor of the victim. Their many case successes are listed on their websites, along with press release examples and a guide on **How to Report a Crime** anonymously.

Parents of Murdered Children® (POMC) is a nonprofit, peer-led membership organization with chapters in many states; it was founded by parents who lost an adult daughter to homicide in 1978. The website has helpful information for all survivors of homicide, not just parents who have lost children. Examples of help are: lists from other survivors of problems survivors face, tips from survivors, legal terms, second opinion services, and more. A major component of this organization is a monthly, peer-led meeting in locations where the organization exists. While not counseling, it is supportive to be with others who share their experiences and support with the criminal justice process and loss.

Mothers Against Drunk Driving (MADD) states its Mission is to Stop Drunk Driving, support the victims of this violent crime, and prevent underage drinking. This organization was founded by mothers who lost children to drunk driving and has been instrumental in education and victim support. You can find locations in your state by going to the website and looking at the listings at the bottom of the website page. Additional information also applicable to other homicides is available, including brochures titled: *Your Grief: You're Not Going Crazy, Men and Mourning, Selecting a Civil Attorney, Guide Through the Criminal Justice System, Helping Children Cope with Grief*, and more.

Survivors of Violent Loss (SVLP) was founded by the author, who is a member of the national **Violent Death Bereavement Society** of professionals who study, research and provide specialized treatment in the aftermath of violent death. The organization's website is a source of useful information for co-victims, including poems and stories of inspiration from survivors, such as: the Homicide Diet, Courthouse Survival Advice, 9-11 Poem, I Never Got to Say Good-bye, and more. ***The Journey Workbook: Ten Steps to Learning to Live with Violent Death*** is available from this organization as well. Victim advocates and professionals will find helpful information on the website.

Survivor Tips

Rose

✔ ***Have someone you trust to be by your side***, *from notification and through the following days and weeks to come to help answer those questions that will come up that you know were explained but have no recollection of. Notes that were taken were very important to me later when I tried to piece those early moments together. You will have a hundred questions after the law enforcement leaves, so write those down, too, because law enforcement is not the best at getting back to you, and you will forget your questions.*

✔ *Don't try to do the funeral planning by yourself; have people you trust help you with those unfathomable decisions you have to make.*

✔ ***Get EVERYONE'S business cards*** *so you have contact information, and keep everything in a large envelope so it stays together and you aren't struggling to try to remember who was who and who does what.*

✔ *Understand from the beginning that the homicide department and the DA's office work for your murdered loved one; they do not work for you.*

✔ *Do your best to get along with those working on your loved one's case, if at all possible. There are naturally going to be times when you get fed up, tired of waiting on an arrest and updates, etc., but if you **can maintain some sort of working relationship, that will always be in your best interest.** (I failed to do that and had no communication or response from the Sgt. for nearly half a year, and for us that is a lifetime.) Basically these people go into homicide because they have a passion to solve these murders, to bring a measure of justice to our loved ones. They want it solved ALMOST as much as you do.*

✔ *Most importantly, as hard as it is to wait for an arrest,* **do not rush the detectives with their investigation.** *The conviction of the person responsible for your loved one's murder depends on a solid investigation by the homicide team, and then the DA's office has to make it into a case that can bring home a conviction. You get one shot at the murderer, and as hard as it is to wait to see them held accountable and convicted, it would be a whole lot worse to see them walk free forever!*

Harrier

✔ *As a survivor, tend to your grief, your emotions. I did not. In a criminal case, it's easy to set that aside while you search for a reasonable explanation for what happened and to see that justice is done. That search consumed me, and 30 years passed before I truly addressed the underlying emotions associated with the deaths of my parents.*

✔ *Law enforcement has a job to do, and rather than stonewalling them, cooperation may be the best course.* **The initial details coming out of a criminal investigation are often murky at best, and may even be false.** *I learned that the gut instinct of the cops turned out to be accurate, and that my brother and sister had intentionally lied to them and to me and to our family to conceal what had actually happened.*

✔ **Acknowledge that when a family member is a suspect, you cannot be objective.** *Even so, be cognizant of that and try to keep an open mind, and listen to what law enforcement is saying. It may turn out that they are wrong, but a kneejerk rejection of their suspicions may not helpful.*

Kaila

✔ **The detectives and the DA are just doing their jobs and can't help the family of the victim.** *The most helpful people in my case were the staff and secretaries at the court offices.*

✔ *Survivors should not expect the detectives or the district attorney to help them with their grieving; seek out information, or tell others that you are not OK.*

Resources

Black's Law Dictionary—The Free Online Law Dictionary http://www.thelawdictionary.org/discovery/.

Crime Stoppers USA; http://www.crimestoppersusa.com.

Citizens Against Homicide—free newsletter http://www.www.citizensagainsthomicide.org.

Mothers Against Drunk Driving (MADD); website has useful information for survivors of homicide, too; http://www.madd.org

Office of Victims of Crime (OVC) has a site to support crime victim and service professionals. https://ovc.ojp.gov.

Parents of Murdered Children, Inc.®; http://www.www.pomc.com.

National Center for Victims of Crime (NCVC) has a number of resources available to assist victims of crime. The Connect Directory provides a way for victims to locate service providers throughout the country and get help articles. http://www.www.ncvc.org.

National Crime Victim Bar Association is a network of attorneys and allied professionals dedicated to facilitating civil actions brought by crime victims. http://www.www.victimsofcrime.org/our-programs/national-crime-victim-bar-association.

National Victims' Constitutional Amendment Project; http://www.nvcap.org.

State of California Department of Justice, Victims' Bill of Rights Act of 2008: Marsy's Law; http://oag.ca.gov/victimservices/marsys_law.

Survivors of Violent Loss (SVL) website has useful information in its support and resource sections and has a link to *The Journey Workbook: Ten Steps to Learning to Live with Violent Death*; http://svlp.org.

U.S. Department of Justice, Office for Victims of Crime (OVC), provides an online directory of Victim Services throughout the country. OVC also provides information about victim assistance and compensation programs available in communities around the country. http://www.ojp.usdoj.gov/ovc.

U.S. Department of Justice, Crime Victims' Rights Act http://www.ovc.gov/rights/legislation.html.

U.S. Resource Map of Crime Victim Services & Information http://www.www.ovc.gov/map.html.

* Some Web addresses may have changed since publication.

Page intentionally left blank. Use it for jotting notes or your thoughts, if you wish.

5

The Homicide Investigation
What, How, Who and Why?

In the United States of America, one person is murdered every 35.6 minutes. (FBI, 2010)

What?

Murder impacts everyone! This fact has been given very little attention. While we know families are impacted, so are neighbors, friends, work and school mates, businesses, social and religious groups.

This includes those who serve in the criminal justice system. One homicide detective imagined the baby was a doll in order to remain emotionally detached and help him objectively investigate an infant's death. But to the survivors, this detachment can be perceived as "not caring." The majority of the time, that is not true. Investigators do care, but they can't let their emotions sidetrack the investigation. They must try to remain as objective as possible.

It is important for you to know who investigates:

> Police
> Prosecution
> Defense counsel
> News media

Our focus in this chapter will be on the investigations done by the police. Most investigations start at the crime scene. Usually, the first on scene is the beat cop. His job is to protect life, safeguard the scene, identify and detain witnesses or suspects, and call for help.

Next come the homicide investigators and their team. These investigators will be looking for everything and anything that may be related to the crime. If the crime scene is at your home, you may be denied access until the police have gathered all the forensic evidence they can identify.

Your life has been thrown into a well-developed system, a paramilitary system: the criminal justice system. More than likely you have had little experience with this system, and no matter how many movies or TV shows you have watched, you probably know little of how the system actually works. Police officers, as well as survivors/co-victims who have endured a criminal investigation, are quick to tell us that **it is not like TV**.

Richard Wissemann, Supervising Investigator for the San Diego District Attorney's office, says, "The real problem is that most people believe CSI is truly real, including the families and, unfortunately, the Jury. DNA cannot be identified in half an hour. [TV watching] can hurt as much as help your case."

Organized chaos takes place and, yes, it is a time of upmost importance to you, while the confusion is difficult to bear. It is important for you to stay on the sidelines and not interfere. Just take comfort in knowing that in most cases a well-organized, well-trained group is in charge.

Many survivors complain that they don't know what is going on, or that no one is getting back to them, and they are getting little information. Investigators do not know you or what happened, either. It is important that conclusions are not drawn too quickly. You may get a distorted view of who is involved and what is happening in the investigation, especially if a family member is a suspect. The situation is fluid and many changes may take place as investigators try to figure out what happened.

It's important for you to remember that law enforcement's primary duty is to the deceased, not to the survivors. In their effort to protect the integrity of the case, law enforcement will share little or no information with you. Respectfulness by all sides will go a long way in helping here.

I was surprised to learn that I knew nothing about the legal system. (Kaila)

The problem for survivors is that they want answers to their questions, but the investigators won't provide those answers if it is premature. Yes, you will become frustrated. But try to keep in mind that this is done for legal reasons—they do not want to undermine their case.

Hold firm to the belief that the details will come out in court and the perpetrator will be convicted and sent to prison. If this doesn't happen, there are other remedies, but while the investigation is active, the best thing you can do is not get in the way.

Tips for Dealing with Law Enforcement

Develop a good relationship with your investigator. You are on the same side. Their style and what they must do may result in only a good but not great working relationship. You may not agree with what they are doing or what they are classifying as important. But it is the best team that you have, and it has experience in matters that you and your friends do not have. They are doing their job, so developing a working relationship with them is important to achieving justice for your loved one. Each of them is accountable to someone. If needed, there is someone up the chain of command to address your concerns with.

> *I had contact with the homicide detectives.*
> *They asked a lot of questions but wouldn't answer*
> *mine. I understood that they were doing their job*
> *and were just trying to help find my sister's killer.*
> (Kaila)

When asked what families can do, a retired, 15-year-veteran homicide investigator says:

> *To assist with the case, families can help by being honest about their loved ones—such as acknowledging promiscuity, substance abuse, financial issues, or other characteristics or behavior. You may not want to share something that is embarrassing, or that your loved one was involved in illegal activities, but this information may lead the police to suspects more quickly. Know that they are not in the business of sharing information they get from you unnecessarily.*

This does not mean you should tell anyone other than the police what you know. In fact, the police advise family and friends **not to share this information with others. The most important thing is to tell the police everything you can**. The police have the broad stroke of investigating everything and everyone.

> *Anything you hear, the best thing to do is turn that information over to an investigating officer. Whether that is one day or ten years later. You never know when that one piece of information can turn a whole case around. Every lead that comes in is worked.* (CalPOST, 2009)

> *The final act must come from law enforcement. Maybe they aren't doing what you want them to. Sometimes you wonder why they are going that way. Do your best to give them what you have. Yours is not the only case they are working on. They are doing the best that they can. Do all you can to help.* (CalPOST, 2009)

Answer investigators' questions to help them eliminate suspects. The reality is that the suspect is usually someone known to the victim. One of the investigators' first tasks is to eliminate you as a suspect. Some of their questions are hard and hurtful when you know you are innocent, but it must be done because the police do not know you.

Ana Billa Vara, an attempted-murder victim and whose father was murdered, says, "They come out and say: Where were you? What did you do? Were you having an affair? They start victimizing you more. It is their job to uncover the truth." (CalPOST, 2009)

> *This was a hard process to watch; it didn't happen quickly at all, which was confusing. I watched a friend of my daughter jump through every hoop they put in front of him because not only did he know her daily routine, he was an active participant in it. He would take her son to daycare, pick him up when needed, take him to the doctor, and they were as close as if he were his father. I wasn't privy to all he went through, but I know it nearly killed him. All he wanted to do was help the homicide team find the real person responsible, but he had to be completely cleared as a suspect because we already knew the*

defense was going to accuse him of these horrific crimes. Homicide had to clear him beyond a reasonable doubt, and once they did, he probably took his first real breath after 5 months of intense scrutiny. (Rose)

In the book *Murder in Memphis* (Porch, 1997), the authors, in telling their true story, say that there were many things they didn't understand about the criminal justice system, including how they should behave when around the primary suspect. The police advised the family: *Please don't try to be detectives yourself, but do act as if you don't suspect anyone. Call neighbors and tell family to not express suspicions of your sister's husband and do not talk to the press.* **At the funeral, before the husband was identified publicly as a suspect,** the victim's dad was seen with a clenched fist, and family members worried that he would hit the husband.

Staying in your lane while feeling a deep sense of powerlessness and desperation can be very difficult. But the compulsion to do something, to fix things, can be detrimental to you. Cases have been lost due to well-intentioned family members and friends. It may be hard to figure out what is in your lane, what you can do, and that is why we are offering so many tips for what you can do. We suspect you will add to the lists in all these chapters.

As much as families want to be inside the investigation, they are not. Although you are deeply invested, you do not have the objectivity, training, and expertise necessary to conduct the investigation.

Steve Moore, retired FBI investigator, says in his blog (2014): "However, regardless of any law enforcement officer's empathy for the victim's family, absent their role as potential witnesses, family members should *never, ever* be allowed to become actively involved in the investigation and prosecution of suspects. . . . Why? For the same reason a doctor should never operate on his own child: Potential lack of both perspective and emotional detachment." The code of ethics does not allow doctors or therapists to treat their own family and close friends for the same reason.

> *I couldn't take the law into my own hands; I couldn't go and confront who I thought killed them, and, knowing where they lived, that was torture. I couldn't be in on the process of the investigation, but mostly I couldn't bring my daughter and grandson back.* (Rose)

Survivors can help by doing things to bring attention to the case.

My daughter's friends were broken and confused, and their lives were in shambles because they had loved my daughter and grandson and were now left swinging in the wind. None of them had any rights. Their pain and their fears were real, and yet society could barely deal with me much less acknowledge that the ripple effect of murder goes on and on, and many people are simply overlooked or ignored for the impact this has on their lives.

I couldn't have that. Because so many different emotions were coming at me from every direction, including my own, it was easier for me to focus on them and the fact that they needed help, too, and I wanted to be the one to give *it to them. No one understood that their pain was valid, important, not going to go away, nor would they be getting over it soon. **We were our own little group of support for each other;** none of us knew what we were doing, but we weren't doing it alone and that made a huge difference on all of our lives. We started going to a support group together; **we did almost everything regarding Victoria and Louis together**.* (Rose)

Take notes and take care of what you *can* do. Although not official, victim families, friends, co-workers, acquaintances, church family, and neighbors are involved in being members of the investigative team. **You all know the victim more than any stranger does.** Information will come fast and furious as to what you know and what you heard. You may be called as a witness and **your notes on dates, times, actual statements and persons**—but not thoughts and opinions—**will be very helpful.**

My supporters helped me stand and breathe when I couldn't. (Rose)

No one deserves to be murdered. The accusations that blame the victim or you (**only the killer is responsible**) can increase reactivity. Input like this can fuel fires from despair to rage. Get in a safe place with safe people when the anger boils up in you. Take a break, go for a walk, listen to a calming song, breathe. Wait for the intensity to pass before you do something you may regret later, then come up with an action plan.

Carrie Freitag, whose brother Bill was murdered in 1998, suggests in her book, *Aftermath* (2003), that although **survivors** are not given a clear role in the investigation, their involvement **can seriously impact the murder case in both positive and negative ways.**

Social media can be a helpful tool for the investigation of a suspect, as can cell-phone records. This can also be a tool for families, while being careful about what they reveal. Remember that what you write on social media can be used by the defense later in a trial.

How?

Families may be upset when they are not allowed to be physically close to their loved one at the crime scene. Investigators can appear cold and uncaring when what they are doing is preserving the situation so that potential evidence is not disturbed. They need that evidence in order to explain in court what happened and who did what. They can be better at preserving the scene than being comforting to families. Every effort is put in place to make sure the situation is safe and the scene is secure. Their job is to collect evidence and not contaminate the scene themselves or by anyone else in order to investigate what happened.

Investigator Wissemann says law enforcement often only has one chance to collect evidence. "This is why we are so meticulous, time consuming and often causing us to look insensitive to the family. Contamination is the demise of any potential incriminating evidence tainted by human error and possibly the difference between guilty and not-guilty (don't want to say innocent) verdict."

Former journalist Wayne Arthurson, in his novel *Fall From Grace* (2011), says:

> The **majority of cops do their jobs with honor and respect.** But the other truth is that there were countless times when good cops let the behavior of the bad ones slide because to call them to task or complain about them was to be labeled a rat.

The risk for human error is carefully guarded against. Scene contamination and errors can cause the guilty to go free or the innocent to be found guilty. The goal of the investigation is to maintain objectivity, to study and research each suspicious death. This is particularly challenging when the investigators get conflicting information from survivors, such as when an infant is murdered, or when a survivor is a possible suspect. You will not see or hear from many of the team members, although some may appear in court to testify about their evidence.

> I learned that some detectives may be great investigators, but they have no business interacting with a grieving family because they don't know how to talk to us in a dignified manner. We become more or less a bother to them, and they would prefer not to have to even see us. (Rose)

There is a "bible" on procedures used for homicide investigations nation-wide written by veteran homicide detective Vernon Geberth (1983). It explains homicide investigative techniques, from arrival at the crime scene through identification of the deceased and the autopsy to management of the investigation.

The investigation process is described in the book *Homicide Special* (2004) by Miles Corwin:

> (LAPD's Homicide Special Unit) scrupulously log every scrap of paper, notebook, photograph, greeting card, note, document, bill receipt, and match-book recovered from the apartment (scene). Then they compile the murder book, a three-ring binder. . . . It contains all the data gathered during an investigation, including evidence lists, crime scene photographs, diagrams, statements from patrol officers, suspects and witnesses, and keep a day-to-day, sometimes hour-to-hour, chronology of the investigation.

Collecting Evidence (Discovery) begins immediately. Every crime scene contains distinctive information that helps provide information on what happened and who was there. It is important to collect as much evidence as possible before an arrest is made. Every gun engraves distinctive groove marks and patterns on the bullet it releases. Everything you say or do that is written or captured is part of the story and must be turned over to the opposing side.

The larger the community, the greater chance to have an increased number of specialists. In our community, there are teams of five that work homicides and the case stays with that team until it is solved. In smaller communities, the job may be referred to a different agency. In some communities the team keeps the case, and in other communities they may have a standard rotation of officers working the case to give a broader opportunity for all staff to work different divisions and to provide a fresh look at the case.

Available today is a much improved tracking system for DNA, called CODIS. This software database allows for the collection of DNA profiles from offenders. CODIS enables state, local, and national law enforcement crime laborites to compare DNA profiles electronically. The success of CODIS is demonstrated by the thousands of matches that have linked cases to each other and cases that have been solved by matching crime scene evidence. (CODIS, 2013; Black's, 2013)

This has helped police identify possible suspects, but in itself does not solve the case, Wissemann says. It is merely another piece of evidence. Without corroboration, it does little. But it can be overwhelming evidence when tied to some other facts of the case. DNA has also freed the innocent who were wrongly prosecuted, often some 25 or more years earlier.

"The search for justice doesn't go away just because it's been a long time," says Carlton Stowers in his book *Scream at the Sky* (2003). He goes on to describe the plan to get a **DNA sample** of someone suspected of killing two or more girls a decade and half earlier. The police decided to use *abandoned interest* or *discarded property* to get the DNA sample:

> *The investigator, John Little, trailed and watched the suspect for several days at a Laundromat across from where he worked. Little washed the same clothes over and over while identifying the suspect's routine. Finally, and nervously, he saw his chance. After watching him drinking, and eating crackers and cheese, Little saw him leave his wife's truck and head back to work. Little approached him, after stuffing a wad of tobacco in his mouth, and said: "I was wondering if you've got a cup or something I can get from you. Yeah, a spit cup."*
>
> *"Oh yeah, sure. Help yourself."*
>
> *At that, Little looked inside the discard barrel and saw lots of cups, but one had remnants of cheese and crackers. "This'll work. Thanks."*

It couldn't have worked better. The fact that the suspect tossed it, and the investigator was allowed to take the cup, is a classic example of *discarded property*. The DNA was a match. Not only did this serial killer murder the two girls, he had killed a total of five women.

Many people wonder why police don't question the suspect first. Here is an example, from Michael Corwin's *Homcide Special* (2004), of the way detectives may proceed to question the list of people who have knowledge of their murder victim:

> *They decide to approach the case . . . in concentric circles, interviewing peripheral players first, then gradually moving inward . . . and finally to potential suspects. . . . Interviewing the suspects (first) would be useless, as the police have no witnesses, no concrete evidence, and no leverage.*

The rule of thumb is, know the answers to the questions before you ask the questions.

Who?

In this section, our focus is on discovering who killed your loved one. Although everyone may be included in trying to uncover this answer, only one team has this as their job and that is the homicide investigator and his or her team.

One of the worries for co-victims is that the investigation of who killed their loved one is shelved or not worked, which they translate as meaning that no one cares about their loved one. **Kaila** suspects that is what happened in her case when she says: *Later, a very rich, famous person was murdered. My DA took the case, and **my sister's case took a back seat** (maybe because she was not rich or famous).*

The truth is, the police may have several cases they are working on—yours is not the only one. While concerns like Kaila's may be true, most times it is not. The size of the community may also dictate how many investigators are involved in the case, as well as when the death crosses over into other jurisdictions.

One time I was doing crisis intervention in a death on a military base in a town that did not have a Homicide Team. My job was to stay with the witnesses and keep them supported, and not talk about what happened until they were interviewed. This took several hours, into the middle of the night, while the jurisdiction was clarified.

While the family may only have contact with the lead detective, **there is a large team** in place that reports to the detective.

> *The Sergeant of the homicide team was assigned to my daughter's and grandson's murders. I believed he was in charge, and if I had any questions I was to direct them to him. There were 5 other officers assigned to our case and although I met 4 of them, they were assigned to different friends and family members who they needed to question/interview, one being my husband. I didn't understand why my husband had some other detective to answer to than I did, but I didn't understand anything that was happening anyway.* (Rose)

Like you, investigators, too, are changed forever. You often do not see that, as they don't want to add to your burden. Each detective has different strengths. Jobs are split up to reflect that internal knowledge whenever possible.

Detectives do not work for you. Rose often quotes her Lieutenant letting her know just that. **They work for the state and represent victims.** She was surprised by the force of him telling her that when she was about to blow the case, but it was an important wake-up call.

If you do not hear updates from the investigators, it does not mean they have forgotten about your loved one. Rose realized she was not a part of the investigative team. She was a mother and had just lost her only child and ten-month-old grandson. The detective was not her employee.

Why?

Why did this happen to my loved one? This question is one of the most difficult for survivors to reconcile and can cause a lifetime of emotional turmoil.

Motive: Why did this occur, or the Motive question, begins immediately for the families as well as investigators. The answer can help provide leads to a suspect or the reason your loved one died. This is one of the reasons that having as much truthful information is so vital to the investigators.

The perpetrator told his son he would get a "29-cent divorce," the cost of a bullet. (Geberth, 1983)

Carol Ellis, director of victim services for the Fairfax County, Virginia, Police Department in 1996, says that within the justice system, "We can answer the 'how' of a person who was killed. But the 'why' is not easily explained. There are hundreds of examples of homicides committed for no valid or justifiable reason. Taking a human life is the ultimate act of violence, an act that is irreversible." (OVC, 2012)

The following are some of the most **common motives** for committing murder listed in a technical manual: abandonment/rejection, altruism, alcohol and drugs, escape, fame/celebrity, fatal abuse, protection of self or others, greed, hate/resentment, honor, insanity/mental illness, media influence, murder suicide, power/control, political ideals, rage, religion, rivalry/jealousy, and unwanted children. (Hickey, 2003)

The reason for my sister's death is a mystery—maybe she jilted him when he made some advances toward her? We will never know, nor would we believe him if he told us.

Here are some replies from the Survivor Writers:

- Money can be a big factor. Trying to stop paying or getting cut off from money. Marina believes her father's murderer was upset about getting cut off from a wealthy suitor.
- Rose believes the reason was to stop having to pay child support for 18-plus years.
- In Harrier's story, was it a way to cover up getting caught having sex with one's sister?
- Or a revenge killing of a sister because the killer could not find the actual target of his rage, as in Kaila's story?

In his book, *Why They Kill* (2003), Richard Rhodes says, ***"We can no longer say a bad seed or he just lost it or so on."*** Instead, many people who commit heinous violent crimes began being groomed at a young age, which he refers to as *violentization*.

People other than trained officials may recognize that a murder has taken place. For example, from the outset a law enforcement agency presumed a 22-year-old female's death was a suicide. The small-town police department lacked the resources to conduct a thorough investigation. All information concerning the woman's death came from her boyfriend. The medical examiner's decision was final, and law enforcement—in spite of numerous inconsistencies in statements from the boyfriend, overwhelming evidence of foul play, and documented reasons for the transferring this case to another agency. However, those that knew her persisted, and they got justice. (CAH, 2012)

The beginning of a criminal death investigation has as many variations as each murder has. One variation is shown in a movie made in India called *No One Killed Jessica* (2011). This movie shows how a rich kid, in spite of many eye witnesses, **got away with murder**. Only after a journalist rallied public support did the legal system eventually take action, many years later, and get a conviction.

When the investigation slows down, agencies and families continue to search for answers. One important agency to work with is Crime Stoppers, which offers a $1000 award for new information. Families can increase the dollar amount with more donations, and Crime Stoppers will hold those funds for a period of time.

When you have a no-arrest situation, what do you do? While most arrests are made right away or within a few days, when there is no arrest, homicide cases remain open, as there is no statue of limitations on murder. If this is your situation, two items will absorb your attention: (1) finding new leads for detectives, and (2) protecting your safety.

Work with your family members and review strategies suggested in Chapter One and have each member select areas to focus on that may bring new leads and potential threats. This may appear to conflict with earlier advice to stay in your lane, but it doesn't. As we have mentioned before, you (all of you) know your loved one the most, and you may think of more things as time moves along. Each part of your support team can carry a notebook and keep a log on ideas, information, and so on.

Questions for This Section

The focus in this section is on the homicide investigation. Each of you have different stories and circumstances, but we hope to help you appreciate the uniqueness of your story and the process you will encounter. This chapter has come together with our team of writers and authors, and interviews from national, state, and local resources.

Survivor Questions: Who was arrested? How soon after the death of your loved one was the arrest(s)? What was the outcome of the arrest?

Write your answers in your notebook.

Rose

Much to my surprise, I received a phone call telling me they had just arrested two people in connection with the murders of my daughter and grandson. I expected the first one to be the biological father of my grandson—but I was surprised to find out that his best friend, who was also his alibi, was arrested at the same time. It took 18 long and torturous months.

Bail was denied to the father, but his friend was originally given a bail amount of $200,000. However, the arraignment judge increased it to $500,000. He was released a few days later after posting bail.

Marina

My dad's girlfriend was arrested on a summer morning in 1999. Her arrest came roughly eight to ten hours after she allegedly killed Dad.

Her confinement did not last very long. She was bailed out the following morning by a girlfriend. Turns out the killer called her little pal ten or eleven times from Dad's phone on the night of the murder. She arranged for bail while Dad lay dead or dying on his own bedroom floor. She spent a night in jail. Then she was set free.

I learned this as I prepared to go to Dad's house for the first time since the murder. The police had concluded their investigation, so we were "free" to enter the house.

But it was a murder house. I didn't want to go. But I HAD to go. Not only that, but now there was the tandem need to change the locks on Dad's doors. The sheriff had advised that we do this as soon as possible. A killer was roaming at will.

Harrier

In my case, **no one was ever arrested**, charged, indicted, or prosecuted. In my mind, my parents never got the justice they deserved.

The FBI kept assuring me that an indictment was imminent and the trial was just a few months away. That dragged on for more than three years. Ultimately, it fizzled and became a cold case, awaiting a witness who would agree to testify truthfully in court. Thirty-six years later, I'm still waiting.

Kaila

My ex-boyfriend was arrested about one month after my sister's death. He denied that he killed her and pled the fifth.

Yvonne

The perpetrator was a neighborhood stranger who lived within a couple miles of our family. The only accurate date and information I can obtain is from related news articles. I am led to believe that it was within a week or two of my mother's attack. I understand that his arrest was within several blocks of our house as he attempted to do the same to a neighbor. Again, he had gained entry into her residence; thankfully, she was able to escape.

As I understand it, he was given 25 years to life, becoming eligible for parole every 5 years.

Halia

One of the two suspects in the abduction, rape, and murder of my sister was arrested. Both suspects were initially interviewed and released after questioning.

The arrest occurred 28 years later. It was a combination of a very persistent detective and the latest forensic technology that led to the arrest of one of the two suspects.

The outcome of the arrest is that we were able to get a 21-year sentence to keep the convict behind bars.

Mary

Six teenage boys were arrested. Five of them were 16-year-olds and one was 17 years old. A couple had been in trouble with the law before and for the others, this was their first time.

They were arrested one month after our son's murder. We knew at Thanksgiving that the police were close to making arrests, but it was hard knowing that the perpetrators got to spend Thanksgiving with their families and we were without our son.

They all were arrested on a Friday and kept in jail until the following Monday when they went for arraignments. Two of them were charged with Murder. Our son had been stabbed 6 times, and he had two slashes across his face. It was believed that a pocket knife and a box cutter were used. (No weapons had been found at that time and it is now believed that some of the parents may have gotten rid of the knives.)

The other four teenagers were charged with Accessory to Murder. The bail for the two charged with Murder was

1.25 million dollars. The bail for the four charged with Accessory to Murder was $500,000. None ever were able to post bail and all remained behind bars throughout the Court proceedings.

JJ

Six teens were arrested on charges ranging from murder to conspiracy/accessory, more than a month later. However, little physical evidence was recovered due to the length of time between the crime and arrest.

All six have received jail time as a result of accepting plea offers from the State. The sentences ranged from 15 to 35 years.

Survivor Questions: What was your/your family's role at this point in the process? What surprises, complications, disappointments happened?

Write your answers in your notebook.

Rose

Long before our investigation was turned over to the DA's office, I went to Victim's Assistance trying to get information because I wasn't getting it from the detectives, and I felt like I was going crazy. Not only did the secretary at the DA's office not answer any of my questions, she asked if I was sure my daughter and grandson were murdered in their jurisdiction because she had never heard of them or the murders. Needless to say that is not the response I was looking for, nor was it helpful in any way.

This is a question I asked so many times I lost count. It was one of the most frustrating lessons I had to learn on this journey. It made no sense to me that someone, anyone, could not be bothered

with updating me much less return my calls. It isn't singled out to any one person; we all get that treatment. The reason they don't call you and keep you updated is because:

A) They keep the investigation private so no one accidently leaks information that should not be known to the public; also referred to as "for the integrity of the case." Often times they hold information back to use in an interrogation with a suspect.

B) As it was told to me, it really isn't their job to call us or even return our calls with an update; they are busy investigating not only our case but many cases at one time. I was told after the trial that they didn't know what to say to me when I called. They said "trust us, we are working on it; no there isn't any new *information we can share with you." They said this so many times that not only was it falling on deaf ears (mine), I was very angry and vocal about it, which didn't help the situation.*

I also learned afterward that it was very hard for them not to be able to tell me more because they were fully aware of how desperate I was for any answers. To which I responded, "You don't know how hard it was for me to wait for your call. I don't care if it was too hard for you to call me and not have anything new to tell me. It didn't change the fact that I sat by the phone day after day, week after week, month after month, waiting for the phone to ring."

Marina

The family had no role in the arrest. The big surprise and disappointment was that the accused spent just one night in jail. She was never incarcerated again.

Harrier

I had defended my brother up to the point of being an observer at the FBI's questioning aboard the sailboat. I wanted to believe what he had told me in terms of what had happened aboard the boat and how our parents had died. But as I witnessed his explanation to the FBI, things didn't add up; it didn't make sense. I began to doubt the veracity of what he told the investigators; I began to wonder if my brother was hiding something, and if so, what?

The next day, the FBI interviewed him again but would not let me observe. Later, as I became aware of more evidence that my brother had lied to me and law enforcement, I could no longer deny that he might be responsible for our parents'

deaths. My sister said he had assaulted and raped her prior to the deaths.

*When the probate court scheduled a hearing to settle my parents' estate, two of my sisters and I filed an objection to the dispersal of the estate, alleging that our brother was the "slayer" of our parents. We wanted our parents to have their day in court. We hoped that enough evidence would come out to aid the criminal prosecution, which was still ongoing. However, **my brother did not contest the allegation**, and agreed not to receive any inheritance. But it was a hollow victory. My parents never got their day in court.*

Kaila

My role was to tell the family of any court procedures and any new developments with the case.

***I was surprised to learn that I knew nothing about the court system,** and I had to put my feelings aside to help the family understand what was going on with the trial. Complications arose when a witness was badly beaten up before he testified for my sister's trial. I was scared that I might be next; I was scared to tell my family. I was not sure what to do. Disappointment came after, when the trial kept getting postponed many times over, due to unclear reasons. The disappointments kept coming.*

*Later, a very rich, famous person was murdered. My DA took the case and **my sisters case took a back seat** (maybe because she was not rich or famous). The disappointments didn't stop there. I was not informed that a detective had had an affair with a witness that was testifying for my sister's trial; basically a lot of information was not presented, and later I found out I was not allowed to say things* that I thought would help the trial. Things like my ex-boyfriend that killed my sister was physically abusive, and because I left him, he couldn't find me so he killed her.

Yvonne

My sister and I were minors at the time. Understandably, my father went to great lengths to ensure that we would be protected during the trial. According to my father's account, of which I recently learned, the killer admitted to his crimes in exchange for a shorter sentence.

Halia

My family interacted with the detectives early on in the case and maintained contact throughout the years to determine if there was any progress in the case. Once an arrest was made, I acted as the family liaison between the court and my family to communicate regarding the legal proceedings.

Mary

At arraignment the police had warned us that it would be better to stay away as there could easily be a large crowd of supporters for these six and it would be difficult for us to see. So the family stayed away and many of our son's friends did go. And, yes, there were many supporters there for our son's murderers. It was a school day and many, many teenagers skipped school to be there. Later, this was addressed by the city and the school board. The police were out in force to keep peace at the Courthouse.

The only surprise I had at this time was when I heard that the reason our son was killed was because six teenagers were bored that night! The complication was that the murder weapons were never found! Later, the surprise was that we heard parents had gotten rid of the weapons!

The police were never able to prove this, so no parents were ever charged. I know parents want to be there for their children, but whatever happened to loving your children but making them stay responsible for their actions?

We were also disappointed that arrests couldn't be made sooner. The team knew who the teenagers were, but had to make the case so solid that if a Probable Cause hearing was asked for, we would win and be able to move forward.

The other thing that disappointed and angered us was the day after our son died, the Public Relations Officer for the police put out a statement that they felt this was a drug deal gone bad and that the city was safe. Our son's friends immediately jumped on this, saying that it was absolutely not so.

The investigation had barely begun and yet the Public Relations Officer was saying that our son played a part for responsibility in his death. The city cried out for justice and let others know that the city was not safe and that the Public Relations Officer should not have put out that statement as the investigation had barely begun. The Public Relations Officer no longer works in this town.

JJ

We had no role in the arrests or events leading up to it other than profiling our son early in the investigation. We participated in the development of the plea offers, which was very stressful. We also read victim's *impact statements at each of the sentencing hearings.*

Learning about the details of sentencing and the limitations on the justice/penal system was difficult and ultimately disappointing. *Initially, we were fully prepared to go to trial for each defendant; in retrospect, given the toll on our family of just appearing for the sentencing, six trials would have been very difficult.*

Survivor Question: What tips and lessons would you like new families to have during the investigation?

Write down your tips and lessons in your notebook.

Rose

Therapy is so important, I think; the sooner the better. But you have to find the right therapist because not all of them have experience with violent loss.

Support groups, where you can be open and in a judgment-free zone. Here is where you learn that you are not crazy, that others are experiencing the same thoughts and feelings, and in some ways that is very comforting.

Do ANYTHING that honors your loved one's life, that can take you out of the horror of the murder.

Marina

*I don't have any tips or lessons. This phase of the process did not last long enough. But **don't imagine that a quick arrest means automatic success** down the road.*

Harrier

Keep an open mind. *When a family member is accused of a crime, especially a crime against another family member, a common reaction is disbelief and being defensive. At the outset, I* refused to believe my brother could be responsible for our parents' deaths. I defended him against the outrageous allegations of the police and FBI agents. But as the evidence mounted, I had to step back and try to be objective, to see it from the law enforcement perspective, and it horrified me.

Acknowledge that when a family member is involved, you cannot be objective. *Even so, be cognizant of that and try to keep an open mind, and listen to what law enforcement is saying. It may turn out that they are wrong, but kneejerk rejection of their suspicions may not helpful.*

Kaila

Do not do this alone, *either families unite, or find an organization that knows what to do when your mind can't wrap around the confusion.*

Yvonne

I guess that it could be possible to isolate any knowledge of the trial process from children. Again, extreme measures would need to be set in place in order to do so. This becomes an enormous challenge, I wish that some tips could be offered; sadly, I can't.

Halia

Patience, *support one another and self-care, self-care, self-care.*

Mary

The day after our son died, we met with the lead detective, the detective who kept us informed, and a few other detectives on the case, as well as the Chief and the Captain of the police force. The lead detective sat us down and for more than 3 hours talked to us about what they knew had happened; they asked us about who our son was and what his lifestyle was (much of the day-to-day things were given by our other son, as he was so close to his brother), and about what the team was doing to find and capture who killed our son.

Over the next week, we had several discussions and knew that each detective was putting in between 12 to 16 hours a day working on this case. They gave us the confidence to know that they would find out who murdered our son. We gave them the respect that we trusted them to find the killer/killers. That allowed us to move forward, making plans for our son's burial.

I guess for me the tip for new families would be to **stay as calm and respectful as possible.** *If you rant and rave, the police will shut you out and not keep you informed. Remember* **that you want their concentration to be on finding the killers and not on dealing with hysterical family members.** *They need to move quickly to get as much information as possible as early as possible.*

But you also want information, so if you stay calm and don't keep getting in their faces, they will be able to give you what they can quickly, then get back to finding the killers. This being said, you also don't want misinformation put out about your loved one. **Stay strong and stay firm about who your family member was.**

JJ

Do not expect a significant flow of information from the investigators; rather, look for more general status reports *that suggest how well they are progressing. Cooperative listening worked best for us.*

Not All Homicides Are Murder

Criminal Homicide: Prohibited and punishable by law, such as murder or manslaughter.

Excusable Homicide: Resulting from a person's lawful act, committed without intention to harm another.

Justifiable Homicide: The killing of another in self-defense when faced with the danger of death or serious bodily injury (same as excusable homicide).

Negligent Homicide: Resulting from the careless performance of a legal or illegal act in which the danger of death is apparent; the killing of a human being by criminal negligence.

Reckless Homicide: The unlawful killing of another person with conscious indifference toward that person's life.

Vehicular Homicide: The killing of another person by one's unlawful or negligent operation of a motor vehicle.

Manslaughter: The unlawful killing of a human being without malice aforethought.

Involuntary Manslaughter: Homicide in which there is no intention to kill or do grievous bodily harm, but that is committed with criminal negligence or during the commission of a crime not included within the felony-murder rule.

Voluntary Manslaughter: An act of murder reduced to manslaughter because of extenuating circumstances, such as adequate provocation (arousing the "heat of passion") or diminished capacity.

> —*Criminal Law Dictionary* and law-enforcement professionals

Murder

Depraved-Heart Murder: A murder resulting from an act so reckless and careless of the safety of others that it demonstrates the perpetrator's complete lack of regard for human life.

Felony Murder: A murder that occurs during the commission of a felony.

First-Degree Murder: Willful, deliberate, or premeditated, or that is committed during the course of another serious felony (often limited to rape, kidnapping, robbery, burglary, or arson). All murder perpetrated by poisoning or by lying in wait is considered first-degree murder.

Second-Degree Murder: A murder that is not aggravated by any of the circumstances of first-degree murder.

The Office of Victims of Crime Resource Paper on Homicide (DOJ, 2012) includes:

Spousal homicide: The killing of a spouse, life partner, or other significant individual of the same or opposite sex with whom one has lived for some time and formed a stable relationship.

Child homicide: The killing of a person under the age of 18.

Shaken-baby syndrome: The violent shaking of a young child that causes permanent brain injury and/or death.

Parricide: The killing of one's parent.

Stranger homicide: The killing of a person or persons by an individual unknown to the victim.

Mass murders: The murder of several victims within a few moments or hours of each other.

Serial killing: The violent acts of an offender who kills over time. The offenders usually have at least three to four victims, and their killing is characterized by a pattern in the type of the victims selected, or the method or motives used in the killings.

Capital case: A murder case for which a possible sentence is the death penalty.

Resources

Citizens Against Homicide (CAH) Newsletter, subscribe online http://www.citizensagainsthomicide.org.

Dare I Call It Murder?: A Memoir of Violent Loss, Larry M. Edwards, Wigeon Publishing, San Diego, CA, 2013; http://www.dareicallitmurder.com.

Murder, Connie Saindon, *Encyclopedia of Trauma,* Charles Figley, Ed., Sage Publications, Thousand Oaks, CA, 2003.

Encyclopedia of Murder & Violent Crime: Murder, Homicide and Trauma, Eric Hickey, Ed., Sage Publications, Thousand Oaks, CA, 2003.

Murder in Memphis: The true story of a family's quest for justice, Doris Porch & Rebecca Easley. New Horizon Press, Far Hills, NJ, 1997.

The Ride: A Shocking Murder and a Bereaved Father's Journey from Rage to Redemption, Brian Macquarrie, Da Capo Press, 2009.

Scream at the Sky: Five Texas Murders and One Man's Crusade for Justice, Carlton Stowers, St. Martin's True Crime Library, 2004.

Why They Kill: Discoveries of a Maverick Criminologist. Richard Rhodes, Alfred A. Knopf, Inc., New York, NY, 1999.

* Some Web addresses may have changed since publication.

6

The Criminal Justice Process

I think it is vital for survivors to know that real murder and its aftermath only faintly resemble what one sees on television shows. (Marina)

The criminal justice system is an adversarial system set up **in the search for truth.** When a complaint or indictment from the Grand Jury has been filed stating that a crime has been committed, **both sides have a right to an attorney: prosecution and defense.** Our country was founded on the constitutional rights of anyone accused of a crime. The fact is, they are presumed innocent until found guilty in a fair, unbiased trial.

For survivors and co-victims, the pressure to follow what is happening in the criminal justice system is of greatest importance. Swings in emotional intensity are expected and may keep you from processing and remembering well. This is normal, as we discussed in Chapter Two, and not a sign of your incompetence.

Keep in mind that **the District Attorney (DA) is not your personal attorney; the DA works for the state on behalf of the crime victim(s).** A Deputy District Attorney (prosecutor) is assigned to prosecute the accused for the murder of your loved one. The Defense Attorney is hired to defend the accused against the charges brought by the prosecutor.

The District Attorneys are on your side and have the same goals as you for getting justice, but your participation in the proceedings will be limited. It is rare that a request to change prosecutors happens. Typically, the DA's office does not get the case until an arrest is made.

Both sides have rights to the information about the case. The prosecution has an obligation to turn over all materials no later than 30 days before the trial starts. Defense attorneys have the same obligation, but they often state that some material cannot be provided as it is bound by client-attorney privilege. The result is that not all of the information that the defense team has will be turned over to prosecutors.

Legal terms, rules, and procedures can add increased confusion. Information provided in this chapter can help you, especially when you can refer to it again and again. Our Survivor Writers, as well as survivors I have worked with, reveal some terms and surprises that were new to them.

As with other sections in this handbook, our inspiration comes from these experiences. Questions you have that are not answered here can be further explored through the recommendations and resources provided. No book, this one included, can cover it all. You may find information on legal terms and the criminal justice process on both your State Attorney General and District Attorney websites.

Victim Advocates

Your first contact with the District Attorney's office is often through a Victim Advocate. You may not remember them nor realize they are part of the DA's team. More than likely you have their contact information, even if you don't remember getting it. If you don't know who they are, you should ask your other key contacts how to reach them. In many communities, this department is within the District Attorney's office.

The prosecutor may not always be available; a victim advocate can be a good source in keeping you apprised of case actions. It is helpful to have another person to reach. While the DA's main responsibility is to prosecute the case and uphold the law, a victim advocate is there to work on your behalf. Additionally, the victim advocate can provide information and resources on entitlements that you may be eligible for.

Keep notes and collect cards.

In addition to other ways victim advocates help, they are an important resource when you are ready to go to court and be at the trial; their job is to provide you with an orientation and information. Their knowledge about the criminal justice system and legal terms will be invaluable. They may also be available for court accompaniments as well.

Make a list of important contacts. Invite family and friends to help with this.

KEY CONTACTS

Victim Advocate
Name: _____ Phone #/email: _____
DA Investigator
Name: _____ Phone #/email: _____
Deputy District Attorney
Name: _____ Phone #/email: _____

Others:
Title: _____
Name: _____ Phone #/email: _____
Title: _____
Name: _____ Phone #/email: _____
Title: _____
Name: _____ Phone #/email: _____

Each criminal justice community has decisions it can make, so no universal process is available in this handbook. Your Key Contacts can help you, so don't hesitate to ask—and you may need to ask more than once. As with Medical Language, you are not expected to either know nor fully understand all of the legal terms. Each occupation has its own language to increase specificity so that colleagues can more finely tune their communications, but it's often confusing to outsiders.

As in earlier chapters, you will have an opportunity to write your own answers to questions that have been answered in this chapter by our Survivor Writers. Your story, like each of theirs, is different. **Take notes all along the way and document details about your contacts and the process.**

A useful page called "My Case Information" is duplicated for you to fill out; this will help you keep track of your case. You will find it at the end of this chapter, before Resources. This page is from the **Trial Book** from the **Arizona Homicide Survivors, Inc.**, which is listed in Resources. Even though this guide fits Arizona, it has lots of helpful information. There are very few manuals or resources available, so use this guide to help you understand the process, and ask your local team when you have questions. There are some things you should know about going to court.

Going to Court

By all accounts, going to court is a daunting, intimidating experience for survivors/co-victims of homicide. I have worked hard to never have to go to court and, like many of you, until I began this work I never knew much about it. Going to court may not be worse than having to identify your loved one at the morgue, but it can be a close second. It is worse than many other "have to do" experiences. No matter how upsetting, survivors/co-victims tell me they must attend court proceedings for their murdered loved one.

The court room is set up to be adversarial, having families sit on different sides. Family members can be excluded from court if they get too emotional.

The truth is, **going to court is a choice**. It just doesn't feel that way, as it is a time to be a presence for your loved one. It is the work of holding someone accountable for your loved one's murder. It is also a way to have your loved one present in the courtroom when he or she cannot be there. Everyone in the courtroom needs to know that your loved one exists as more than evidence, that he or she was loved and valued.

Some things to know about when going to court. The courtroom is set up to be adversarial, having families sit on different sides. Family members can be excluded from court if they get too emotional.

If you want to avoid some of the activities that take place in the courtroom, ask your Key Contacts which meetings are more important than others. This might be a good time to ask those who want to support you to attend to help reserve time and energy for when you really need to be there. Court procedure can be very confusing; your advisors can guide you.

On the next page is a chart of the role and responsibilities of some of the criminal justice professionals that will be involved with your case.

Criminal Justice Professionals
Roles and Responsibilities

Police (Proof—probable cause)
• Enforce specific laws
• Investigate
• Search people, vicinities, buildings
• Arrest or detain people

Prosecutors (Proof—beyond a reasonable doubt)
• File charges or petitions for adjudication (going to trial)
• Seek indictments from the Grand Jury
• Drop cases
• Reduce charges
• Investigate
• Prosecute the case
  • Present evidence
  • Argue
  • Present rebuttals
  • Keep victims informed

Judges or magistrates
• Set bail or conditions for release
• Accept pleas (guilty, not guilty, and plea bargaining)
• Dismiss charges
• Impose sentence
• Make decisions on motions, hearings
• When a bench trial, determine guilt or innocence
• Are an unbiased presence

Source: professionals within the criminal justice system.

Survivor Questions: Who informed you that the case would be prosecuted and kept you updated? What mistakes did you make? What mistakes did others make? Can we ask for a different prosecutor?

This set of questions will frame the experience and confusion that can take place as a case proceeds. Think about the answers that you know so far and come back to this when you know more about what's going on. Write your answers in your notebook. Be as honest as you can, as each of our writers have been.

Rose

*I don't know if we had a role as far as the police and prosecutor were concerned; but I do know that in my mind, **my role was to represent my daughter and grandson with as much grace and dignity as I could.** I knew that if there was going to be a court hearing, be it a 5-minute hearing or a lengthy one, I was going to be sitting in my daughter's seat, and my husband would be in our grandson's seat. I wanted the court to know that my daughter and grandson had beautiful lives and they were senselessly, brutally murdered. It was well known early on that I would be in that courtroom every second that those monsters were in court. I believed then as I believe now that we were there to be Victoria's and Louis's voices because they could not speak for themselves.*

I was surprised that the person who gave our murderer an alibi (solid alibi, I was told) was also arrested and charged with "conspiracy to obstruct justice." I didn't understand that charge, but then again, after 18 months, I still didn't know 1/10*[th]* of what happened the night my daughter and grandson had been murdered. I was disappointed that I didn't get any real answers, either. I was semi-surprised at the satisfaction I felt seeing them both enter the courtroom in shackles and hand-cuffed. I was surprised and extremely disappointed at the people who came in support of the two accused. Seeing his family wasn't surprising, but friends of theirs that went to school with them as well as with my daughter, that knew my daughter, and yet they were there supporting a person accused of murdering her and her son—his biological son— was more than I could comprehend. Who supports people like that? I was disgusted with all of them.*

Marina

There are many things I don't remember because of the trauma involved. I do remember that some functionary from the DA's office called to advise us of the arraignment date. That was a perfunctory hearing. The prosecutor assigned to Dad's case wasn't able to attend because he was tied up in court.

About a month after the arraignment, I received a call from our prosecutor. He spent half an hour on the phone with me. I liked him immediately because he demonstrated a genuine passion for the case. He attended the murder scene and vowed to put Dad's murderer away for a very long time. He urged me to call any time I had a question. Accessibility is highly desirable in a prosecutor, so I was thrilled about that.

I met him several weeks later. He had the murder book on his desk. He answered many of my questions—protocol and confidentiality forbade answering others. The book was a good seven inches thick, but his grasp of the case was such that he could access any page he wanted within a couple of seconds. His intellect was prodigious, but he had an easygoing, warm personality. He knew how to tell a story, which made me very happy as well. Juries don't like to be bored. Court is boring enough already.

During the first year, little happened, so there wasn't much reason to talk with him. The preliminary came and went, and he did very well. I could almost hear the sound of the cell door closing upon the murderer forever. This prosecutor was that good.

Then the unthinkable happened. One day the prosecutor called to tell me that he was no longer on the case. A sixteen-year-old female witness on a gang murder case accused him of sexual harassment. He was put on administrative leave pending the outcome of an investigation. Ultimately he was exonerated, but it didn't matter, because another prosecutor had already been assigned to our case. I cannot convey adequately my sense of devastation. It was yet another profound loss in a year of too many of them.

After I met with the new prosecutor, I was not happy, but I quelled my fears. I remained doggedly optimistic even though the new man made it clear he did not want the case. He felt it had been foisted upon him.

When I asserted that he did not care, he impatiently gestured at all of the case files in his office. Clearly, I was just a face in the crowd to him. While the first

prosecutor believed the case to be a strong one, the second prosecutor thought it was weak and way too circumstantial. He said he was worried. He was not confident of winning. I hated that—how could he convince a jury of the murderer's guilt without a strong display of conviction?

Plus, he was not particularly well-dressed, and had no personality. He was all business. You might think I'm being petty, but the things I just mentioned matter to juries. I desperately wanted a different prosecutor. But in criminal, families do not choose who prosecutes a case. Families do not determine the charges, either—that would constitute a conflict of interest. The DA's office determines the charges after the police investigate the murder.

With the coming of the second prosecutor, we pretty much ceased to matter. The man answered my calls promptly, but that was it. He did the bare minimum that he was required to do by law. To be fair, I would guess that he was overworked and underpaid. That possibility didn't make it any easier to be treated as a nuisance.

I didn't make many calls. I was polite and helpful. It didn't matter because I didn't matter, and Dad didn't matter.

During the second year, a victim witness representative handled updates. He was a very young and sweet man. His inexperience showed, but he compensated for that with kindness and a strong work ethic. He was wonderful. During the trial, he was very supportive and professional.

He later quit the DA's office because he was so disgusted with the outcome of our case. The person who followed him was a young woman with the personality of a mollusk. She wasn't very bright and didn't like to talk, so I wondered why she was chosen as a victim witness representative in the first place.

Harrier

Following the death of my parents, the local police conducted a criminal investigation. They alleged there had been a "melee" on the boat and, most likely, my brother had killed our parents, and our youngest sister may have been involved as well.

Two days later, the investigation ended and my brother and sister were free to go. It was over. Or so I thought. The following day, I was summoned back to police headquarters. The boat had been impounded and I had to turn over my passport. The police captain then showed me a telegram—FBI agents were on their way. Four days later, the investigation began anew, with increased intensity. Because the deaths occurred on the "high seas," it was under federal jurisdiction rather than the local police and district attorney's office.

Although the FBI refused to disclose everything, they gave me unexpected information and even allowed me to observe one of their interviews with their prime suspect in the murder investigation.

As the investigation dragged on, the primary agent on the case agreed to meet with me periodically to update me and pass along bits of information pertaining to the investigation. He believed my brother was guilty and vowed to get the case to court. However, months would go by without any word and I had to pester him. But I also had to live with the fact that he had other cases to work on besides my parents' case.

Three years after the deaths, the case stalled, and I met with the U.S. attorney assigned to prosecute the case. He explained why there would likely be no prosecution, no trial—the case was circumstantial; there were no bodies; there was little forensic evidence; and my sister was not a reliable witness. He did not want to risk incurring jeopardy by losing the case. The case never went to trial and remains unresolved.

Kaila

I got a call from a detective saying that they had the murderer in custody and therefore the prosecution began. My biggest mistake was in not staying in the same state where my sister's murder took place. I feel that if I was in the same state that I could have easier access to information, and I could have been there at all times.

The mistake others made was in not informing me of events that were happening as they were unfolding. One time I walked into the DA's office and on his wall was a huge poster of him and two other prosecutors with the words "the dream team." The poster was about a high-profile case that put my sister's case on the back burner. It made me feel that this was just a job to them and they didn't really care about my family's pain. It seems like the office women in this case cared about keeping me informed more than the men in this case—a weird observation, but I felt that it was just a job to the men, which happened to be the detectives, DA, and other prosecutors. The women I spoke to seemed to be more compassionate and informative, while getting information from the men seemed to be heartache.

Mary

We had a detective who kept us informed weekly until the arrests were made. This same detective also called us monthly after the arrests to ask how we were doing, and he called us on the anniversaries of our son's murder. He has always shown us great compassion.

We went through two Prosecutors. The first one was very forceful and let us know that he would convict these killers and make them stay in prison for a very long time. But at the same time, he introduced us to another Prosecutor who would be taking over the case as the first Prosecutor was retiring in a few months.

In the State Attorney's office, we were assigned a Victim Advocate. This is the person who was supposed to keep us updated. We had two over the course of the two and a half years. The first one saw us through a Probable Cause hearing four months after our son's death. I didn't feel he kept us informed, and since I was still reeling with grief and in shock, I wasn't constantly calling him. The detectives were the ones I reached out to. My daughter did connect more with this Advocate and developed more of a rapport.

The second Victim Advocate got me through the rest of prosecution. She called and kept us informed. She is a warm person who instilled sincere caring about who our son was and just what we were going through. She has done all that she could to ease us through the proceedings. I have always felt comfortable calling her with questions and concerns. She answered all my questions, and if she didn't have answers she went and found them and got back to me promptly. She was my liaison to the Prosecutor. I greatly admire this service and how we were dealt with.

As I thought our first DA was very good and tough, the DA we got six months later seemed weaker. We were always

unsure about whether he was tough enough to get a conviction. We were concerned about staying in good graces with the DA so that we wouldn't be shut out of knowing what was going on with the case.

 **JJ**
The detectives were very clear early on that they couldn't give out much information on an ongoing investigation. However, we were blessed with having a personal friend on the force who kept in touch with us daily initially, and then weekly throughout the investigation. What he had to tell us was rarely shocking and most often had been present in social media or newspapers beforehand. But having that connection to talk about the investigation made us feel a part of the proceedings and much more satisfied with the police effort. We felt like we were on the same team. I would encourage survivors to rally for a consistent and frequent connection rather than demanding information.

The best information we received came from the Victim Advocate. We had several meetings with the State's Attorney but more often were able to get additional insights or communicate back to the State's Attorney most effectively through the Victim Advocate. We did not get any information that was invalid, but the prosecution did change over time and resulted in plea offers instead of trials.

We would have preferred a more aggressive State's Attorney. The prosecutor seemed equally satisfied with a plea for a reduced sentence than a guilty verdict with a maximum sentence. He emphasized the uncertainty of a jury trial, and the trauma on the survivors associated with a trial.

The Out-of-Town Burden

Under the best of circumstances, attending court proceedings can be a problem for family members. This problem is magnified when you live out of town. For example, a family lived in South Carolina and the case was in Alaska, while another family lived in California and the case was in New England. Harrier's story took him to a foreign country, where his parents were killed; later he moved from San Diego to Seattle, where his family originated and where the FBI was handling the case.

Halia experienced a similar problem:

> *In our case, the Victim Advocate initially acted as the go-between interceding on behalf of the family and the District Attorney. At one point I vented frustration to the Advocate regarding lack of clarification on a particular issue and quickly learned by her swift corrective tone that a more cooperative, even-keeled tone would be required in future communications with her. After about six months into the nearly two-year process, we were able to communicate with the DA directly, and she called us to update us on occasion as well.*

Travel

Keep in touch with your KEY CONTACTS for any anticipated schedule changes and make travel reservations that can be changed.

Travel to court incurs expenses that the family usually has to bear. When you are paying for your own travel, consider travel that can be rebooked. Ask your Key Contacts about any anticipated schedule changes. Know that even with all this preparation, changes can and do happen at the last minute. If you have been subpoenaed to testify, you may get some help with these expenses. Talk with whoever issued the subpoena, as they must ensure you get to court to testify. Let them know about your constraints and ask how they can help.

If you are the one who confirmed the identity of your loved one, you may have to testify at trial. If so, the prosecution should cover the cost of travel just as they would any other witness. Your local victim compensation board may cover some of the court transportation expenses.

Surprises

More surprises that co-victims have experienced and want you to know about are:

Investigators want to interview you. They may say they are investigators or **officers of the court**. In fact, both sides of this adversarial team (prosecution and defense) are officers of the court and have investigators. Prosecutors will usually tell you in advance when they send an investigator. If the investigators are from the defense team, you may want to check with the case prosecutor first, then decide if you want to speak to them. Look at their identification and find out who they are. If you are unsure, schedule a time to get back to them. Check with the case prosecutor to find out if an investigator was sent.

> *Something upsetting happened to us after we met with the DA. One Saturday afternoon, we heard the doorbell ring at our house, and repeated*

knocking on our front door. Because we did not recognize the man and woman standing there, we did not open the door.

We thought they had walked away, and we went about our business. I went outside to continue watering the plants in the back yard and noticed the same two people approaching our back-yard gate. Curious, I asked them what they wanted, and I was surprised when they introduced themselves as an Investigator and Attorney from the Defense team in the case. They attempted to ask me questions about what we said to the District Attorney regarding our death penalty preferences. I asked them to leave.

This unexpected encounter left me very shaken up. We learned that this tactic of trying to catch the victim's family off guard to acquire information is often used by the Defense. It is a despicable one, in our opinion, and done without regard for the degree to which it rattles those who are already dealing with so much. (Valeria)

Subpoena arrives from the Defense Attorney for you to be a witness for them. When you are on the defense witness list, you are kept out of the courtroom until after your testimony. Even then, if the defense expects to call you back, you will not be allowed back in the courtroom. This is a strategy the Defense may use to keep you out of the courtroom for the entire trial, especially if they think you will pull sympathy for the prosecution's case.

I was not allowed in court because I was a witness. I can't really say what happened in court. I can only go by what I was told. . . . He made sure I never made it to the stand, and on the first day of trial he wrote fake subpoenas on hastily ripped up pieces of notepaper for nearly all of the people on our side of the courtroom. Almost everyone who was sympathetic to our side was effectively banned from court. (Marina)

Is there any place safe? Someone had a tape recorder going inside a bathroom stall to capture unsuspecting conversations in private moments between two sisters. Save conversations for your notepaper or when you are home with others you can trust.

Some investigators say they're from the DA's office and do not make clear to the unsuspecting and vulnerable that they are actually from the **Defense Attorney's** office, not the District Attorney's office. In one case, none of the testimony of witnesses was allowed to be presented in court because of this misleading behavior.

Some **investigators** say they are from the "PD" when in fact they are from the Public Defender's office, not the Police Department. **Ask always to see proof** of who they are. When you are not sure, delay when you talk with them. It is to their advantage when they catch you off guard and vulnerable. Review the chapter on dealing with the media, as some of the strategies will work here as well.

Why are there no Miranda Rights for co-victims? According to the law, once someone is in custody they must be given their Miranda Rights; that is, warned that *"everything you say can be used against you."* Co-victims/Survivors are not in custody, therefore they have no Miranda Rights or anything like them. They often believe that their conversations, some that are quite personal and emotional, are protected. Those conversations are not protected and can be used in court.

Everything you post online or that others post on your page or that can be found online in regard to the victim, you had better be prepared to defend on the witness stand! Moreover, this activity will most likely keep you out of the entire trial, or at least until you have testified, and that will usually come at the very end of the defense's case. (Rose)

Everything that you have said, and everyone in your family and friendship network have said to the police, victim advocate, prosecutor, news media, and social media is part of the record of this case. Unfortunately, there are no "crime victim Miranda rights" for you. You will not be told that anything you say can be used against you. Nor will an attorney be hired for you if you cannot afford one. This information can be subject to cross examination in court. These conversations, like others, can be part of the Discovery (evidence) that is required to be turned over to the defense team, which includes the defendant.

Don't ever email your prosecutor or homicide team, because during the discovery phase of the trial, all of that is turned over to the defense attorney and the client—the murderer. The very thought that they had access to my inner thoughts, frustrations, pain, made me sick to my stomach. The fact that some of my personal thoughts or conversations could be used against me when I was subpoenaed to the stand, [as a witness] for the defense no less, was just plain wrong. (Rose)

We state it here for you because many co-victims before you have been surprised and betrayed when heartfelt conversations appeared in the court room.

Everything you say or do can be used against you, including communications and activities with family, friends, co-workers, neighbors, and the prosecution.

Prosecutors cannot tell you what to do or say. You, nor the prosecutor, want to do anything to jeopardize the case. Tell them your ideas and plans before you do anything, and ask them whether they think it will help or hurt the case.

We have talked about the new world you have been thrust into. Most of us do not have knowledge about how this works except for what we have learned on TV or in the movies, and generally that is not accurate. Even if you do have personal or work experience, you are still not prepared for your loved one's court case. You will find this in Marina's story. She may have been familiar with most legal terms, but she was not familiar with the process she had to go through after her dad's murder. Most of us are ignorant about what this system is all about, and it isn't what you see on TV.

Co-victims may not be allowed to wear buttons, shirts, or other items depicting the deceased, as the defense will argue that it is prejudicial to the jury. The court room is a very sterile environment. (Saindon, 2013)

The CSI effect. Prosecutor Tracy Prior teaches classes on the "CSI effect" for in-coming prosecutors where she works. There is good news and bad news here. We see TV commercials on medications and their promises, and we pressure our doctors to prescribe the latest and what we think is the best medicine. Similarly, the attraction and proliferation of TV crime shows, especially about murder cases, sets up unreasonable expectations for co-victims. Instead of the few hours on TV it takes to get back forensic information, in real life it can take months. In one investigation, it took five months for a top FBI computer forensics specialist to find the information that was significantly persuasive in one case.

Coverage of real trials is compressed out of necessity, so don't expect things to move as quickly or efficiently as they seem to on the news. (Marina)

Feeling safe: If you have knowledge or suspicion about being unsafe, or if you or your family have been threatened by the accused or their network, let the prosecutor or your victim advocate know immediately.

Under the Fair Treatment Standards for Crime Victims (New York), the court shall take steps to ensure that, whenever possible, victims and other prosecution witnesses awaiting court appearances have been provided with a secure waiting area separate from all other witnesses.

I felt that he had more rights to be protected than I did, and that was proven when a witness that was testifying against the killer was severely beaten after he arrived at his hotel. (Kaila)

The Wait, Postponements and Delays

I don't think any of us can talk too much about the **WAIT**. The WAIT would be different if it made sense to survivors and you were kept informed all along the way. The WAIT includes the changes in dates and timelines. One aspect is planned for by survivors, support is rallied, flight reservations are made, then the court makes changes and all that planning and preparation has stopped. Know that these changes must be approved by the judge, and there are usually good reasons for them. Nonetheless, they disrupt our lives.

I would like to tell you that you can count on dates, schedules, and the process to move in a way that you can plan your life and attendance better, but I cannot. There is much that can and needs to happen before the final and actual trial date. For example, Prosecutor Tracy Prior drew a stairway with many steps of different sizes to symbolize what must be accomplished along the way. Under the defendant's right to a speedy trial, prosecutors always have to state they are ready or time will be charged against them. The defense does not have this concern.

Postponement hearings: This is a term I made up. By saying "postponement hearing," it can remind you that the date set for a hearing may change many times.

A family coming from Africa had enough funds to travel one time to attend the court proceedings, only to have the time changed. They lost their only opportunity to attend the trial of their loved one's murderer. As tragic as the loss of a loved one is, events like this add more wounds to the family. The zigzag of life's plan and intensity deepens the scars for the bereaved, who are without a rudder.

One of the delays that can occur is that the defendant can ask for a new attorney. It is up to the judge to determine whether the defendant's request has merit and grants the request, or denies it as having no basis. If the defendant is granted a new attorney, expect everything in the case to stop for at least six months as the new attorney gets up to speed.

> *There were so many pretrial motions where either the prosecutor or defense attorney would argue over what could be presented in the case. We were present at every one of these, whether it was for five minutes or the entire day. There were also so many continuances that took a major toll on all of us.*
>
> *We would get our hopes up that soon we would be going to trial just to find out it would be continued another 6-8 weeks, and we would start the process all over again. This went on until we finally got through all the various motion hearings, pretrial hearings, preliminary hearings, and continuances until we heard the magic words . . . the Judge had set a trial date . . . for 18 months AFTER THE ARRESTS.* (Rose)

There are reasons for the delays and continuances that few survivors understand or know about. One group of survivors remembers too well that one of the delays was for a vacation, while they could not plan any such activity for their own family. Their lives are on hold for years to be available to go to court, while having no say in these decisions.

Something many families don't know is that investigators have to act on every tip. The more tips that come in, the more time it will take to follow up on all the leads. Attempts to be helpful can sometimes overload their system, so it is important to weigh the value of a new tip. This is when your team of supporters can help. You may want to discuss with others before you forward a new lead, especially when it looks like the police have identified the suspect.

Multiple trials are a burden for families. Bonnie and John endured two trials for the same defendant. If there is a hung jury or mistrial, there can be another trial.

Some families have had to endure four or five trials. JJ and Mary's son was murdered by six gang members on his way home from work. The son was living near his brother, 3,000 miles away from his parents. JJ and Mary traveled those miles to attend multiple hearings, and they gave *victim impact statements* six times. When there are multiple defendants and the court decides to have multiple trials, the family will have this extra burden.

Hiring your own attorney. When things do get underway and a trial is planned, you will want to know about the court process and what you need to be prepared for, as well as what you can and cannot do. This is the role of a victim advocate. They should be doing this. Survivors do not know they can have their own legal counsel, preferably one that is familiar with criminal law. An attorney can be helpful in explaining the legal system and can help later if a civil case is pursued.

This question is an important one, as many survivors have been confused about who the prosecuting attorney works for. As we discussed earlier, the prosecutors have been mistaken for the family's attorney. Survivors have attempted to influence the direction of the prosecutors or want to replace them when they follow a path the survivors don't agree on. Survivors find they cannot do either. The prosecutors in the District Attorney's office represent the State on behalf of the deceased, not the survivors. The prosecutors are assigned by the District Attorney.

The care, commitment, and expertise of prosecutors is rarely undeniable, but survivors have had varying relationships with them and their Key Contacts, as you can read in the survivor writings.

Co-victims cannot have their own attorney prosecute the murder of their loved one, but an attorney can help with advocating and understanding the legal system, and if the co-victims later file a civil complaint, as was done in the OJ Simpson case. Unfortunately, this is expensive.

Deafening Silence. Silence is eloquently clear to those waiting to hear the next news in the case of their loved one. The silence and not-knowing gets translated into "no one cares." Co-victims can take action and call someone, when they want answers. If you are very stirred up, which will happen many times (again, this is normal), you may want to write out your questions and discuss them with a friend, family member, or trusted advocate before you make the call. Use your most professional, medium-pitched voice, the voice you would use in a delicate situation. Practice taking periodic deep breaths to help you keep calm and professional. Don't be surprised if you become frustrated or angry (it's normal). Take a break if that happens, especially if you experience anger or rage (normal). And don't forget to write down the replies as well. Add the date to help you keep track of your calls.

From murder to trial, it was over 3 years of excruciating pain, confusion, and lack of knowledge that this was really how long most murders take to get to trial. (Rose)

The wall of silence needs to change. Families of murder victims are recognized by the National Center for Victims of Crime as *co-victims* in cases of murder. They need to hear what is going on. What they at least would like to hear is: "We have not forgotten your loved one. We are making progress and the details involve many technical specialists and community organizations. Thanks for your patience and understanding."

Even if co-victims hear this every time, they tell us it is much better than silence. They fear being cut off from hearing anything, even though they have a right to be respected and informed all along the way with what they have a legal right to know.

"Protecting the integrity of the case" is a phrase families hear often, especially when they don't get their questions answered. An investigation is fluid and has many potentially changing parts. Protecting the integrity of the case can mean making sure information does not get out while the case is still being investigated. This is information that could inadvertently slip out during a conversation, so it is protected. It could be information only the killer would know or is still being substantiated by DNA testing or other research.

The pressure to want to know is understandable; after all, this is about your loved one. You may believe that any new information cannot be any worse than knowing your loved one was murdered. You may also believe you have a right to know. The pain of not knowing can add more wounds to existing ones. However, it's important to understand that the long-term goal of a successful prosecution has to take precedence over your immediate desire to be fully informed of every detail.

Sometimes a specific question can be answered. We all try to imagine scenarios, and try to complete the "what happened" in our minds. This is a natural thing to do. Let your prosecutor know what that question is and perhaps, without jeopardizing "the integrity of the case," he or she can provide the information, suggests San Diego County Deputy District Attorney Tracy Prior.

Courthouse Survival Advice

Once a trial date has been set, your next challenge is attending court proceedings with its rules and protocols. Bonnie and John had to endure this twice after their 80-year-old mother was raped and killed in 1995. They wrote *Courthouse Survival Advice* in the hopes that it would help others. Their heartfelt, practical advice continues to help families everywhere.

Bonnie and John start out by advising what to wear, not only to help give a good impression but also for comfort and ease. They know the stress you will experience. You can tell by their tone that they are speaking from the heart in wanting to help you from their own very difficult experience of having to go through this process twice. This guide is several pages long and worth every word. Send copies to everyone you know who is following your case. Below is just a sample of the document. It is a must read.

- ✓ **Clothing**—first of all, if you are clean and look halfway neat, you look better than most of the people at the courthouse. If you want to be dealing with the press, dress accordingly. **They will put slobs on TV, but they don't like to. Like it or not, there is often a lot of PR necessary in getting justice for your loved one.** The lawyers will be wearing suits. The criminal may too. You don't have to go so far as high heels or coat and tie, but stay away from the cutoffs and T-shirts.

- ✓ **Line up at least five (Monday through Friday) "easy-to-care-for and easy-to-live-in" outfits.** I'd suggest an emphasis on comfortable clothing that you can sit in for hours, if necessary, without a lot of fussing, tucking, pinching and riding up.

- ✓ **Find a non-fussy hairdo and non-fussy makeup, etc.** Pare down as much primping as you can in the morning, since you'll be needing more sleep than you are used to needing. Fair warning—even good-quality eye makeup tends to run when you cry—and there's nothing like courthouse proceedings to reduce you to tears.

- ✓ **Start taking VERY GOOD care of yourself, if you aren't already.** Work your schedule to allow you to get more sleep, take your vitamins, and get some calm exercise. Avoid caffeine, take it easy on junk food. You may find you will be more prone to colds, stomach upsets, etc. **Stress will do you in.**

There is so much more to their very helpful article, read more of it online and add your own pieces to it. The article is available on the Survivors of Violent Loss Program website and listed in Resources at the end of this chapter.

Survivor Questions: What is your experience of the court process? What are the rules of behavior in court for you, for the accused, your family, their family and friends? What surprises did you have?

You may want to answer these questions at a later time and add your own tips.

Rose
There were to be no outbursts in the court room. *In addition, we were not allowed to speak to anyone while in court. There were to be no facial expressions that could be misconstrued or influence the jury.* ***There was to be no talking in the hallways or bathrooms, as the jury was in the same vicinity as those attending the trial.*** *We were not allowed to look over at the other side of the court where the defendant's supporters were, no dirty looks and certainly no verbal exchanges. The rules were pretty much the same for all parties involved.*

You should dress appropriately whenever in the court room. ***Some judges will allow you to wear a button depicting your loved one and some judges won't.***

Surprises in the court were the fact that the judge seemed to grant all of the defense's motions and very few of ours, which was extremely frustrating until it was explained to me. The judge allowed the motions so that in the future the defense couldn't use any of those types of excuses when seeking an appeal. Just knowing that made a huge difference while sitting there and listening to all the falsehoods that the defense tried to use to get his client off.

I was surprised and appalled when on the first day of trial the defendant turned around and looked me straight in the eye and smiled at me. I brought it to the attention of the prosecutor immediately and it never happened again.

Marina
In the course of my experience with the court, I didn't really learn any new terms. I was already pretty familiar with the criminal justice system because I had worked within the child dependency system for years. Sometimes child abuse involves murder, so I knew how the criminal justice system worked already.

I think it is vital for survivors to know that real murder and its aftermath only faintly resemble what one sees on television shows. *Coverage of real trials is compressed out of necessity, so don't expect things to move as quickly or efficiently as they seem to on the news. Commercial television is even worse. I call programs like "CSI" and "Law and Order" "Death by Disney." What you see on television may contain elements of reality, but it is merely entertainment. Throw out all of your preconceived notions of crime and punishment. In my experience, the criminal justice system is simply a legal system. Justice is not a given, not by a long shot.*

Compounding this is the fact that the "Busted System" has irritable bowel disease. Sometimes nothing happens. Sometimes it seems like something is going to happen—then nothing happens. Sometimes everything comes out all at once. Predictions and plans are useless, so it's important to at least try to stay flexible and fluid. It's impossible to be ready for every eventuality because there are just too many emotions and expectations involved.

Try to expect the unexpected. I wasn't ready for failure, and it almost killed me.

Try as well to live some semblance of a normal life—you'll need it whether you get justice or not. Do not live your life for the outcome of the criminal case. Yes, it's easy for me to say that, so many years after the fact, and it's almost impossible to do, but you must try. **Do not let the murderer take yet another life.**

Honor your loved one by continuing to live yours.

Harrier

My parents' case never went to criminal court, but my sisters and I did file a petition in civil court to block our brother from receiving any inheritance from our parents' estate. This process tears at one's gut, especially when family members not only disapproved, but turned their backs on us.

One of my favorite aunts wrote to me and said she never wanted to hear from me again because of "what you did" to your brother.

Kaila

Prior to court I was told how I should act and dress. I was told to refrain from losing my mind and trying to kill this murderer, or at least that's what I heard. I dressed nicely and answered the questions, but if looks could kill, I was trying . . . it didn't work.

I was surprised to see other inmates at the last trial when I did my impact statement; I was advised not to mention in detail what he did to my sister, as if protecting him again. I reached a point where I didn't know who to trust anymore and that is true for so many victims. I wished I had access to autopsy and forensic reports, because at some point I felt that I had to do my own investigation because of the lack of information that I was given.

One thing I learned in court is that you will feel like you are being judged (and the last thing you need to do is also be treated like a criminal). I also learned "postponed trial," which kept happening in my case. **There are people in the DA's office that are willing to help; it just needs to be more clear on where to go and whom to speak to.**

For me it was Mary, the DA's secretary; she offered help that I never would have thought on my own to get. That's how I met SVLP, the best thing that happened to me in this case. I didn't know that after the storm it can be calm.

Trials can be complicated; there should be someone assigned to the help victims with court language that not everybody understands. I was young and I went through the courts by myself.

Because the courts did not want me to tell my side of the story, I never dealt with the fact that I was a victim of domestic violence . . . it just took a back seat because my sister's homicide was more important. I felt that he had more rights to be protected than I did, and that was proven when a witness testifying against the killer was severely beaten after he arrived at his hotel.

Halia

Twenty-eight years after the death an arrest was made. After two years of court hearings, a plea agreement was reached for second-degree murder.

These are the hard, cold facts. The story sounds like something one reads in the newspapers or hears about in the evening news that happened to a distant neighbor somewhere. Except it happened to my sister, to our family, and to our friends, who loved her dearly. It gutted

time, particularly at the more pertinent hearings such as arraignment, plea bargaining, or sentencing hearings.

*What is extremely frustrating is that all the rights seem to be extended to the accused, and the family members are expected to sit quietly in the background. In our case, **the suspect spoke Spanish and had an interpreter who spoke at the same time** the judge or prosecutor was speaking. This made it extremely hard to hear the court proceedings. This was very upsetting after traveling from out of town, staying in a hotel, and then*

All the rights seem to be extended to the accused, and the family members are expected to sit quietly in the background. (Halia)

---

our family and it gutted our lives. It tore open deep caverns in the fabric of our souls.

*[**Before you attend a hearing or trial,] drive the route to court and scout out where you plan to park**. Do this on a similar day and time to ensure there will be space available and gauge the timing. Security and elevator lines can take 20 to 30 minutes each. Entering court even five minutes late can mean missing a hearing. This can be costly both emotionally and financially if you have taken time off work or traveled from out of town and paid for hotel expenses*

*In the court process, things move very quickly and often more than one person is talking at the same time. If there is an interpreter, the interpreter will often be speaking while the other individual continues the conversation. If this occurs, you have the right to speak to the Victim Rights Advocate or District Attorney **and request that one person speak at a***

being in an 8 min. hearing to be unable to hear the proceeding!

*On the other hand, showing up early and sitting very quietly in the courtroom will afford you the ability to hear conversations that are occurring between attorneys in the room as they are having a bit more relaxed conversation. **Don't be surprised if you see the defense and prosecution attorneys smiling at one another and conversing in a very friendly manner.***

***It is very important to know which side of the courtroom that the victims or family members of victims are to sit on,** and which side those who are there for the defendant are to sit on. This is important because if you sit on the wrong side, you may just be sitting next to the family member of the person who took the life of your loved one. The Court Officer has the responsibility to ensure people sit on the correct side when they walk in; however, this does not always happen.*

Evidenced by the fact that two ladies wailed and said to me, "Oh, he looks so frail" when the person who took my sister's life was called forward for his hearing.

Turning cell phones off is an absolute must. *Some Judges will ask the individual to exit the court.* **Gum chewing and eating in court is not allowed**. *Coffee is allowed in most courtrooms. If an individual is diabetic, they can get permission to bring necessary foods ahead of time, as hearings may occur early, may last all day, or may get cancelled and rescheduled; it is quite unpredictable.*

Prepare for the long haul. *Expect the unexpected. Know that this is a very emotional and physical process and self-care is very important during this time. Nutrition, exercise, and surrounding yourself with what brings you some peace and support will sustain you through this journey.*

Don't be surprised if the nature of your relationships change *as you go through this metamorphosis. It's OK. You will survive it and you will be stronger for it. Some people will stick with you and some may fade away. Be willing to let them go, at least for now. Your wings will be lighter when you emerge from the cocoon and you're ready to fly.*

Mary

As these 6 defendants were teenagers, the law in this state says they must each be seen in Court every month. In the initial hearings that were held for each defendant every month until trial, the Court is called into session as the judge comes into the room. We all stood and then sat when told to do so. The judge starts by asking questions of the Defense

Attorney and the Defendant, then the Prosecutor. After some discussion, another hearing is set for the next month. As this was a very sensitive case, the hearing was always the last of the morning session. All stand until the judge leaves the room. This all lasts about 5-10 minutes. This was done 6 times a month for over 2 years.

We understood that dressing respectfully and behaving respectfully was an expected rule of behavior. *I didn't feel the defendants' families and friends always understood this. Sometimes there were outbursts by the defendant's friends. Someone kept bringing a baby to Court (and it was a little distracting). We were treated very well by the second Victim's Advocate, and she did all she could to shield us. She met us in the lobby and was with us while waiting to go into Court. The guards kept the front two rows available for our family (behind the Prosecutor). We were then able to see, from the side, the face and demeanor of the defendant. (Only once did the defendant's family hurry in and take those rows and refuse to leave for the guards). We didn't press the matter that day.* **While waiting to go into Court, it does get awkward with the family and friends of the murderer right nearby. Early on they would sneer or try to intimidate us (and actually did scare some of the younger supporters of ours).**

In Court, we could sometimes hear the other side making inappropriate comments and sometimes laughing about the case. A few times the parents did reprimand these friends and told them to be quiet. The only surprise I guess I really had was how many friends of these defendants came to the Plea Offer Hear-

ings and Sentencings. It was like they still believed that their "friend" was innocent.

JJ

We did not have a court trial, only sentencing hearings. The court officers enforce decorum as best they can. We did have reported outbursts of support for the defendants from other hearings. Initially, there was a large community gathering outside the court house supporting the defendants at their arraignment. As more information came out and the courts did not schedule more than one defendant a day, this became less and less of a problem. Seeing that initial support from the local high school indicating that these "good boys" could not have been involved was hurtful.

Valeria

I found it essential to bring to the court anything that would be of comfort and help me get through the delays and stressors of each day. [In the list below, see the items Valeria recommends that you have on hand in the courtroom.]

Courtroom Survival Kit

Survivor writer Valeria recommends you bring these items with you to the courtroom:

- ✔ A notepad and pen or pencil for taking notes during the trial. If we had any questions or concerns about what we heard, we could refer to our notes and receive clarity from the Prosecutors.
- ✔ Many bring iPads/iPhones that connect them to their work during breaks. Of course, all electronic devices must be silenced in the court room.
- ✔ Have a protein bar or some crackers on hand to calm hunger or a nervous stomach.
- ✔ Some cash to use to buy small items at the food kiosks in the court throughout the day or you can bring your own items.
- ✔ Consider wearing comfortable clothes for sitting long hours, and shoes for walking—or bring an extra pair of shoes for walking.
- ✔ Courtrooms can be either too cold or too hot, so a warm scarf to use as a wrap, or a cardigan sweater you can take on or off easily, can make you more comfortable as you sit for hours listening to evidence.
- ✔ Bringing bottled water is also helpful. The water fountains in the courthouse were often out of order.
- ✔ For women, a hand lotion to use at breaks—mine was almond coconut scented, and the soothing aroma helped me relax and breathe.
- ✔ Anything else that is comforting—maybe a meaningful trinket or card someone gave to you, which you can take with you and look at during the day.
- ✔ Of course, nothing can take the place of being lifted by the grace and support of family and friends who attend court with you.

Survivor Questions: Legal terms can be confusing. What legal terms are you learning and what ones do you want to know?

Write your answers in your notebook.

We have added additional legal terms here for you as well:

Adjudication: the legal process overseen by a judge.

Discovery: evidence.

Hearing: any time the prosecutor and defense attorney meet before the judge regarding your case. It can take as little as five minutes to a couple of hours, depending on what needs to be discussed.

Objection/sustained: the prosecutor or defense attorney may object to something said or shown in court. When the judge says "sustained," it means that he or she agrees with the objection and the information will not be used in the case.

Post-conviction relief: a prisoner's request for release, a new trial, modification of sentence, or such other relief. One family got a conviction in Arizona 30 years after the crime. The convict then applied for post-conviction relief to enable him to leave prison earlier than what he was sentenced to serve.

Probable cause hearings: If the defendant asks for one, the DA must be ready to go to court quickly and have enough evidence to prove there is probable cause that this defendant did the crime. If the judge feels there is sufficient evidence, then they proceed to a trial.

> *We learned that a probable cause hearing is a right afforded the defendant to see what evidence is available against him. The judge determines whether there is enough evidence to go to trial. Not all evidence is required to be disclosed. (JJ)*

Representative from the court: it could be anyone involved in the legal process, from your victim advocate to the prosecutor, defense attorney or the judge.

Subpoena: a court order to appear in court on a certain day and time. The subpoena can come from the prosecutor or the defense attorney, regardless of what side you are on. If you are subpoenaed you cannot be in the court room prior to your testimony; afterward you can stay, if you so choose, unless you are told you may be called back to testify again.

Without malice aforethought: one did not think and plan to kill before the death.

Wrongful death: a situation where a person has not been found guilty in criminal court of taking a person's life, but can be sued in civil court for being responsible for the death and liable for monetary damages. This is what happened to O.J. Simpson.

> *My sisters and I filed a petition in probate court, alleging that our brother was the "slayer" of our parents and should not benefit from their deaths by receiving a share of their estate. The "slayer" statute was new to me, although the principles involved were not. (Harrier)*

More information is available at the Victim Law website (see Resources). This is a searchable database of victims' rights legal provisions, including federal, state, and territorial statutes. You can find particulars for your state as well as a list of legal terms defined.

My Case Information

Case #_____

Judge:_____

Courtroom#_____

Prosecutor:_____

Paralegal:_____

Phone #: (_____)_____-_____

Email:_____

Victim Services Advocate:_____

Phone #: (_____)_____-_____

Email:_____

Important Hearing Dates:

Initial Appearance: _____/_____/_____

Notes_____

_____

_____

_____

_____

Arraignment: _____/_____/_____

Notes_____

_____

_____

_____

_____

Case Mgt. Conference: _____/_____/_____

Notes_____

_____

_____

_____

_____

Case Mgt. Conference: _____/_____/_____

Notes_____

_____

_____

_____

_____

Pretrial Conference: _____/_____/_____

Notes_____

_____

_____

_____

_____

Trial: _____/_____/_____

Notes_____

_____

_____

_____

_____

Resources

Courthouse Survival Advice, article by Bonnie and John
https://www.svlp.org/courthouse-survival.

Homicide Survivors, Inc., Tucson, Arizona
https://homicidesurvivorsinc.org.

National Center for Victims of Crime (NCVC) 800-FYI-CALL
http://www.ncvc.org.

Navigating the Criminal Justice System, Los Angeles County District Attorney's
Office; https://da.lacounty.gov/navigating-criminal-justice-system.

Victim Law; https://www.victimlaw.org.

Parents of Murdered Children® website; http://www.pomc.org.

Email your tips and comments to: **cdsnetwork1@gmail.com**.

* Some Web addresses may have changed since publication.

Page intentionally left blank. Use it for jotting notes or your thoughts, if you wish.

7

Prosecuting the Case

The FBI had a prime suspect in my parents' deaths. They wanted to prosecute, but the U.S. attorney's office refused, saying that without bodies, with little forensic evidence, and having an unreliable witness, the odds of a guilty verdict were too low to risk incurring jeopardy. (Harrier)

Pursuing or Not Pursuing Prosecution

Family members demand swift results in the prosecution of their family member's murderer, but prosecutors only have one shot. Every step, from what law enforcement does at the first moment of its investigation to the very moment the prosecutor and defense rest during trial, is scrutinized by the family, the Prosecution, the Defense, the Judge, the Jury and the public through the news, says Richard Wissemann, Supervising Investigator with the San Diego County District Attorney's office.

Thus, when a District Attorney (DA) or U.S. attorney (in federal cases) considers issuing a criminal complaint or indictment against a murder suspect, they do so only after they have examined every bit of information that both the homicide team and their own investigators have gathered. The homicide team presents its case to the DA or U.S. attorney (also know as a prosecutor) when they feel they have enough evidence for an arrest. When the case is presented to prosecution, every piece of evidence, every interview, every document is closely examined, which takes time.

The prosecutor often times will give the police a list of items that still need to be investigated. The homicide team may present the same case to the prosecutor more than once. Prosecution and the police departments work closely to ensure there are no other reasonable leads. Defense often uses the third-person culpability defense—someone else could have committed this murder. The family is also often quick to come up with who could have committed this crime. They may even argue with the investigators. It is the job of law enforcement to not let this sway the investigation. "All other reasonable leads need to be followed up on to eliminate the third-person culpability claim," Wissemann says.

The prosecution team makes sure that every "i" is dotted and every "t" is crossed, that there are no loopholes. Every lead must be checked, witness statements verified, forensic evidence catalogued, and any other possible suspects must be cleared prior to an arrest. There can be over one hundred pieces of evidence.

This takes time. To the survivors, to the co-victims, this passage of time can be excruciating. But criminal prosecution moves slowly, not only to ensure a thorough investigation, but for technical reasons as well. For example, one DNA sample can take weeks to get test results, another can take months. If prosecutors don't think they can get a conviction with the evidence they have, they will continue to do their "due diligence" until they have tracked down every lead. The investigation continues until the prosecution team is satisfied the evidence will get a conviction.

If there has been an arrest and the prosecution is not ready to issue an indictment, they can hold a suspect for up to 72 hours. If the prosecutors decide not to issue an indictment at that time, they must release the suspect. The suspect may be rearrested in the future, if and when more evidence supports it.

When the case stalled, I met with the U.S. attorney assigned to the case. He explained why there would likely be no prosecution, no trial—the case was circumstantial; there were no bodies; there was little forensic evidence; and my sister was not a reliable witness. He did not want to risk incurring jeopardy by losing the case. (Harrier)

When indictments are not issued, it is because prosecutors are not convinced they have enough evidence to get a conviction. They only get one shot at it. If the defendant is found not guilty, it's over. They do not want to risk not being able to prosecute if and when more information comes in.

The distress for families is very high when this occurs, but it is necessary. You read in Halia's story the number of years she and her family waited before the actual prosecution took place. Dee Dee's niece's case took thirteen years before it went to trial. (Stowers, 2003)

If prosecutors decide they cannot prove the case beyond a reasonable doubt, then the investigation stays open within the police department as an unsolved case. You can read in Harrier's story an example of a case with little forensic evidence to support it.

What You Can Do When Prosecutors Do Not Prosecute

Realize that the case is still open and your local Crime Stoppers may be significant in getting the word out on key dates, such as the one-year anniversary of the death, to encourage new leads or tips to help solve this crime.

Survivors should get the help they need, be it therapy, support groups, something that will help them for the long haul and to be better prepared mentally when the case is ready to go to trial. Put the focus and energy to better use, such as finding different ways of honoring your loved one's life—scrapbook, make a website where people can go and leave messages, etc. We really need to stress to a family that even with a trial and a conviction/or not, that nothing really changes for them. Your loved one is still gone, and there is a huge vacuum that occurs even when the legal fight is over. If you have some of your focus on the honoring or volunteering, the vacuum can be less intense, although it will still be there. This is really the first time that the reality hits. Without anything there to buffer the pain, there is nothing left to fight for. (Rose)

First Step When Prosecuting (Adjudicating)

Most cases proceed after a complaint has been filed or an indictment by a grand jury has been handed up. It can take many months before this process starts. In Rose's case, it took 18 months. The prosecutors we interviewed say one of the reasons for the delay is that they are obligated to prove "beyond a reasonable doubt" their accusation against the defendant. Police only have a "probable cause" obligation to make an arrest. The burden of proof is higher for prosecution.

Investigator Wissemann describes the difference between the burden of proof of the police and that of the prosecution. "Local law enforcement uses probable cause—is it reasonable to believe that this person could have committed the crime? For prosecution, 'beyond a reasonable doubt' is a giant step beyond probable cause. Proof must be a preponderance of evidence to lead a reasonable person to believe this person is the only person who could have committed the crime."

The prosecutor can elect to use the grand jury to review evidence and listen to witnesses. Only the prosecutor and subpoenaed witnesses attend a grand jury hearing, and all are sworn to secrecy. Grand jury records typically remain secret and do not become public records. Families often are not informed right away if this takes place. Most of the time in murder cases the defendant has been arrested and is in jail.

The court has two days to set up an **arraignment hearing**, which calls the defendant to the court to hear and reply to the criminal charge(s). This is when the defendant is given information about the complaint and his or her constitutional rights to counsel, to a trial, to cross examine witnesses, and so on. The defendant typically enters a plea of guilty or not guilty. If the case is not "dismissed" or if the defendant pleads "not guilty," and the crime is serious and violent, the court usually sets a substantial amount of bail. The defendant stays in jail until the next court appearance, unless the bail is paid.

Your relationship with the Prosecution will be a long-standing one, because of the many years it takes to bring a death-penalty case to trial. All the legal wrangling from both sides will be overwhelming at times. You have no idea how each motion filed and each decision by the Judge will affect the case at trial. Often it will feel like it is more about the system than it is about justice. It will seem like every consideration is being given to the Defense, on behalf of the Defendant. Because the stakes are high for the Defendant, all parties in death penalty cases, especially the Judge, are exceedingly careful to follow the letter of the law and listen carefully to both sides, dotting every "i" and crossing every "t," which reduces the chances of future appeal on their judgments. Patience, and reminding yourself that even though it is complex and frus-

trating process, it is a tried-and-true system—the only one we have—and that is the most you can hope for. (Valeria)

Review Your Rights

You have the right to attend all proceedings except the grand jury proceedings, and jury selection. This includes arraignment and most pre-trial hearings, readiness conferences, round tables, sentencing, and so on, prior to and during the trial. However, you will not be allowed to attend in-house planning and discussion meetings.

If you are not getting attention or answers to your questions, first ask your Key Contacts, then whoever is up the chain from there. Everyone has a boss and are all accountable to someone. It may be helpful to go up the ladder to address your concerns. You may have met more of the key people who are part of the prosecution team at an early conference you participated in. It's important to get their business cards and keep track of who is who and what part they have in prosecuting the case. **You have a right to be respected, to ask questions and get a reply**. The reply may not be much, but you have the right to get a response. "We cannot tell you" is much better than silence.

The family of the victim and the defendant are allowed to attend all of the meetings except grand jury hearings; they are usually not at jury selection, mostly due to space limitations.

In my case, the Advocate and DA told me that it was not necessary for me to attend the hearings and encouraged me not to make the trip from out of town. My sense was that it is easier to not have family members present in the courtroom. (Halia)

You have a right of access to resources, which includes the prosecuting attorney, crime victim or community advocate, and peer supporters. For example, in San Diego, you would have assigned to you an advocate that works out of the Victim Assistance Department within the District Attorney's office. Your advocate can offer you court accompaniment, definitions of legal terms and procedures, help with getting time off from work, referrals to counseling services, application for victim compensation, and peer-support services.

Clarify with your victim advocate what his or her job is. If you don't remember who the person is, ask your Key Contacts. You will find a lot of information locally on the website of most District Attorney offices. The Attorney General's office will have helpful information for crime victims as well. If you can't get help locally, contact the state office, which may be able to steer you in the right direction.

Survivor Questions: What charges are filed? What voice can I have here?

Write your answers in your notebook.

Rose

Prior to charges being filed, the prosecutor has done all his homework along with homicide, and they won't make charges they feel they may not get a conviction on. They want the perpetrator to get the stiffest sentence possible, but they won't jeopardize a conviction by adding a charge the jury may not convict on. They have a great deal of input from the homicide detectives and others who may have seen the evidence, such as a team of other prosecutors, often times the Grand Jury, but in end it is the DA who makes the final decision. **Surviving victims have little say on the charges unless the death penalty is on the table.**

Kaila

Who decides the charge? And does my voice count? These are questions I asked myself, but I never asked in court. I wish I would have asked. I always wondered why I was not allowed to speak about the domestic violence I suffered while in the presence of the person that murdered my sister. I felt that the jury would have seen what type of person this monster was, and he would have gotten a stiffer sentence. I was told that my telling of domestic abuse was not relevant to the case, but I feel that it was the reason my sister was murdered, because I left my abusive boyfriend, and he couldn't find me, so he found my sister and murdered her.

Mary

During the Probable Cause hearing, we didn't feel the forcefulness with the second Prosecutor as we did with the first. Then, after he took over the case, he informed us that even though he felt he could get a Murder conviction for the main murderer who stabbed our son to death, he didn't feel there was enough evidence to convict the others on the Murder charge or the Accessory to Murder charge. So he reduced the charge to Manslaughter.

He also said that in this State every homicide case got plea offers, and if that wasn't taken, then we would go to trial. And in the case of teenagers, the maximum sentence could only be 60 years in prison.

There was a lot of talk on Facebook and newspaper (blogs related to stories about the crime) about whether this was racially motivated. Our son was Caucasian and the six teens were either Black or Hispanic. But it was never really believed by us or the police and Prosecution team that this was racially related. They were just six teens who were bored one night and decided to beat someone up. It was never proven to be racial.

JJ

Our charges were worked out behind closed doors with input from the Judge. We were advised up front that the justice system did not allow tailoring charges to increase the available sen-

tencing options. We were given a voice only in the crafting of the plea offers, and then it was advisory in nature. We did, however, feel that the State took into account our perspective and the degree of concurrence we expressed was communicated to the judge at sentencing.

 Valeria
A few months after our Preliminary Hearing concluded, the victim's families were invited to meet with the District Attorney of our city to discuss our preferences regarding the death penalty for the Defendant in our case, and whether or not we wanted this case to be death-penalty eligible. Those family members who could not attend wrote letters expressing their views to the DA. Ultimately, it was the DA's decision to make, after considering the totality of the input received. Within a month, the Prosecution was informed of the DA's decision to make this a death-penalty-eligible case.

Evidence Only

Prosecutors consider evidence only, not what the public or family believes happened. It takes as much time as it takes to make sure that the prosecution is ready. This wait, although necessary, can be excruciating for the victim's family. Prosecutors know they must have all the evidence they need to prove beyond a reasonable doubt that the person they have charged is in fact guilty of the crime. Prosecutors submit their evidence (discovery) to the Defense team in spurts over time. They don't delay because the delay can be a reason that the judge agrees to postpone a trial date to give defense more time to review the evidence.

"It is not an even playing field," Wissemann says. "Prosecution is required to present all evidence 30 days prior to trial (Discovery Rule). Defense does not have this burden. If, during their own investigation, the defense finds a piece of evidence or a witness statement that does not help their case, they are not obligated to turn it over. Nor are they bound by the 30-day-prior-to-trial rule. In fact, we often learn of a surprise witness moments before testimony. Sometimes prosecution wins the battle to exclude this witness due to discovery rules, but it does not always happen."

Plea bargain is also known as an agreement, deal, or "copping a plea." In a criminal case, this agreement is between the defendant and the prosecutor. The defendant agrees to plead guilty to a particular charge in return for some concession.

This may mean that the defendant will plead guilty to a less serious charge, or to one of several charges, in return for the dismissal of other charges; or it may mean that the defendant will plead guilty to the original criminal charge in return for a more lenient sentence. (Black's, 2013) For instance, if there are two charges on the criminal complaint, and the defendant pleads guilty to one of the two charges, this would be a plea bargain. The reason it is called a plea "bargain" is that both sides are "giving up" something for the end result of the case resolving, prior to a jury trial.

"Plea bargaining is absolutely necessary for the criminal justice system to proceed. If every case were to go to a jury trial, we would probably need thousands of jurors in every courthouse daily, and cases would be stacked in line for months, waiting to get to a trial department," says San Diego County Deputy District Attorney Tracy Prior.

Although you may not agree with a decision to go to trial versus making a plea agreement, the prosecutor is obligated to make that decision, but in many jurisdictions, they have to meet with you and hear your views. They also have to inform you of their decision. Check with your sources about rights you have to be there if a defendant should take a plea. Your Key Contacts should be able to advise you what fits where your case will be heard.

Means, Motive and Opportunity

The prosecution of a case does not mean motive has to be proven, but the jury does want to know why it happened. Did the defendant have the means, motive, and opportunity to do what he or she is charged with? In our Survivor Writer stories, the motives they believe were:

Rose: *Prevent having his life disrupted by his son's existence; it would ruin him . . . child support was secondary.*

Marina: *Oldest motive in the book. Dad planned to end his relationship with his abusive girlfriend, and she was enraged at the loss of a wealthy man to support her lifestyle! During a five-hour videotaped interview, she gave a homicide detective cold shivers up his spine when she growled, "Five years, and I got NOTHING!" She punished Dad for leaving her.*

Harrier: *He got caught doing something wrong.*

Kaila: *"Revenge." How dare I leave the man that loved me. He murdered my sister because I left him.*

Yvonne: *Random act, opportunity, found someone alone and vulnerable.*

Halia: *Sadism, Fantasy, Anger, Sexual Gratification & Thrill Seeking.*

Mary: *I do personally feel that these six teens were stupid and immature. I believe they were bored and thought it was okay to get their kicks that night by beating someone up and causing someone an injury. They may not have left the house with the intent of murdering someone, but they thought it was okay to hurt people. Stupidity, immaturity, boredom, and the kind of friends they hung out with may have all led to our son's death. I know they didn't all come from the best of homes, but I do believe that not all the parents were to blame for the actions of their children.*

Examples of Potential Charges and Penalties for Murder

These examples are from California. Check with your Key Contacts for clarification as to the charges and potential penalties used in your case and state. A "count" is one charge, which could be murder; additional charges may also be filed, such as burglary. There can be one to dozens of charges. For example, the Ariel Castro case had up to 900 charges for crimes related to his holding three girls hostage for more than a decade. (CBS, 2013)

Homicide Types and Charges

Homicide is the killing of one human being by another, **either lawfully or unlawfully**. (Lawful would be a killing in legal self-defense.)

Homicide includes both Murder (A) and Manslaughter (B).

A. **Murder** is defined as the unlawful and unjustified killing of another human being, with malice aforethought. "Malice Aforethought" is defined as an intention to unlawfully kill a human being. Malice can also be implied when someone does an act that is so obviously dangerous, knows the risks, and proceeds anyway; for example, shooting a gun into a crowd of people. Most murders are second degree, and only those with extra qualifiers will "graduate" up to being a first-degree murder.

　　1. **First-Degree Murder** is defined as being willful, deliberate, or premeditated, or committed during the course of other certain felonies (often limited to rape, kidnapping, robbery, burglary, or arson).

　　1 a. Capital Murder is a term reserved for only those first-degree murders that have an additional aggravating element, called a "special circumstance." In California, Capital Murder is reserved for murders carried out for financial gain, serial murders, defendant has a prior murder conviction, murder by means of destruction (e.g., a bomb or explosive device), murder committed for the purpose of avoiding arrest, murder of a police officer, murder of a federal law enforcement officer, murder of a firefighter, murder of a witness to a crime intentionally killed for the purpose of preventing testimony, murder of a prosecutor, murder of a judge, murder of an elected official, murder by lying in wait, murder in the commission of a robbery, kidnapping, rape, sodomy, or child molestation, burglary, arson, and some other crimes, such as murder by poison, murder of a juror to retaliate against a verdict, murder when the defendant was actively participating in a street gang.

　　2. **Second-Degree Murder:** Murder that is not aggravated by any of the circumstances of first-degree murder. Murder's main element is "malice." It is "malice" (express or implied) that makes a killing a murder.

B. **Manslaughter** is the unlawful killing of a human being without malice afore-thought.

　　1. **Vehicular manslaughter** occurs when a person drives a vehicle and unlawfully kills another human being.

　　2. **Voluntary Manslaughter** occurs when a person kills another in the heat of passion, or with "imperfect self-defense," without planning beforehand. An "imperfect self-defense" is when a person kills and believes it is self-defense, but objectively, society would not think the killing was reasonable. (For example, a

drunk comes out of a bar, sees a pack of skinheads, one has something shiny, so the drunk pulls out a gun and fires, killing a person. Then it turns out the shiny object was a cell phone.)

3. **Involuntary Manslaughter**, also known as criminally negligent homicide, occurs when a death is an indirect result of recklessness or negligence.

Examples of penalties:

- First-degree murder with special circumstances ("capital murder") is punished by either life without the possibility of parole or the death penalty.
- First-degree murder is punishable by 25 years to life in prison.
- Second-degree murder is punishable by 15 years to life in prison.

When the numbers that the defendant is to serve are revealed at sentencing, co-victims rarely see the math as fair. One life gone does not equal any amount of time the defendant gets to live. It doesn't meet the "eye for an eye" fairness doctrine that so many hold dear. Not only has the murder victim received a death sentence, all those who love the victim get a life sentence. The number of years the convicted must serve in comparison to the loss of all the years for the loved one does not compute. This reality cannot be reasonably reconciled. Penal codes determine the maximum and minimum time served as well as the provability of the evidence beyond that "reasonable doubt" standard that determines what the court can do. It is very difficult to reconcile this reality in both prosecuted and unsolved cases.

Death Penalty cases (also referred to as Capital Punishment) are different for families. One of the important differences and surprises is that these cases usually take four or more years before they go to trial. One family I worked with did not know that, nor did I. This delay takes its toll on families, especially when they don't know this important distinction.

Death-penalty-eligible cases are longer because they consist of a Criminal Trial and an additional Penalty Phase if the defendant is found guilty by the jury in the criminal trial. Only if the penalty phase results in a unanimous punishment verdict by the jury will the judge impose the death penalty.

Though you can never really be prepared for the unique challenges that will come your way, we hope that by relating our experiences and what we learned in our journey through a death-penalty trial, you will gain insight and confidence by which to navigate the process, should you ever have to. (Valeria)

The District Attorney, who is elected by voters, often interviews the family about their wishes but makes the ultimate decision whether to seek a death sentence or life in prison without the possibility of parole. When the sentence is death, the case is never over for the family due to the many appeals. The first appeal in California is mandated by the state.

In **Rose's** case, the defendant was convicted and is serving two life sentences without the possibility of parole. She says:

*Surviving victims have little say on the charges unless the death penalty is on the table. That is when a decision to go for life w/o parole or death is up for debate. In our case, we knew that the majority were hoping for the death penalty. We were not. In the long months between murders and arrest, **I did my homework on this topic**. I always thought I believed in the death penalty, and I don't know that I don't believe in it; just not in our case. It warranted the charge, but after reading everything I could get my hands on to see what it entailed vs. life without parole, I was adamant that I didn't want the death penalty.*

__I was unsure if I would survive one trial much less the numerous appeals afforded those on death row. I already had a life sentence__ without my loved ones, and numerous appeals would have given me another one along with the person who murdered them. With life without the possibility of parole, the murderer was given one shot at an appeal and that could take years. Fortunately, it didn't take that long, and his one and only appeal was denied, and I never have to see his face again. He will rot & die in his prison cell, alone and forgotten.

The Judge is the courtroom manager and will negotiate disputes and let everyone know what is expected in the courtroom. Prior to trial, Wissemann explains, there are pretrial motions where the judge decides what can and cannot be introduced in trial. "Some family members ask during and after the trial why the prosecution did not go into detail on certain topics, such as the defendant's lifestyle, or the prosecution did not introduce a piece of evidence or even the interview of the suspect. There is often a legal reason for not introducing that piece. Either the defense objected to it, or it was not legally allowed to be presented."

Watch out for running into the defendant and his or her supporters. They will be there. Survivors say they are surprised at how close in proximity they are in the room and how upsetting the supporters' facial expressions and gestures can be. One survivor said in a Massachusetts court room, the defendants came in like "Rock Stars."

Most judges will not allow you to wear T-shirts, ribbons, or buttons to represent your loved one in court. I have heard of a few exceptions, but be prepared to put away what you are told you cannot wear. You are not expected to know what is allowed in court nor how the criminal process is run. Ask what is expected of you and what is allowed, especially from your Key Contacts we asked you to list in Chapter 6.

The Victim is not in court. A major difference in murder trials is that the defendant gets to sit next to his or her attorney. However, the victim, unlike the accused, is not sitting next to his or her attorney. Prosecutor Tracy Prior explained her keen awareness of this and works with the judge, whenever allowed, "to have a photo in a small frame always in the courtroom for the jury to see the victim."

Prosecuting Attorney: Prior to the start of the trial, the prosecutor usually invites the immediate family in to review the case and answer questions. Although prosecutors are representatives for the state, remember they are on the same side as you. All of you are interested in holding accountable the person who murdered your loved one. Be prepared to ask questions and know that some questions will not be answered if there is a need to "protect the integrity of the case."

Prosecutor Prior writes the following questions on the back of her business card and encourages the family to ask the questions each time they meet:

- When is the next court date?
- What can I expect?
- Will anything new happen?
- Is the case still going as planned?
- What can I do to help?

The Defense Attorney: We add this section due to the many reports of additional surprises and stressors that many co-victims report regarding the defense team. Having a better understanding of their job and strategies may help. Their real duty is to protect the rights of the client, the defendant. But that does not mean they have to play fair. They have the ability to poke holes in the case, to confuse the witnesses testifying, sometimes getting conflicting answers presented to the jury, causing doubt, but they cannot introduce false or fictitious evidence.

"Families do not like to hear negative remarks about their deceased family member, and they don't like it when this information is presented by the prosecution," Wissemann says. "But the prosecutor's job is to present the evidence, good or bad, because if they don't, the defense will. Not all homicide victims were angels, and the prosecutor cannot hide the fact that the victim may have been involved in criminal behavior or just was not a nice person."

Either way, no one deserves to be murdered. Being in court, you may become upset or even angry when this happens. It is better to hear it from the prosecution side rather than the defense attorney's interpretation. The defense attorney's rendition of the victim will be much worse.

Some of the issues expressed here are from families I have worked with over the years and more have been expounded on by our team of Survivor Writers. Services to victims have changed over the years, so some of these concerns have been addressed. The experiences and tips of Survivor Writers may reduce some unnecessary confusion and help you be better prepared.

Remember, the defense attorney's job is to get the case dismissed or a Not Guilty verdict. One of the surprises can be that you find out you may not be present in court if you have been subpoenaed to testify by the Defense. You may be allowed only after you testify. The defense may attempt to use this strategy if they think your absence will help them in some way.

The defense does not have to prove innocence or not guilty; it just has to poke holes in the prosecution's case so the jury will decide that the prosecution did not prove its case beyond a reasonable doubt. The defense team will use every means possible to achieve this goal. Some of these tactics may upset you or even seem unforgivable.

Your emotions are understandably close to the surface, which is quite normal for what you are dealing with. It won't take much to stir up that pain. Use information in this guide even when you see the opposite behavior by the defendants' supporters. Their focus is on life and freedom. Your loved one is the victim and the team representing them are the accusers. You have seen the icons of our Survivor Writers. Bring with you a symbol of your loved one as a reminder of what the trial is about and what you are doing there to help you get through these most difficult times. If you're not allowed to display it on your clothing, you can keep it in a pocket or purse.

Survivor Questions: In dealing with defense attorneys, what do you need to be prepared for? Are there any pitfalls or tips you want to impart for new survivors?

Write your answers in your notebook.

Rose

You have to be prepared to hear made-up stories about your loved one, attacks on their character, out-and-out lies, and alibis that are false, people taking the stand and swearing to tell the truth and hear them lie through their teeth.

Don't ever email your prosecutor or homicide team, because during the discovery phase of the

Marina

The medical examiner who determined the cause of Dad's death had performed thousands of autopsies. He was the chief medical examiner on a famous 1997 case involving the murder of 10 young women. Some of the victims died from manual strangulation. A perfect witness for the prosecution, right? Wrong. Not perfect. Not when he was kept on the stand for three days in a row. He was battered with

---

The very thought that the defendants had access to my inner thoughts, frustrations, pain, made me sick to my stomach. (Rose)

---

trial, all of that is turned over to the defense attorney and in turn their client, the murderer. *The very thought that the defendants had access to my inner thoughts, frustrations, pain, made me sick to my stomach. The fact that some of my personal thoughts or conversations could be used against me when I was sub- poenaed to the stand for the defense, no less, was just plain wrong. The defense attorney's investigators often interview witnesses under the guise that they are from the DA's office: the Defense Attorney's office. Not only is that tactic illegal, any information they obtain as a result of false representation is not allowed to be presented at trial. Always ask for identification prior to speaking to anyone.*

the same repetitive questions, over and over again. Friends in court told me that on the third day he said aloud, "I have never been treated like this." Friends said the judge often just sat there quietly, looking both confused and bemused, as if he couldn't quite understand what was happening. The prosecutor made the coroner the cornerstone of his case—along with a five-hour video of the police interview of the murderer. In the end, both were thrown under the bus. The video never saw the light of day.

The defense attorney wore everybody down until no one cared anymore. The judge just let it happen. The prosecutor "papered" the judge after the trial, meaning that he lodged a complaint regarding the judge's performance. That and twenty-five cents won't buy a cup of coffee.

Harrier

In my parents' case, there was no trial, so I did not have to deal with a defense attorney. However, when my sisters and I alleged in probate court that our brother had slain our parents, our brother hired an attorney to represent him. The attorney's response to our allegations did not surprise me, but when he issued a press release to the news media, it caught me off guard, and I failed to immediately respond to his outrageous comments and the "spin" he put on the case. He and others accused me and my sisters of trying to cover up what actually happened to our parents when, in fact, the opposite was true.

Be prepared. Attorneys for the opposition can and will be vicious. You should try to anticipate what they will say in court and to the news media, and be ready to counter with your own statements and rebuttals so your voice gets heard. Often, law enforcement and the prosecution will discourage this, claiming it might hurt their case. You need to weigh that, because it is important to cooperate as much as possible. But at the same time, it's important not to do what I did—I gave the defendant sole possession of public arena.

Halia

The defense attorney will try every dirty little trick in the book, using every loophole they can to delay the trial. In our case the defense attempted a subpoena to the FBI to obtain the National DNA Database to disprove its efficacy. Another favorite is to claim the defendant is mentally incompetent to stand trial, relocating them from the prison to the mental forensic unit.

The Judge reviews the evaluation and 9 times out of 10 the defendant is found competent to stand trial. Next, the defense can remand the hearing back to the Grand Jury, claiming the case lacks enough merit to proceed to trial. If the Judge denies the request, the defense can request a review by the Supreme Court. There is a time limit set by the Judge for the trial and all delays by the defense stop the clock; therefore, they will use this to the fullest extent for their advantage. It requires great patience and good communication with the Victim's Advocate and District Attorney.

You will get through this!

JJ

Initially, at the probable cause hearing, I was angered by the questions directed at witnesses as the defense attorney tried to obscure or weaken their testimony. However, after reflection, I did want the defense attorney to explore all avenues to ensure that there would be no grounds for a mistrial.

One of the defense attorneys spoke to us before a sentencing hearing and said he was in complete sympathy with our loss and shared some other personal information; he said he planned to speak at the hearing.

We did not expect extensive speaking at a sentencing hearing. He spoke for more than a half an hour about how he had badly represented his client and that he should have been given an opportunity to cooperate with the investigation. He additionally tapped into the argument that teenagers don't have a fully developed brain and cannot always discern correctly between right and wrong, an argument now supported by the

Supreme Court. It was very upsetting to hear him lament the circumstances that his client found himself in, while our son was dead at his client's hands.

Valeria

When the trial started and the Prosecution began presenting its Case, we noticed that several supporters of the defendant filling the defense side of the courtroom, especially on days when important prosecution witnesses were scheduled to testify. We learned that because defendants technically "assist" their attorney in their own defense during their trial, they receive the witness list of people who are scheduled to testify, a day in advance. We assumed the defendant was contacting his supporters to come to court for the purpose of intimidating the witnesses scheduled to appear during the prosecution's part of the case. Once the prosecution's case rested, there were fewer supporters of the defendant who came to court.

Crime Scene Photos

The trial and the evidence presented may impact you as much if not more than the murder itself. There will be photographs and testimony by both the prosecution side and the defense side, all of which is gruesome in itself. Your relationship was very personal, and hearing and seeing evidence can be very difficult.

One of the surprises we want to prepare you for is **seeing the graphic details in crime-scene photos.** We also recommend that you ask someone on the prosecution team to let you know when the photos will be presented so that you can look away or leave the courtroom. If pictures are being displayed as evidence, an advocate can request the prosectuor to inform the family in advance when these are going to be viewed as well as when the medical examiner is going to testify. This gives you and your family a choice to be present or not.

Listening and imagining what happened is hard enough. Images can sear permanent stains in your mind; you will see them over and over again. You already have many difficult images to deal with, and you may want to avoid adding these.

When you disagree with what is going on, do talk with the people most directly involved, starting with the prosecution. They know the law and the evidence they have, and best understand why they are pursuing that course. They live in a world of specialized language, like a medical doctor, mechanic, or a computer geek. You are not expected to know their world. You have a right to ask them questions and be treated with respect.

Having pretrial conversations and input from other victim's families has helped in many instances. Find a peer support group, as it too can be crucial as you navigate the criminal justice community.

More surprises will come

Expect the unexpected; examples include:

- Request to change the venue (location) of the trial.
- Attempts to keep witnesses from testifying.
- Your loved one is described in discrediting terms. This may have already happened during police interviews. My dad told us of a time when he reached over the desk to try to punch the police chief when the chief suggested that my sister was promiscuous. Other police officers held my dad back.
- Disappointments can occur when the prosecutor does not take into consideration what the family wants. One mother was convinced that her son's murder was a hate crime. She remained angry at the prosecutor for not adding this to the charges. She believed the penalty would be greater if hate crime was included.

Trial Timeline

When the trial actually starts the timeline may go like this:

Pre-trial Conferences: A judge may "sit in" on conferences during negotiations between the prosecutor and the defense. If there is a plea agreement, both sides and the judge must agree with the decision. Unless the charges are dismissed or an agreement has been made, the case goes forward to trial. Although the plea can be changed any time going forward, it is rarely done. Families should be informed that plea bargaining is happening or is a possibility, and be asked to express their views.

Twenty-eight years later an arrest was made. After two years of court hearings, a plea agreement was reached for second-degree murder. (Halia)

Jury selection is overseen by a judge and is conducted by the prosecuting and defense attorneys. The defendant is present at these proceedings. Twelve people (usually) and alternates are selected after both sides ask questions and accept or excuse people, if they determine any bias. The rules allow each side a set number of jurers they can excuse in order to get the best possible jury. These are called "preemptory challenges."

Remember that from this point on, the hallways and restrooms are not a free zone for you to let out your raw pain. **Use your notebook to record your reactions. Draw images if you need to, but continue to show respectful decorum wherever you are**.

Prosecutor Tracy Prior says: "The jury will note your appearance and behavior both inside and outside the courtroom."

Set up safe people and places to debrief with afterward. Watch out for your facial expressions, glares, and stares, as your face is the window into your pain.

Prior to court I was told how I should act and dress; I was told to refrain from losing my mind and trying to kill this murderer, or at least that's what I heard. I dressed nicely and answered the questions, but if looks could kill, I was trying . . . it didn't work. (Kaila)

Timeline of a trial

- **Pre-Trial Conferences**
- **Jury Selection**
- **Trial Starts**
- **Opening Statements**
- **State Presents Its Case**
- **Defense Presents Its Case**
- **Rebuttals by Prosecution and Defense**
- **Closing Arguments**
- **Jury Instructions**
- **Verdict**
- **Sentencing**

Trial Starts: We discussed before that there can be many delays or changes in trial start dates. Families need to be prepared for this. If the defense declares it is not ready, the judge is prone to support this change to prevent appeals later. The defendant can ask for a new attorney, discussed previously in Chapter 6.

When court comes into session, they ask if the judge, the recorder, the prosecutor, the defendant, and the defendant's attorney are present. They don't even care or ask if the victim's family is there. In a lot of cases, I think the defense would be very happy if we were not there. (CalPOST, 2009)

Opening Statements: These contain the "Table of Contents" that will be presented over the course of the trial by both sides.

State Presents Its Case: The prosecution presents its evidence and witnesses to prove "beyond a reasonable doubt" that the defendant is guilty.

Defense Presents Its Case: The defense presents its evidence and witnesses to prove the defendant is not guilty as charged.

Rebuttals by Both Sides: Each side has the opportunity to present more convincing forensics or witnesses to dispute the opposing side's evidence and witness statements.

Closing Arguments: Each side summarizes its position before the jury (or judge) deliberates the case.

Closing arguments have to be based on the facts that have been presented, but the jury is instructed that closing arguments are not evidence. (Rose)

Be prepared to hear the defense make a request to the judge to dismiss the case after the prosecutor rests the case, claiming that the prosecution did not meet its burden and did not put on a prima facie (sufficient for conviction) case.

Jury Instructions: The applicable law is given by the judge to guide the jury during deliberations. The jury in a trial does not decide if there is probable cause, but whether they are convinced that the accusations have been proven beyond a reasonable doubt. Right before the jury gets the case to deliberate, the judge will charge the jury, explaining the charges and what the jury should consider. Once this starts, no one is allowed to enter or leave the courtroom.

Verdict: The results of the jury's decision are presented in court. Possibilities are: guilty, not guilty, unable to reach a verdict (the finding is never "innocent"). If there is a mistrial or hung jury, the prosecution will decide whether or not to refile charges and retry the case.

A mistrial is called when the judge determines that procedural misconduct has occurred; for example, attempts by the prosecution or defense to influence jurors. More than likely, the case will be retried.

A hung jury occurs when the jurors do not all agree on a verdict. The only benefit, if there is one, is that the case may be retried, and the prosecution knows where the evidence was lacking for one or more of the jurors to be able to come to a guilty verdict.

Sentencing: If the finding is "guilty," a sentencing date is set. Depending on the charge, there is a minimum and maximum penalty based on the penal code; the judge may have some leeway in terms of the severity of the sentence. Each side will present information to support what they want this decision to be. The vicitm's family will usually have an opportunity to present **Victim Impact Statements** at sentencing. This is the first time co-victims are able to talk about their loved one and his or her value in court. Victim impact statements are covered more thoroughly in Chapter 8. Go there to get guidance and a sample statement.

Survivor Question: What is your experience of the court process?

Write your answer in your notebook.

Rose

In our case, there was an arraignment hearing where the judge asked the defendants to plead guilty or not guilty. This happened three days after the arrests, which occurred 18 months after the murders. Of course, the murderer pleaded "not guilty." Bail was denied for him. Bail was set for the defendant charged with "Obstruction of Justice." Although we had little inside information to the evidence, I wondered why the second one wasn't charged with "accessory to murder."

There were so many pretrial motions where either the prosecutor or defense attorney would argue over what could be presented in the case. We were present at every one of these, whether it was for five minutes or the entire day. There were also

so many continuances, which took a major toll on all of us. We would get our hopes up that soon we would be going to trial just to find out it would be continued another six to eight weeks, and we would start the process all over again. This went on until we finally got through all the various motion hearings, pretrial hearings, preliminary hearings, continuances until we heard the magic words . . . the Judge had set a trial date. The jury selection started about a week before, and ***that was the one time we were not allowed to be in the courtroom.*** *However, once the jury is selected, the trial starts immediately; for us, the actual trial began—18 months AFTER THE ARRESTS.*

From murder to the end of trial, it took over three years (18 months until the arrest and 18 months more

Then came

the moment

of truth:

The defendant

was going

to take

the stand.

(Rose)

until the trial) of excruciating pain, confusion, and lack of knowledge that this was really how long most murders take to get to trial.

Opening statements started with the prosecutor, then the defense. I was completely caught off guard, first of seeing the murderer in a suit like he was a normal person, and then seeing the Jury file in and take their seats.

There was such tension in the room; or maybe it was just that I could feel the anxiety inside me and from everyone around me. I was able to follow along with the opening statement of the prosecutor; some of what he was saying I was already aware of; it was the other stuff he said he would prove throughout the court process that I was really confused about. I guess that may have been when the light went on in my head that I really had little idea of all the facts surrounding the case.

Then came the defense's turn to do their opening statements. Not only did I have trouble with what he was saying, because so much of it was untrue, but I kept hearing something the prosecutor had said to me many times over the course of investigation and preparing the case for trial, **"They have a story; we have the truth."**

Once both sides were done with the opening arguments, the prosecutor began putting on his evidence and calling witnesses. I was caught off guard at how quickly (day 2) the prosecution dove right into the deaths. We had been asked not to attend or to excuse ourselves when this portion of testimony was presented, because it would be gruesome. We always said we wouldn't leave the courtroom; we would be sitting in place of Victoria and Louis. I gave everyone else the chance to leave and really had hoped my father would, but instead we all sat there in horror.

The medical examiner's testimony was clinical, technical, words I didn't understand, but I felt sick because it was as if he was speaking of a dead carcass and not human beings, my babies. And there were the horrific photos of them in death on giant big screens that you couldn't help but glance at. We just stared down at the floor with tears streaming down our cheeks for what seemed like an eternity.

The defense gets to cross examine each witness, and I remember him asking stupid questions that had already been answered, but I guess he had to at least make an attempt to discredit some of what was being said. I wondered how he thought he could attempt to try to make this look like anything other than what it is was: a premeditated double homicide. I don't remember much about the order of witnesses taking the stand, but I know the prosecution had gone to the ends of the earth to prove the defendant's guilt.

There were cell-tower forensics that boggled the mind, cell-phone forensics that took months to get back information that had been deleted and told a story all on their own; there were the witnesses that I knew who had been friends of Victoria's, her two roommates, one of which had found the bodies and called 911. The tapes that played that call were devastatingly painful. The other roommate that had known Victoria for years, now on the stand shaking and crying.

Then came the witness that had been Victoria's best friend, and the man that the defense was using as their third-party culpability . . . who they were trying to frame for these murders. He was on the stand for two days; it was torture for him and for his family and all of us to watch him go through this. The defense went at him with all that they had; they made jokes about his virginity and how Victoria was his first. They were horrible to him, but when he stepped off that stand, he came straight to me and sat right next to me. He had lost all innocence he had had over the years I had known him; he had been through hell and back, and he stood his ground on the stand and told the truth . . . not a story like the defense had.

By the time the prosecution rested, I was overwhelmed at the length to which they went to prove the case, and the endless information I had had no idea about. Every attempt that the defense had made to discredit any of the witnesses fell short, and I felt pretty good about how it was going.

Then came the moment of truth: The defendant was going to take the stand. I wanted to throw up throughout his testimony as he spoke about my daughter and grandson. *The lies he told, the composure he had as he was telling these lies worried me.*

It was

the longest day

and a half

of my life,

waiting for

them to

come back

with a verdict.

(Rose)

167

When they played his interrogation tape, he stuttered through most of it, and now he was not stuttering and had an answer for every question posed to him by his attorney. I went home that night afraid because he hadn't missed a beat. The next day, the prosecutor got a hold of him in cross examination and any fear I had previously was wiped away within the first hour.

It dawned on me that of course he was composed with his own attorney; he had 18 months to study the questions and

defense and that in the notification process the day I found out they were dead, those confused answers could come back and be used against me and work for the defense.) The prosecution cleared it up under cross-examination and it was over.

Now it was the defense attorney's turn to put on his case. It was all I could do to sit in my chair and not scream out at him because he was using his own witnesses that were all clearly lying; their testi-

---

The hard work and time we had put into gaining mastery over our emotions and grief was challenged on a regular basis, especially during the trial. (Rose)

---

rehearse his answers. Not so when the prosecution went at him. The prosecutor didn't go in a linear line of events leading up to the murders; he went from one question to a completely different one about something completely different. Quickly the defendant began to lose his cool; he began to stutter like I now knew he did when he was nervous, and he got tangled up in his own lies. **If this was a boxing match, the prosecution TKO'd him in the first round.**

Finally the defense called its last witness: me. Why was I a witness for the defense? It was his way of trying to keep me out of the courtroom throughout the trial until I testified; it had backfired, however, because the judge ruled I could be in the courtroom as I had been in every other hearing leading up to trial. The defense attorney had no real questions to ask me; **he had me read my initial statement to the jury (one I had no idea would be turned over to the**

mony was staged and had no basis in fact.

The closing arguments began on September 8th and were really a synopsis of the evidence presented in the case. The prosecutor had proven his case (we believed beyond any reasonable doubt) and reiterated that for the jury. The defense still stuck to their original theory that there was third-party culpability, and he was the actual murderer, even with all the evidence that proved that to be untrue. That afternoon the Jury was given instructions and sent back to deliberate. They got the case at 3 P.M., were deliberating the entire next day and on the third day.

It was the longest day and a half of my life, waiting for them to come back with a verdict. Now it was ready to be heard. I was sick, shaking, and afraid I might faint.

When I got to the courtroom, the hallway was already full of supporters, *friends of mine and of Victoria's, my sister, all the detectives and Sgt. on the case, and media galore. Once the courtroom was full, the rest had to stay in the hallway and watch the proceedings on a monitor. The jury filed in, the defendant was red-eyed and sweaty.*

When the verdict was read, **he was found guilty of two counts of first-degree murder and one count of obstruction.** *I remember hugging and*

Everything was stop and go, stop and go. *I felt like we were constantly being pulled in different directions, re-focusing our energy on this one, then that one, and back again. In the end I know we got as much justice as we were going to see on Earth, and I know that so many others never get that, so I should be grateful. The truth is, justice is great and all, but it isn't really all it is cracked up to be. The one thing I couldn't get was*

It was our only opportunity to bring our loved-one into focus as a once living, breathing human being who mattered to us and to so many. (Valeria)

---

crying into my husband's arms and then into my sister's. I remember looking over at the murderer, and his head was in his hands; I felt no rage, certainly no sympathy, just grateful that he would finally for once in his miserable life be held accountable for what he did.

I whispered "thank you" to the jury as they were ushered out the back way and escorted to their cars. I remember a roar of screams and shouts, but it wasn't in the courtroom; it was from everyone in the hallway! For a brief moment I saw his mother and fiancée and felt nothing for them either. I knew that would come later, but it wasn't going to intrude on the overwhelming sense of gratefulness I felt. Victoria and Louis could finally rest in peace.

It was one of the worst experiences of my life, and it wasn't over yet. Sentencing was set for November 6th, another two months away.

This case took somewhere around four and a half years from the time of the murders to sentencing. Years that are forever engrained in my mind, years that took away so much of my grieving time.

Victoria and Louis back, and that was all I really wanted in the first place.

 Valeria
No one in our family had ever been involved with the judicial system to the extent that our loved-one's murder forced us into. Other than participating in minor jury duty service, we had not spent much time in any courthouse. Now, we were forced into an unknown situation of having to endure a death-penalty trial, unsure of how we were going to come out of it, on the other side. It was a time when our private and public self felt so disconnected, and the hard work we had put into managing our emotions and grief was challenged on a regular basis throughout the trial.

Each time we listened to details of evidence from witnesses we had never heard of before, looked at upsetting autopsy photos we had never seen before, prepared and delivered testimony on behalf of our son, or heard a decision by the Judge that was not in the Prosecution's favor, the range of emotions from anger to sadness erupted and, once again, our spirits collapsed.

When a Prosecutor was assigned to the case after the capture of the suspect in 2008, the lead Detective Investigator on our case arranged for our family to meet with him. He gave us a general roadmap of how things were expected to proceed to trial, and addressed many of our concerns. We were reassured by his stated commitment to keep in constant contact with

family members as they were guided by the Prosecutors questions in delivering their own testimony—all while facing the person responsible for the murder.

It was our only opportunity to bring our loved-one into focus as a once living, breathing human being who mattered to us and to so many.

At the conclusion of the Penalty Phase, when the Jury submits its Sentencing recommendation to the Judge, the

---

One of the most difficult moments was during the Penalty Phase, when each one of us were called to the witness stand to deliver our testimony . . . (Valeria)

---

us from the day we met him to the conclusion of the case. Throughout the lengthy four-and-a-half-year process of our case, we were grateful for, and buoyed by the abiding support we received from the Prosecution Team, and from the cooperative relationship and excellent communication we had with them.

We witnessed the skill of the Prosecutor, whose intellect, professionalism, and calm demeanor were qualities that assured us that the victims in this case were going to receive the best representation. This put us at ease going forward.

One of the most difficult moments for our family was during the Penalty Phase, when each one of us were called to the witness stand to deliver our testimony about who our loved one was and the impact their murder had in changing our family and our lives forever. While it was difficult to think about what we wanted to say and bring all of our emotions to the surface five years after the event, it was equally gut wrenching to hear and feel the pain in the voices of each one of our

Judge orders a Sentencing Report to be put together by a member of the Sheriff's Department. It is a complete evaluation of the trial, crimes committed, charges, verdict(s), and corresponding guidelines for Sentencing for each guilty count, Restitution requested by victims, State-owed Restitution to be paid by the convicted, and victim's testimony in the Penalty Phase.

Prior to submitting this report to the Judge, the Probation Officer will contact each one of the victims to ask them what Sentence they desire the Judge give. When we were asked, we desired that the convicted receive nothing less than the maximum Sentence allowable on each one of his convictions handed down by the Jury, to be served consecutively. Requesting this, we know that there is no punishment here on Earth severe enough for him to serve for the atrocities he committed and the wake of destruction he has left in society.

TIP: The victim's family is entitled to receive a copy of the Sentencing Report at Sentencing. I strongly encourage you to request this for its valuable information.

When Is the "End"

A Director of Victim Services tells us that survivors should not expect that even after the case turns out the way they want it to, there may be a "crash, a mental let down" once the criminal justice system piece is over and there is nothing left for them to do but grieve for their loved ones. They expected that this would make them feel better, but they still go home empty handed and without the one thing they wanted, their loved ones back.

Prosecutors typically say they are not done with a case until four to five years after sentencing, when the first appeal has been denied. If the appeal is granted, then they would retry the case.

The criminal justice system is for the accused. It is made up of human beings, and it is true that it has a lot in place to protect a defendant from being wrongly convicted of a crime. None of us want a person to go to jail for something that he or she didn't do. However, a universal complaint from survivors of murder victims is that the court system is set up for helping criminals, not them.

Parents of a murdered son traveled cross-country six times to present victim impact statements. They were pleased with the verdicts for the murder of their son. That is, until they got the news just two months later that all sentences were reduced by 60 percent due to a new law just passed in that state, which had reduced sentencing for anyone who was a minor when they committed their crime.

Everyone on both sides of the aisle makes the same complaint: There is not much protection and support for crime victims. As sad as this is, we will not give up and will continue to have folks advocate for changes and fairness in the criminal justice system. We must work together and continue to make changes to recalibrate this wrong. Many survivors have done just that and made significant changes in honor of their loved one.

Jan Maurizi, Bureau Director, LA County District Attorney, says: "Even after sentencing and they are in jail, you still wake up and think of your loved one. It affects every aspect of your life. It is the most horrendous experience that anyone could go through." (CalPOST, 2009)

The promise is that after the verdict is rendered, life will be back on track and normal again. Co-victims are surprised when this does not happen. They realize again and again that soon after the criminal justice system process is over, they are not back to normal at all. Their lives have been on hold, waiting for the relief that they believed a verdict and sentencing would give them. But their lives never go back to that "old normal." Instead, they must deal with the "new normal."

That being said, we know it is still important for you to attend the proceedings that you can. Just have it in the back of your head that your journey will continue in unique ways for you, your family, and community.

Survivors ask you to not put all your hopes and expectations in the Verdict Basket! Keep some reserve and focus on other aspects of your life, even if you are often just going through the motions.

Public Records

When a charge has been decided, the information and records regarding the case become public record and survivors have the right to acquire them. Your Key Contacts can help obtain these records.

An adjudicated case, even homicide, becomes public record. **Some family members want to know the whole story and request a copy of the investigation. I do not recommend this.** *There are witness statements often talking poorly of the deceased, but the most devastating are the photographs. Having been to many homicide scenes, overseeing scenes, collecting evidence and photographing, no person should have to see what we as investigators have seen. We become callous, sometimes unemotional, but deep down, each scene plays a toll on us. I can close my eyes now and go through a photo album in my head of many, if not most, of the scenes. As I have told many victim's families, family members need to remember their loved ones as they once were, not how they were found.* (Wissemann)

However, if a case is never prosecuted, there are limits on how much information can be released. Harrier learned this when he got the records regarding the deaths of his parents:

Another term I learned was "redacted," which means information in official reports, such as peoples' names and testimony, has been removed so I could not have access to it. This included witness names and, in some cases, the entire statements of some witnesses.

Other public records include the autopsy reports. These are very graphic and written in medical language. Like seeing the crime scene photos, they can be very difficult to review, and it may not be in your best interest. If you do review them, please consider doing so with a medical professional so you understand the terms being used.

You may have to pay for the records you request. Some agencies can put them on a computer disk and reduce the cost.

As all six of our cases were settled with defendants taking plea offers, there was no trial where the detailed autopsy report was made public (it was not needed in the Probable Cause Hearing). JJ and I talked about the report and have chosen not to request a copy. We did go to the two hospitals our son was taken to and requested and received medical records. That was very painful to have to read the medical details of his condition that night. But we were told when we asked that if we wanted to see the full details of all records the prosecution had, we would be shown them at the end of the sentencing. We were also told that there were many, many boxes that we would have to go through. At the end, we decided not to go through them. (Mary)

Resources

Books

Dare I Call it Murder? A Memoir of Violent Loss, Larry M. Edwards, Wigeon Publishing, 2013.

Murder in Memphis: The True Story of a Family's Quest for Justice, Doris D. Porch and Rebecca Easley, New Horizon Press, 1997.

Scream at the Sky: Five Texas Murders and One Man's Crusade for Justice, Carlton Stowers, St. Martin's Press, 2003.

The Ride: A Shocking Murder and a Bereaved Father's Journey from Rage to Redemption, Brian MacQuarrie, Da Capo Press, 2009.

Online

ACLU of Northern California: *The Truth About Life Without Parole: Condemned to Die in Prison*; https://www.aclunc.org/article/truth-about-life-without-parole-condemned-die-prison.

Arbitrary Death: Rick Unklesbay of the Pima County Attorney's Office in Arizona, explains why he wrote the book *Arbitrary Death*, which deals with how death-penalty murder cases impact the surviving family; https://homicidesurvivorsinc.org/arbitrary-death/.

Death Penalty Information Center: Victim's brother says execution left him with "horror and emptiness" https://deathpenaltyinfo.org/news/new-voices-victims-brother-says-execution-left-him-with-horror-and-emptiness.

Death Penalty: Working on Alternatives to the Death Penalty http://www.deathpenalty.org/article.php?id=56.

Murder Victims' Families for Reconciliation: advocates for the repeal of the death penalty; http://www.mvfr.org.

National Center for Victims of Crime (NCVC), 800-FYI-CALL http://www.ncvc.org.

ProCon.org: Death Penalty: Is Life in Prison Without Parole a Better Option Than the Death Penalty? http://deathpenalty.procon.org/view.answers.php?questionID=001017.

Victims of Crime Resource Center, University of the Pacific-McGeorge School of Law; http://www.1800victims.org/

Victim Law: The Justice System Explained http://www.victimlaw.org.

* Some Web addresses may have changed since publication.

Page intentionally left blank. Use it for jotting notes or your thoughts, if you wish.

8

Victim Impact, Justice & Unsolved Cases

> *One thing we are certain of . . . anyone who has lost a loved-one, then goes through a criminal trial, whether it is a death-penalty case or not, knows that, in the end, there are no winners, no closure, no "happy endings." What was done, can never be undone.* (Valeria)

Victim Impact Statement

Today, judges are compelled by law to give co-victims an opportunity to address the court. All states guarantee the right for those who have been most affected by a crime to present a written or oral statement in court. This is the **Victim Impact Statement** (VIS).

Most of the time this opportunity is at "sentencing." The decision is up to the judge, but you will probably have an opportunity to read your statement in court. These reports become part of the record for this case. The judge may allow several Victim Impact Statements to be submitted from different people who have been impacted. Check with your Key Contacts (Chapter 6) as to what is allowed in your circumstance.

Up to this point, the voices of co-victims have not been heard unless they were witnesses. An impact statement gives them an opportunity to speak on behalf of a loved one. This one chance to be the voice puts great pressure on co-victims to make sure it is complete and right within the limited time they have to speak.

I have heard several co-victims lament over what to say and worry they will be unable to read their statements in court without breaking down. **You may appoint someone to read it for you.** Again, check with your Key Contacts about what is allowed in your situation and have a backup plan.

Whether or not your case gets to a Sentencing Phase, this type of report will provide a family report and is valuable psychologically. Writing down the story of your experience can be of great value to you and others over time. Once written down, you can edit it and refer to it so that you will not need to tell the story over and over again to new people in your world. Fill in the form included in this chapter to prepare for your court report or your personal records. Your story is important, and this is one of the few times you have to tell it.

The sample Victim Impact Statement form in this chapter may be different than the one provided you in your community. The questions will ask who your loved one was and the cost of their loss to you and those around you. The costs may be emotional, financial, and physical. Contrary to the initial belief by many co-victims, this is not a time to give the killer hell. It is the time to tell the judge what sentence to impose. By learning more about the victim and the surrounding loss factors, the judge is more informed about what sentence, within what is allowed by law, he or she will hand down.

Mothers Against Drunk Driving (MADD) also has a workbook that you can refer to when filling out your Victim Impact Statement. Look under the Supportive Literature section

Consequences and Costs of Homicide

According to a study by the National Institute of Justice (Miller, et al., 1996), a single homicide costs close to $3 million. Tangible costs are the dollar amount calculated from losses such as medical and property expenses. Intangible costs are double this amount and less easily measured items such as pain, emotional trauma, reduced productivity at home and school, and long-term suffering. Below is a list of some of the costs and consequences of the crime for you and your family to consider including in your victim impact statement:

Homicide	$2,940,000
Rape/sexual assault	$87,000
Assault w/ injury	$24,000
Assault w/o injury	$2,000

- Family's involvement in the criminal justice system
- Physical/property damages or loss
- Lost days at work or school
- Time and financial costs to you and your family
- Life course changes
- Relationship changes
- Health problems—medical and/or mental
- Angry outbursts
- Diminished quality of life
- Family dysfunction
- Increased fear of crime and safety issues
- Social and leisure time changes and losses
- Career changes
- Loss of faith
- PTSD, depression, and substance abuse
- Job loss
- Social isolation

of the organization's website for the Victim Impact Statement Workbook or contact MADD directly. The workbook contains thoughtful and supportive questions. (See Resources at the end of this chapter.)

When the day of Sentencing arrived our family was prepared to give our individual Victim Impact Statements to the convicted, telling him how what he did changed the course of our lives forever. One of our family members took off several days of work to fly from the east coast to deliver his statement in court. Just before we were to be called, there was one last unexpected and unsuccessful motion to the Judge by the Defense Attorney to prevent all of us from giving our Impact Statements (even though there is a law in our state constitution which allows crime victims the right to do this). The Prosecutor argued vehemently on our behalf, and the Judge allowed us to give our statements. (Valeria)

On the next page is a modified example for you to work with. You will find a template for children to use in Resources at the end of this chapter.

When you prepare your own impact statment, **please make it as long or short as you need. Use your notebook for this exercise. Make copies of the template for others to use in completing their statements as well.**

Feel free to add anything beyond the suggestions to describe the impact on you and your family.

Survivor Sample: Victim Imact Statement

Use the accompanying template to prepare your own victim impact statement.

Rose
Your Name: <u>Rose</u> **Your age:** <u>53</u> **Date of Loss:** _____
Type of Loss: <u>Murder</u>
Victim's Name: <u>Victoria</u> **Age:** <u>22</u> **Relationship to you:** <u>Daughter</u>
Victim's Name: <u>Louis</u> **Age:** <u>10 months</u> **Relationship to you:** <u>Grandson</u>

1. How has the crime affected you and those close to you?

It changed anything & everything. I lost my identity as a mother and grandmother, and that is really how I defined my life. The world as I knew it stopped on a dime; it has never looked the same since. I questioned every belief I had had prior to the murders. I went through stages of shock, disbelief, anger/rage, denial, confusion, frustration, bitterness, and envy. I couldn't make sense of anything. The world was still turning but mine was frozen in time. I lost 30 lbs., then gained 50 lbs. Everything was out of balance, and I didn't care about anything but getting that arrest. It changed my husband in ways that I didn't notice at first, but they became crystal clear as time went on. He was angry all the time, devastated at the loss, and the details tore him up.

continued on page 179

Co-victims of Murder Impact Statement

Your Name _____Age _____

Date of Loss _____ Type of Loss_____

Victim's Name_____ Age _____

Relationship to you_____

Victim's Name_____ Age _____

Relationship to you_____

Suggestions for completing this crime impact report: Write in your own words how this crime has affected you and those close to you. Please answer as many questions as you wish. If a question doesn't fit or is too upsetting for you, skip it for now.

1. If you wish, please tell what kind of person your loved one was and what he or she meant to you. You may wish to tell about some of your loved ones interests, hopes, and dreams.
2. How has the crime affected you and those close to you? Please feel free to discuss your feelings about what has happened, and how it has affected your general well-being.
3. How has this crime affected your relationship with any family members, friends, co-workers, and other people?
4. What physical injuries or symptoms have you or others close to you suffered as a result of this crime? You may want to write about how long the injuries/symptoms lasted, or how long they are expected to last, and if you sought medical treatment for these injuries. You may also want to discuss what changes you have made in your life as a result of these injuries.
5. What has been the effect of this crime on your (or family members') ability to work or do any of the things you normally do, such as going to school, running a household, or any other activities you perform or enjoy?
6. What future events stand out that you no longer can look forward to?
7. How has this death caused financial losses for you (or family members)? Some examples of expenses you may have paid or owe include medical bills or expenses; counseling costs; lost wages or loss of support; funeral expenses; crime scene cleanup; relocations ; the repair or replacement of door locks and security devices.
8. How much time off from work have you (or family members) had to take? You may want to include relatives that have had to travel for funerals to provide support and to attend legal meetings, such as court hearings.
9. How is your (or family members') sense of safety different since this loss?

Impact Statement for Children and Their Parents

1. How has this crime affected your life as a parent, your child's life, or the lives of those close to you?
2. How has life changed between your child and his or her friends, both at school and in your neighborhood?
3. How has the loss changed your child's behavior or schoolwork?
4. Write about the medical treatment or emotional counseling your child or other members of your family have received or expect to receive in the future.

continued from page 177

He was supposed to protect her and his grandson, and he felt he had failed. He also felt like he was losing me to the unknown, and he couldn't save me either, so he felt like even more of a failure.

2. Has this crime affected your relationship with any family members, friends, co-workers, and other people?

My father lost all faith in God. He was always such a strong man but this broke him. He had 4 strokes between the murders and the arrest. He survived long enough for the trial, but passed away from complications of the strokes a year and a half later. I lost my mother in the process; although she is still alive, she has no relationship with me nor I with her. After three months she said, "You should get over it; now you are just milking it."

I became extremely close to two of my sisters in the process, much closer than we had ever been in our lives. My oldest sister called me every day to check in on me, and she was my sounding board for every thought and emotion I had. We still talk almost every day and that has been one of the blessings in my life. She also flew out here from Florida many times for different events we had for Victoria and Louis prior to the arrests. She was also here off and on during the trial; staying a week at a time. My youngest sister also was here from Minnesota for different events, and she was here for the trial when my other sister wasn't, so I always had family with me.

I am blessed to say I still have many of the friends I had prior to the murders and even more because Victoria's friends came to support me; they have become my friends now.

3. What physical injuries or symptoms have you or others close to you suffered as a result of this crime?

I was diagnosed with PTSD and depression, panic attacks, and high blood pressure. In the beginning I would see Louis hanging from a bridge, a tree, a wire, just about everywhere. To this day it still happens occasionally, and it feels like I am back to square one. I would see Victoria without the back of her head walking somewhere or driving in the car next to me and although that part of her head was missing, it wasn't bloody; it just wasn't there anymore. Although there was blunt-force trauma to her head, the death certificate says the actual cause of death was strangulation. I don't know why I don't see that part of it; just the head stands out in my thoughts.

My husband suffers from depression, although he has a hard time admitting that; but I see it very clearly. He doesn't believe in medication, and although therapy helped us deal with the grieving process, it didn't help with the depression we both suffer from now.

You may want to write about how long the injuries lasted, or how long they are expected to last, and if you sought medical treatment for these injuries.

According to my doctor I will always suffer from PTSD, and there really hasn't been a time frame for the depression, but the medication on both has been reduced as time went on, but not until a few months after the trial was over.

You may also want to discuss what changes you have made in your life as a result of these injuries.

I have educated myself on these conditions, and I do know that at any given time something could trigger something, and I have to be prepared to deal with it head on. If I have a panic attack, I now know I am not having a heart attack and that it will subside. I do deep breathing to center myself; sometimes I have to put my head between my knees so I don't pass out. I don't go to the cemetery as often as I did in the beginning. Instead we built a serenity garden at our home, and I usually will spend time there gardening or just being with my plants and memories of Victoria and Louis.

4. What has been the effect of this crime on your (family members') ability to work or do any of the things you normally do, such as going to school, running a household, or any other activities you normally perform or enjoy?

My husband lost his job a few months after the murders. After that he did enroll in night school, and for the next 4 years (including during the trial, which he attended every day) he got his Associate's & Bachelor's degrees. I never went back to work; my job as an Account Manager was extremely stressful prior to the murders. There was no way I could have handled that stress when I could barely function day to day. I needed help doing the simplest functions, like grocery shopping.

If you wish, please tell what kind of person your loved one was and what he or she meant to you. You may wish to tell about some of your loved one's interests, hopes, and dreams.

Victoria was the love of my life, my best friend, my greatest contribution to the world; she was my everything. She was perfectly flawed, and she was the perfect daughter for me.

Victoria was strong in a quiet sort of way; she didn't mince words, but she was kind in her delivery of them. She was extremely funny in a sarcastic sort of way and sometimes the things she would say would make you do a double take because she had a baby face, and her humor didn't always fit into that mold. She had a real sense of who she was; she wasn't interested in being in the "in crowd"; she didn't give in to peer pressure; she followed her own path. She was fiercely loyal to her family and friends; she didn't care if you liked them or not; that had no bearing on her whatsoever. She was blossoming into a wonderful mother which was a beautiful sight to see, a grown woman in the prime of her life with nothing but beautiful things ahead of her.

Louis was the missing link that we never knew we were missing until he arrived on Earth. He was beyond beautiful, he was a sweet baby that was always smiling, and he loved everyone around him especially his mom and his grandpa. When you looked into his beautiful baby-blue eyes, you saw his innocence, purity, and I believe I saw a glimpse of Heaven through those eyes. I was so proud to be his grandma.

5. What future events stand out that you no longer can look forward to?

Watching Victoria grow as a mother and as a woman in her own right. The dreams she had, the goals she had, watching her get married, the lifetime she had in front of her. For Louis, his first day of school, sports, graduation, Halloween costumes, who he would be as he grew day by day and into the man he would one day become. Every birthday for both of them, every holiday throughout the year. Everything is tainted now. I do something for each one of those days to honor them.

6. How has this loss caused financial losses for you (or family members)?

Financially we lost everything: our home, our savings. We simply could not afford anything. What little money we had put aside we live off now. The funeral costs were covered by the state, but we paid for a memorial bench in lieu of a headstone. My insurance covered our counseling costs and doctor bills, and when it ran out my doctors continued to see me for free so there would be no lapse in my care.

7. How much time off from work have you (or family members) had to take?

You may want to include relatives that have traveled from other states for funerals, to provide support and to attend legal meetings.

My husband took off four weeks before going back to work, but then he got fired a few months later. I never went back to work. My dad was retired, so he didn't lose time off work, but my sisters were here for a week for the funeral planning, and then after for a few days. They each took off a week here and there to visit and participate in things we were doing for Victoria and Louis. Then they each took off a total of three separate weeks, alternating each other so we always had support during the trial.

8. How is your (or family members') sense of safety different since this loss?

I guess this seems to be more of an issue for my sisters, and my father when he was still alive, than it ever has been for me. Prior to the arrests, my husband tried to go to the cemetery with me as often as possible because we were always followed home when we went there. It happened with my sisters, too, which I think contributed to their sense of safety for me, not themselves as they live in other states. As for me, I have zero fear for my safety. I guess I have an attitude of "nothing can hurt me worse than I have already been hurt, so bring it on." Perhaps not the healthiest attitude to take under the circumstances, but it is what it is.

Justice

Justice requires more than holding offenders accountable. Yet we minimize a victim's pain and suffering, and pretend that criminal convictions are a sufficient balm. We must meet our obligation to victims, not just because we are a compassionate society, but because helping victims rebuild their lives is an essential component of justice. (Herman, 2010)

True justice cannot really be achieved.

I hear this again and again, listening to so many of you: that when all the legal process is over, and the sentence you hoped for has occurred, true justice is not possible, as there is no getting our loved one(s) back. The perpetrator may be held accountable by the legal system, but he or she has already "gotten away with murder." Co-victims are challenged with having to reconcile this fact and rebuild their lives in spite of this reality. This is hard work.

It's justice for them; my ex-husband's life does not compare to my father's life. It will never be over; there will never be justice. (CalPOST, 2009)

"Getting closure" usually means only that an aspect of the journey after a murder will not be repeated, such as when there is a trial and someone is found guilty. Usually, but not always, that work is done and there is closure to that activity.

Some of us will have to face the additional burden of putting our lives on hold for what can take years and years of waiting for the wheels of justice to turn, while bearing witness for our loved one—unsure if we will ever receive the judicial closure we are so hoping for. (Valeria)

Most of the time when folks are talking to you about "getting closure," it misses the mark. They usually want you to get over it and not feel badly anymore. The hope is that this is like other deaths, natural deaths, and you eventually "get over it."

This journey is about learning to live with what has happened to you. You will not get closure nor "get over it." An amputee learns to adapt to a missing leg. The leg is never returning. Co-victims of murder have to deal with their loved one dying by the volitional act of someone in a violent and purposeful way. The loved one is not coming back. We do not get over it. When successful, we do learn to live with this loss and how our loved one(s) continue in our lives through their memories and what they stood for, with some purpose in life that is meaningful.

Susan Herman, the Executive Director of the National Center for Victims of Crime from 1997–2002, authored an important book, *Parallel Justice* (2010). In it, she proposes changes for crime victims that include:

- All victims deserve justice.
- Victims should be told that what happened to them was wrong and that every effort will be made to help them rebuild their lives.
- Rights should be implemented and enforced.

Survivor Question: Justice is defined as a penalty for the perpetrator, the killer of your loved one(s). What was your experience of justice being served and your thoughts about it?

Write your answer in your notebook.

Rose

For the person who actually murdered Victoria and Louis, we got the sentence we asked for, which was two life sentences without the possibility of parole. As for the person charged with Obstruction of Justice, I don't think we got justice at all. He got a mere slap on the wrist of 3 years and only served 9 months. Then he was on parole, which he violated and was resentenced to do the remainder of his sentence, but with good behavior was out in less than a year. I never agreed to his charges as I thought he should have been charged as an accessory to murder and served 25-to-life, so justice doesn't fit at all in my mind when it comes to him.

I think that people think that if you receive the sentence you asked for then justice was served. However, in reality they got away with murder because Victoria and Louis are still dead. I find no justice in that. I thought that when I heard the words: guilty, guilty, guilty, and I left the courtroom, in some way I would feel differently. I didn't. I took a small measure of pleasure that he was going to have to spend the rest of his life in a cage; that he didn't get to walk out of the courtroom a free man.

Marina

I am very bitter about my experience with the justice system. Statistically, it is a system with a fifty percent failure rate. That is unacceptable, yet we are taught that the American system of justice is the

best in the world. Really? Would you buy a two-story house with a missing second floor? Would you ever climb on a jet if you knew it might crash fifty percent of the time? Would you keep your money at a banking institution with a fifty percent default rate? You can call it a justice system if you please, but I call it the Busted System. So what if some people think it's the best system in the world? That may or may not be true—it's a big planet. But to me, the American legal system is merely the cleanest dirty shirt in the closet.

*I grudgingly admit that I feel better when I see a murder trial result in a conviction. Keeping company with other survivors has shown me that some murderers do pay for the lives they take. Seeing the joy of vindication on the face of a survivor can be heartening. But it's a double-edged sword. Sometimes my joy lasts for about as long as it takes to burn a Kleenex. If I'm in a dark place, happiness can turn into bitterness and melancholy. **Eventually I pull myself back from the abyss by reminding myself that this murder has not gone unpunished.***

Witness: the criminal attorney who defended Dad's killer became a murderer himself. Two years after the trial, he shot his embezzling paralegal to death. Then he shot himself. What a banner day that was! I rejoiced for a month. The paralegal was a paroled kidnapper and extortionist with a nasty gambling habit. He turned to embezzling from the elderly to cover his losses. When that wasn't enough, he embezzled a large amount from the criminal

> *In the end,*
>
> *there are*
>
> *no winners,*
>
> *no closure,*
>
> *no "happy*
>
> *endings."*
>
> *What was*
>
> *done can*
>
> *never be*
>
> *undone.*
>
> (Valeria)

attorney. Ha—that made the criminal attorney a crime victim! I hooted with savage glee when I read that the local criminal attorney community was "devastated" at the loss of one of their own.

Then there's the alleged murderer. I was deeply disappointed when newspaper articles about her disappeared from Google after a number of years—but this is the Age of the Internet. Information never truly disappears. The homicide detective assigned to the case told us the alleged murderer was a parasite: she lived off what she could glean from the men she targeted. In spite of being middle-aged, she had no employment history whatsoever. I can only hope that her lack of gainful employment continues indefinitely. Potential employers run all sorts of computer checks. She'll be lucky to get even the most menial of jobs, but I don't think she can—at least not for long. I want her life to be one of penury and desperation. By her own actions, she is gradually making my dream a reality. I feel no guilt in gloating over the facts.

She must have shelled out at least 50K to pay for the attorney. Attorneys don't take rain checks, so that's gone. She lost her house several years after the trial. As far as I'm concerned, she doesn't deserve to occupy a hamster cage. She can't afford to move out of the town where the murder occurred. It's not a huge town, so if she somehow loses herself, her obscurity never lasts for long. Through the years I have heard bits and pieces that point to the following: Every time she tries to present herself as an upstanding member of the community, she is ultimately found out.

I have to assume that the kind of justice I dream of will never take place. The reality is that this creature might go through the rest of her days with nothing more than a bad cold. I have come to the conclusion that there is no karma in this world—many killers and mass murderers have gone on to live out frictionless lives—history bears me out.

But I will always nurture a hope. For the most part, I have achieved my goal of living her into irrelevance. I have willed myself to step aside. It took tons of hard work, but I did it. That doesn't mean I wouldn't have the party of the century if something awful were to happen to her—why wouldn't I? It just couldn't be at the expense of *another innocent human life. That would be horrific.*

Kaila

In my sister's case I don't feel that justice was served; the killer had committed crimes in California previous to killing my sister, and he conse-quentially got 30 to life. Which means same time, two crimes in two states.

Valeria

One thing we are certain of: any-one who has lost a loved-one, then goes through a criminal trial, whether it is a death-penalty case or not, knows that, in the end, there are no winners, no closure, no "happy endings." What was done can never be undone. Our loved one is never going to come back, and their murder will continue to hover over the edge of everything we do, think, feel, and every relationship we have.

Sometimes it all feels like an exercise in futility. It is not something we ever wanted to do, and the last place we thought we would ever find ourselves. At the same time, we were compelled to do the one significant, last thing we could do to honor our loved one, and that is, to be there in the courtroom to reject the mind-less, reckless violence and harm caused by the killer.

Survivor Question: Has there been a silver lining, a way that your life has changed for the better or that life has rebalanced in some way?

The founders of the National Organization of Parents for Murdered Children started this organization after their daughter was murdered by her ex-boyfriend. Justice was not served as he only got 16 months in jail. Unfortunately and sadly, he killed another girlfriend a year later. The silver lining here may have been that by this time he was found guilty of murder and sentenced to death. He died at his own hands before that sentence could be carried out.

Write your answer in your notebook.

Marina

If Dad's alleged killer had been convicted, I might have never gotten involved in helping other survivors. I might have decided that justice had been done; I may have left well enough alone.

Things didn't work out that way, so I was compelled to seek out my own version of a satisfactory resolution to tragic loss. I continued to speak with my therapist from time to time, but I still felt mired and bereft of hope. Now I know that I needed to feel that way in order to discover the next step toward healing. I just didn't know it at the

time. I confirmed and reconfirmed the fact that from the moment my sister called, on that morning of all mornings, Dad had already been dead for hours. His story was written; his agony, no more.

Occasionally I attended survivor events, seeking some sort of release or epiphany.

I slowly became involved in projects with my therapist and my fellow survivors. My aspirations were as yet undefined. I continued to involve myself as I felt up to it. **When I spoke to survivors, and saw their faces light up in recognition at my words, I felt a rush like no other. I had information and skills, and I had** *earned them the hard way—why not use them in a constructive manner? That would be the ultimate triumph over a vicious murderer!*

It's important to note that I gave myself permission to pull back from involvement at any time. I still do. The "new normal" has to be serviced and nurtured as well. Coming back to life feels pretty damned good, and I don't want to lose that feeling.

Some survivors fill their lives with various types of survivor work. I admire their courage, but I am not like that. I enjoy long periods of not thinking about the murder at all. Unless you are a survivor, you cannot understand what an astounding accomplishment this represents, and I am very proud of what I have achieved. It gives me the strength to go on, even during those ghostly visits in the early morning hours.

I have learned how to lick honey from the razor's edge. It's a special ability, and I like to think that in some small way, I am helping my fellow survivors to learn how to acquire it. I will do it until I die—I can't help it. It's a drive, and it is my mission. In helping to heal others, I heal myself—and leave behind something that will endure.

Kaila

The silver lining for me is that I have peace in my life now; the dark gift is that I lost my family that blamed me for my sister's murder and could not get past the grief. **My mother has taught me how NOT to be when tragedy strikes.** *She still blames me, and I have no relationship with her.*

Unsolved Cases

Cold-case homicides are one of the most significant challenges facing law enforcement agencies nationwide. Murder cases can go unsolved not only for decades, but for centuries. For co-victims, this fact is just as disconcerting as the murder case itself. It is an extra-special torture and burden. Never forgotten, this unfinished story weaves in and out of focus in their lives until that status changes. Someone comes forth, new technology emerges, unknown evidence is found, someone discovers a new pattern to make a case active again. Families may become increasingly active in trying to find new leads to rekindle the case. This is a tremendous burden for co-victims who take on role of investigator when they worry that "no one cares" about getting justice for their loved one(s). Ask your Key Contacts about the status of your case and whether it has been put in the cold-case department. Your case may still be active and just taking a long time to get all the evidence together.

Larry Edwards's story, an unsolved case since 1978, is an example of this torture for him. He tells us it has affected many of members of his family and their life course. He is still waiting for justice for his parents.

He has written a book, *Dare I Call It Murder?: A Memoir of Violent Loss* (2013), detailing more about what he knows and what he has experienced. Will someone come forward now? He can only hope.

When the investigation has exhausted all leads and no new leads appear, the case moves to a cold-case status. Unsolved cases are never closed for families or investigators. Cold-case investigations are about more than seeing a case solved and getting a conviction. They are also about having protocols in place to ensure sensitivity to co-victims' needs during this time. Doing so improves outcomes by solving more cold cases. Some cold cases are solved, even decades later.

- Survivor writer Marina has no hope of getting justice in the legal arena but finds ways to direct her rage and finds hope.
- Dee Dee's family waited 13 years for detectives to find a pattern in the death of five women. Looking at their cases together led to a suspect and convictions. (Stowers, 2003)
- Joselyn Martinez (2013), a 36-year-old actress, cracked a cold case by tracking down her father's killer 26 years later, and handed her work over to detectives.
- The movie *No One Killed Jessica* (2011) tells the true story of model Jessica Lall, who was shot dead while tending bar in a New Delhi restaurant. Although a trial was conducted and dozens of witnesses testified, the suspected gunman was acquitted. But media outcry and petitions to India's president by her sister and a journalist led to a reopening of the case and subsequent conviction.
- Actor Dylan McDermott solved the mystery of his mother's tragic murder 45 years later, after he discovered police had covered it up. He was just five years old when it happened. (Rand, 2012)

When a new angle is identified, or a new timeline has passed, Crime Stoppers can help bring public attention to an unsolved case. For example, The *Pasadena Star News* agreed to publish pictures and background information on any unsolved homicide case in Los Angeles on the newspaper's website. Additionally, the newspaper highlights an unsolved case weekly. It only takes one person, one call, to turn an unsolved case to solved.

Survivor Questions: How has your case been stalled? How long has it been that you have sought justice and accountability for your loved one(s).

If applicable, write your answer in your notebook.

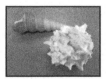

Harrier
My parents' case has been stalled since 1980.
For three years I stayed in contact with the FBI agent in charge of the case, hoping for justice for my dead parents. Since then, I have reviewed the case and the evidence, and written a book about the case to disclose information that had never before been made public.

When a case is reopened, survivors may find they re-experience both the events and emotions with its accompanying intensity. While this occurs intermittently in their lives when they are triggered after the loss, it is most certain when a case is reopened. This leads to an opportunity to put in place the additional supportive activities such as peer support groups and clinical services. Planning a meeting with the investigation team as well as family and friend gatherings will help buffer the additional strain of this time. Going it alone, toughing it out, is not recommended in most situations.

Survivor Questions: Is there an identified killer? What has gotten in the way that has kept this an unsolved case? What strengths have you discovered about yourself and those around you? How has this unsolved situation changed your life and those connected to your loved ones?

If applicable, write your answer in your notebook.

Harrier

*The FBI had a prime suspect in my parents' deaths—my younger brother. They wanted to prosecute, but the US attorney's office refused, saying that without bodies, with little forensic evidence, and having an unreliable witness (my youngest sister, who failed two lie-detector tests and vowed to lie in court), that . . . **the odds of getting a guilty verdict were too low to risk incurring jeopardy.***

When I got the news, it left me devastated. The investigation had dragged on for three years, and the FBI agents handling the case repeatedly assured me

*they were going "nail him." Then one day an agent met with me and other family members, and he told us there would be no prosecution, no trial, unless our sister agreed to testify truthfully. Over the years, I tried to get my sister to come forward and tell the court what she had told the FBI and me in private. But she has repeatedly refused. **I am still waiting.***

The lack of justice for my parents has tormented me for three decades, and that has been a contributor to post-traumatic stress, which in turn has negatively affected my life, my career, my family, my marriage.

Survivor Tips: What mistake do you want to help others avoid?

Write your answer in your notebook.

Rose

*No matter what kind of job you think the homicide team is or isn't doing, **you cannot try to solve the case yourself**. Do not speak to people that may have information. Once you have spoken to this possible witness, the defense will have a field day with your personal involvement, and their testimony could very well be thrown out of court. But if you get information, give that person's information to your detectives and stay out of it after that.*

Marina

Six years before the murder, Dad had a stroke. As he lay in a hospital bed—in a strange city, in another state—I wondered what I could do to make things better. At first he was glad I showed up, but eventually he chafed at my solicitude. He had no way of knowing that the weather outside was foul when he urged me to explore one of the many fish restaurants which dotted the nearby seashore. I suppose my visible concern was unbearable for a "man of action" who had nowhere to go.

*Well, I was appalled. How could he talk about seafood and earthly pleasures when he was disabled and lying in a hospital bed? Wasn't I supposed to maintain a bedside vigil like a good, responsible daughter? Didn't he appreciate what I was doing? I didn't know it then, but **he gave me a tremendous gift I did not recognize until many years had passed.***

In that moment he was telling me that life is to be savored. He didn't want me holding constant vigil at his bedside—it was annoying. He wanted me to be out in the world, enjoying what he himself had once enjoyed. He was trying to share his joy in life itself.

I never did visit those seaside restaurants, not in bitterly cold, stormy weather.

But four years after the trial, as I gazed down upon the desert he loved from the austere, beautiful mountains above, I knew in my heart that he would not want me to waste my comparatively young life in perpetual mourning of his loss. I had his word on it.

Harrier
*At first, I dealt with it by not dealing with it. I buried it deep and tried to get on with my life. I self-medicated. At times dinner consisted of an entire six-pack or bottle of wine. I did not seek professional counseling. **After all, I was a MAN. I didn't see no stinkin' head shrinker.** I just popped another beer. In hindsight, I can see that I made a big mistake.*

Survivor Lessons: What do you want to impart to others who have a cold case?

If applicable, write your answer in your notebook.

Rose
***Although your case may be labeled a cold case, it doesn't mean there will never be an arrest.** It means at this point in time the homicide team has exhausted all their leads and must wait for something new to develop. If and when that happens, the case is active again.*

Marina
***Don't count on the justice system to fix things—or you.** It's natural and human to imagine that all will be well once your loved one's murderer is convicted and behind bars. Do what you must, but know that at some point you must leave the murder behind and stop immersing yourself in death. Your loved one's murderer may go free, as did the woman who I believe slaughtered Dad. It's unthinkable, but it happens. Unbelievably, my deceased father was the one to show me that life goes on.*

As I write this, I feel the warm summer breeze coming through an open window. I feel the warmth and weight of Philo, my Amazon parrot, as he sits patiently upon my shoulder. He loves the feeling of being on my shoulder as I write. It is good juju. Later, I will grill a piece of chicken and savor the sandwich I make with it. Philo will surely get a piece of chicken, too, and I will chuckle as I hear his little squawks of gustatory pleasure.

Maybe later, we'll sit outside with a book and watch the lizards sun themselves on nearby rocks. This is life! You cannot bring your loved one back from the dead. I should know. I tried. It cannot be done. Your life is here right now. Don't waste it. Honor the dead, but do not spend too much time trying to inhabit their world. You do not want to see that wish realized.

do that for yourself, in your own unique way.

Harrier

I don't think anyone can prepare for such an even-tuality. It is too unpleasant to think about or consider. We not only want justice for our deceased loved ones, we expect justice. There is an implicit promise in the rule of law in our "civil"

Let someone make you smile, let someone make you laugh, allow yourself to be happy. (Kaila)

The justice system will not heal your pain. **Oh, yes, I envy those survivors who see justice done, but it's all a matter of degrees.** They would tell me that a conviction does not erase the pain of murder, even though it might bring some measure of relief. I have met other survivors who envy the fact that I got to see Dad's alleged murderer brought to the courtroom. She didn't "get away with it." The whole town knows what she did. Some survivors don't even know who murdered their loved one. Some do know, but never see the murderer brought to any sort of justice. Some loved ones disappear, never to be seen again. **Someone will always be better or worse off than you.**

It's a compulsive and ghoulish comparison game, and it's unavoidable. But don't get in too deep. Every case is different. Every person is different, different as the fingerprints on a human hand. Tend to your own garden. **Your responsibility is to heal yourself.** The legal system will not do that for you. You must

society that justice will be served. But the sad fact remains, justice is not always served.

My advice to other survivors is that they seek professional counseling immediately and learn how to deal with the grief, anger, depression, and post-traumatic stress that accompanies not only the deaths, but especially the lack of justice that a cold case brings with it. Professional therapists specially trained in working with survivors of violent, criminal death can provide support and techniques that help survivors develop their innate resiliencies and learn to cope with potentially debilitating emotions so they can lead productive lives and experience moments of joy.

Kaila

Let someone make you smile, let someone make you laugh, allow yourself to be happy. You could be a blessing that someone else needs.

Resources

Books

Dare I Call It Murder?: A Memoir of Violent Loss, Larry M. Edwards, Wigeon Publishing, 2013. http://www.dareicallitmurder.com.

Parallel Justice for Victims of Crime, Susan Herman, 2010. National Center for Victims of Crime, Washington, DC. www.paralleljustice.org.

Shattered Assumptions: ***Towards a New Psychology of Trauma***, R. Janoff-Bulman, New York: The Free Press, 1992.

Scream at the Sky: Five Texas Murders and One Man's Crusade for Jus*tice, Carlton Stowers, St. Martin's True Crime Library, 2004.*

Victim Impact Statement Workbook, Mothers Against Drunk Drivers. http://www.madd.org/victim-services.

Online

Crime Stoppers USA; http://www.crimestoppersusa.com.

Citizens Against Homicide, free newsletter http://www.citizensagainsthomicide.org.

Exploring Life's Mysteries, ***Unsolved Murders*** http://www.exploringlifesmysteries.com/unsolved-murders.

National Center for Victims of Crime (NCVC) has a number of resources available. The Connect Directory provides a way for victims to locate service providers throughout the country and get helpful articles onthis subject. http://www.ncvc.org.

Parents of Murdered Children, Inc.® (POMC); http://www.pomc.com.

The Pasadena Star News, ***Cold Cases*** https://www.pasadenastarnews.com/2006/09/03/tracking-the-cold-cases/.

Serving Survivors of Homicide Victims During Cold-Case Investigations: *A Guide for Developing a Law Enforcement Protocol*, prepared by National Sheriffs' Association, Justice Solutions, and National Organization of Parents of Murdered Children, Inc. https://www.ojp.gov/ncjrs/virtual-library/abstracts/serving-survivors-homicide-victims-during-cold-case-investigations.

Victim Impact for Children example can be found on this website in Alaska http://www.correct.state.ak.us/pnp/pdf/1000.01C.pdf.

Movies

No One Killed Jessica, Raj Kumar Guptam, director, 2011.

* Some Web addresses may have changed since publication.

Page intentionally left blank. Use it for jotting notes or your thoughts, if you wish.

9

Long-Term Consequences

Bravo. PTSD is a topic that needs to be discussed more, because the conventional attitude has always been "get over it." But mental health professionals and scientists have recognized that PTSD can cause irreparable damage to the brain and change a person's behavior—not for the better.
—**Larry M. Edwards** (2012)

What now? What is in store for us now? How can we adapt to things we cannot change and become stronger with the changes that have taken place? These are important questions.

It ain't over when it's over!

This section is in response to the mistaken idea that once a criminal case has closed or had its day in court, you will "get over it." Survivors and clinical research tell us this is not so. Research on soldiers returning from war tell us this, too. Larry Edwards writes in his blog about a story on National Public Radio with the headline: *PTSD Not Just War Wound, Young People Suffer, Too.* (See Resources at the end of the chapter.)

A legal or partial closure occurs when a verdict and sentencing takes place, or the case is placed in a cold-case file waiting for new leads.

When the verdict of "Guilty" was read in court, we experienced an immediate sense of relief. That step was finally over. But it seems that within minutes, a feeling of emptiness came over each of us with the realization that we still wouldn't get our daughter back. I hadn't consciously had this thought before and of course my mind knew it was impossible, but the emptiness prevailed. We hadn't discussed as a family what our next step would be, but we all felt the need to go to the cemetery where we could tell our daughter about the outcome. We stopped and bought some flowers, then proceeded to that saddest of places. We felt each other's support and each in our own way dealt with our feelings. (Evelyn)

At this same time, the interaction between the criminal justice system and crime victims is significantly diminished. The quiet and absence of activity can be a difficult adjustment. There is no official description of what happens next. During this period, co-victims take their first deep breaths, yet it may have the biggest surprises and disappointments.

The chaos has subsided and now you begin to see the landscape of what is left. There may be employment changes, health issues, life transitions. Children's reactions get noticed more, and you may have more triggered reactions while still disbelieving what has made a wide swath in your life.

Will I ever wake up?
When will this nightmare end?
Some are surprised that they survived, that they did live through it.

Changes Co-victims May Experience:

- Continued involvement in the criminal justice system

- Missed days at work or school

- Time, financial and life-course changes

- Relationship changes

- Health problems

- Angry outbursts

- Diminished quality of life

- Family dysfunction

- Increased fear of crime and safety issues

- Social and leisure time changes

- Career changes

- Loss of faith

- PTSD, depression and substance abuse

- Job loss

- Social isolation

When it was all over, we came away with a combination of feelings. We were strengthened by having endured more than we ever thought possible after being strained beyond belief by layers of physical and mental tension, and put though a situation that had the potential to destroy us, our relationships, and even affect our careers. We were also empowered by having been part of a team working in a united effort for justice on behalf of all the victims in this case. We were grateful for the hard work of everyone in law enforcement. **For better or worse, it was an experience that left us battle-hardened.** (Valeria)

In this chapter, Survivor Writers describe what longer term changes occurred for them in three areas: their involvement in the criminal justice system, how they and their families were changed, and what missions or tips they want to pass on to those who will take this difficult journey.

Criminal Justice System Involvement

Victims' Rights and Services Do Not End at Sentencing. Changes have been made so that the former victims' rights and services that included only front-end services now include back-end rights and services, such as the right to be notified of the prisoner whereabouts.

> . . . *their (co-victims) need for support and assistance may even increase when an offender is sentenced. . . . Victims' rights to information, notification, restitution, and participation are an integral component of community corrections. The "voice of the victim" can and should have a powerful influence on how offenders are supervised. . . .* (APPA, 2012)

VINE Link (Victim Information and Notification Everyday) (see Resources) is an online national network that allows you, 24 hours a day, to obtain timely and reliable information on prisoners. Most states have this service. You can register to be notified by phone, email, or text message when an offender's custody status changes. Rose was surprised, though, that **they don't notify you if the prisoners are transferred to a new prison.**

Contact VINE for clarification and with questions you may have. Some states have additional websites that will locate an inmate. Contact the Department of Corrections in your state. You can usually get this information and sign up for VINE if you have the offenders name or ID number, or Corrections number. Ask your Key Contacts how to get the information you need. Some states have forms available that you use to request the type of information you want. Resources at the end of the chapter has links to two forms (CR-110 and CDCR 1017) used in California that help crime victims ask for information.

Survivors and the public mistakenly think that once a case has had its day in court then life will be okay. Families can start getting their lives back on track. It is true that, once a case has reached a conclusion and there is nothing more to do, families have more time to call their own again. They do work to get their lives going in a different direction and realize much has changed.

However, co-victims may be drawn back into the system due to appeals, parole hearings, restitution, or other procedures that inmates have a right to. Some survivors describe it as "life in prison *without* the possibility of parole."

In Rose's case, she gets an infrequent and unpredictable trickling of small restitution checks from money deducted from the killer's prison account. It is a double-edged sword. Each time she gets it, it is a stab in the heart for her. *This is the value of their lives?* She rationalizes the checks as funds to pay for some of the gasoline costs for her crime-victim advocacy work.

When a case results in the death penalty or life without the possibility of parole, the convicted have a right to appeal that decision. This often takes years and many court appearances that families participate in as well.

There are strong advocates for and against the death penalty. It may sound straight forward at first with the old idea that death warrants a punishment of death. Not so simple, says a group of murder victim family members that advocate against the death penalty.

**Tips for Preparation for
Parole Hearings:**

1. Make sure your name and address is on file with the prison so you will be notified of any hearings or changes.
2. When you receive a letter informing you of an upcoming parole hearing, schedule an appointment with the appropriate person in the District Attorney's office.
3. Engage the support of your family and/or friends to help you through the procedure.
4. At the meeting with the Deputy District Attorney who will be presenting at the hearing, talk about your loved one so the DDA feels in touch with her/him as well as with your family.
5. Obtain the correct names and addresses for letters to be sent objecting to parole.
6. Ask for copies of sample letters.
7. Some people request that copies of letters be sent to them as well as to the officials. This is your choice. Also, the DA's office usually wants a copy. Get the information you need for this. Reading the letters might help the DDA in presenting the argument for parole denial.
8. Know the date by which letters must be submitted.
9. Allow plenty of time prior to the hearing. If it's a long drive, go the day before and stay overnight.
10. Take your personally written statement, about how this murder affected your life, typed and printed in large enough font that you will be able to read it even when you are nervous and emotional.

(Evelyn)

There is a moral issue at play here and a high cost to families and taxpayers for years of having a lengthy court process involvement that takes an additional toll on families. Rose explains how she changed her perspective to favor life in prison without the possibility of parole rather than death. The final decision is up to the District Attorney, and in California, the family's wishes are taken into consideration at the time of sentencing.

In his book *The Ride* (2009), author Brian Macquarrie chronicles how a father actively sought the death penalty, but later he changed his mind. His young son had been killed by a sexual predator, a pedophile. One of the convincing experiences came from a father of an Oklahoma bombing victim.

When the sentence is life **with the possibility** of parole, the inmate has a right to a legal hearing to determine if time should be reduced. The first hearing in California is one year before the killer's first eligible release date. Check with your Key Contacts for your state's information.

After the trials, our contact with the criminal justice system changed. The personal relationships that developed during the long ordeal have continued. Since it was a First-Degree Murder conviction, the appeal process seemed to start rather quickly. Support for the conviction was handled by the State Attorney General's office. We had no contact with them that I recall but were permitted to attend the Appeals Court proceedings. This was another stressful time as the defense attorney pointed out all the "defects" in the case, and we just had to hope that the objections were groundless. (Evelyn)

The opportunity and burden for the family's involvement continues as they are allowed to appear at parole hearings. In some communities, the original victim impact statements have been videotaped and are shown again at these review hearings. The parole hearing usually takes place where the prisoner is incarcerated. Families may have to travel to many different places. Families of the victims, along with others, state why the convicted should or should not have prison time reduced. Many factors are taken into consideration, including the prisoner's behavior and accomplishments while incarcerated.

> *Parole hearings are tremendously stressful. Entering the prison is like stepping into a movie set, yet it's like nothing you have ever imagined. We have had 3 parole hearings, the first 14 years after my daughter's murder.*
> *The most important advice I can give is to have plenty of support at the hearing. It is imperative to meet with the Deputy District Attorney who will present the case to the Parole Board. Make an appointment as soon as you are notified of the upcoming hearing and take your family with you to discuss the procedure.*
> *Discuss what to expect, ask details about your roles, and accept any help that is offered to guide you. Talk with the DDA about your loved one so he/she will be able to feel the immense void that was left by this murderer. The points that will be made during the hearing by the District Attorney will be points of law, but the feeling for the victim should be felt as well. (Evelyn)*

On the next page, Evelyn provides you with a sample letter asking for support to deny parole.

Marsy's Law (California) provides specific rights to victims and next of kin regarding parole hearings, including: to be informed of all parole procedures, to participate in the parole process, to provide information to the parole authority to be considered before the parole of the offender, and to be notified, upon request, of the parole or other release of the offender.

The Parole Board oversees this process and specific prosecutors are assigned to represent the District Attorney at hearings. Your Key Contacts are an important source to find out who will be managing your case.

Death Row Experience: Twenty-seven years and eleven months after a serial killer was sentenced to die and placed on death row, one of the victims' families got the news that he had died of natural causes at age 54. This was the news in the summer of 2013. Poor health did what the justice system failed to do in 28 years.

Family members of one of the victims, a grandmother, gathered to celebrate this day but realized that closure would never happen. A grandson said that wouldn't happen until he gets a chance to hug Grandma in Heaven.

A granddaughter said, "This news was a sudden and unexpected reminder of how the pain and grief from suffering the loss of my grandma 28 years ago to this horrific killer is

continued on page 199

Sample Letter to Parole Board

[Date] _____

Dear Family and Friends,

We are preparing for another parole hearing and are asking your help to keep the monster in prison, where he belongs. This will be the third parole hearing since _____. Our family has attended both previous hearings and will be there to fight his release as many times as necessary.

The opposition letters from the public have been truly pivotal to the decision of the Parole Board to deny parole. The laws have recently changed making it more plausible that he could be released. Your letters are more important now than ever.

The Board reads every letter and considers the content. It is no longer a requirement that the prisoner admits guilt or shows remorse. The Parole Board considers the gravity of the crime and psychological evaluations.

Personally written letters are the most effective. It is suggested in the "parole suitability handbook" that letters describe your personal feelings or emotions about how the crime affected you, your family, or your community. **The primary consideration for release is whether or not the prisoner is a danger to the public. If you would be fearful having him free, express those fears!**

Another change in the law allows for a longer interval before the next hearing. The maximum length of time between hearings was previously 5 years, but it is now 15 years. The pain and agony of these hearings is a TRUE LIFE SENTENCE to our family. It seems so unfair that we must continue to be punished every few years. A longer interval between hearings would be helpful.

Be sure to include his name and Inmate Identification Number (required):

Name: _____   *Inmate #:* _____

Send your letters, with the salutation "Dear Commissioners of the Board of Parole Hearings," to:

Address of inmate: _____

_____

Please take a few moments today to send your letter. We would be most appreciative if you will ask your friends and neighbors to write one as well. Letters must be received by December 31, _____.

Remember, EVERY LETTER COUNTS!

Thank you for any assistance you can provide!

[signature]

continued from page 197

never far from me. In fact, grief only becomes a sleeping monster tucked away inside and often awakened by a multitude of triggers."

She continues with: "I made a promise to myself many years ago that I would no longer allow her death become bigger than her life. She lived sixty years, her death lasted only a few minutes."

The iCAN Foundation provides victims' services, free of charge, that include advocacy. The foundation has a booklet about the parole system for victims. Although the group is based in California, it can help in your location.

> *Nineteen years later, I have survived the experience of working with the criminal justice system to see my offender caught, tried, and sentenced. However, now I am faced with yet another challenge, one which at the moment seems the most difficult to face: the reality of my offender's release. . . . (iCAN, 2013)*

I can speak to this reality, as in my own family the offender was released after serving less than eleven years of a life sentence. He was released to his home, which was in a small town where my family lived. Running into him was a real and steady possibility. There are many examples of life going on for the killer, when your loved one's life has been stopped forever.

Some families find that there are many ways that the convicted get released. One of our writers, Halia, was faced with a Post-Conviction Relief appeal right after sentencing. Post-conviction relief is a court proceeding where a criminal may challenge a conviction. (Black's, 2013) This is a general term related to appeals of criminal convictions. This may include release, new trial, modification of sentence, and such other relief as may be "proper and just." Post-conviction relief is governed by federal and state laws, which vary by state. (USLEGAL.com, 2013)

Unsolved Cases

Many cases alternate for several years between being open, then closed. Open in that the crime could still be prosecuted, or cold, as there are no new leads. This experience keeps the family in continued contact with the criminal justice system and keeps them active in pursuing new leads for investigators. A role as participants in the investigation can become more realized than the earlier investigation allows for.

"We got the life sentence," say many co-victims, and it's quite apparent to families who have an unsolved case.

There is no end in sight here. The "life sentence" impacts the entire family in varying ways and gets transferred to younger generations as well. Their loved one is still gone, whether anyone paid the price or not. Adjustments must include this reality.

In unsolved cases, the question plagues families as they worry if anyone will ever be arrested and face a court of justice. Like the character Pigpen in the Charlie Brown comic strip, life moves along with dark clouds hovering over your head. Unfortunately, you can get an occasional brick thrown at you that gets you off track, and you have to work to get back to your routine again. The number and size of the bricks will determine the time it takes to reestablish your journey.

Families in waiting: The forlornness of those who wait, but never give up, for someone to be charged and prosecuted is a burden co-victims bear more heavily than anyone else involved in the case. Every minute, day, month, and year that passes adds incrementally to this heavy load. Lives are impacted; each family member endures this. A wrong has not been "righted." Some cases have an identified suspect but lack enough evidence for a successful prosecution.

Many co-victims do not understand prosecutors' explanations to not prosecute when their appears to be a defendant. Families may proclaim that is just an irrational, wrong decision. This tension can result in the prosecution taking the brunt of the family's blame, which is directed away from the actual killer.

The cost to families in waiting takes its toll. The longer the time frame the more difficult it can be. It is hard to get on with one's life, a life that is now changed forever. As you read the writers stories you can add to the ideas you may have yourself of what to do in the interim. This is indeed a very personal path.

Survivor Questions: What follow-up contact do you have with the criminal justice system regarding your case? What has been your experience with parole hearings? Have you signed up to keep tabs on the prisoner(s) What is this like?

Write your answers in your notebook.

Rose
As for the Appeal process, that is key in to why we asked for two life sentences without the possibility of parole so we wouldn't have to continue to go to court every time he filed an appeal. Not only did he have the means financially to file appeal after appeal had he been sentenced to death, he would have been able to manipulate the system and us in the process by having to return to court for another hearing every 5 years. With life without the possibility of parole, he is given one and only one appeal.

Almost a year and a half later, I received a call from the prosecutor that the appeal the killer had filed was denied.

I have since read the appeal, and it was almost as ridiculous as his case was in court. **I took a deep breath because I knew I would never have to see or deal with him again. He would spend the rest of his life in a cage.**

For the second defendant, we had to go to a probation hearing when he violated his probation and was resentenced. To me it felt like another day connected to the convict, whom I wanted nothing to do with.

I did sign up with the VINE program, not because I thought he would ever get out of jail, but so I would be notified if he was ever moved from one prison to another. I recently found out that **the prison system doesn't notify you if the prisoners are transferred to a new** *prison* because that is not uncommon. The system only notifies you if there is a parole hearing, if he escaped, or if he died. I did check out his new prison and will continue to periodically check on the website to see if he is transferred in the future.

I still feel the need to keep tabs on what he is doing; I am trying to learn to let go of that because the only one who really is affected by this is me. When I heard he was obese, had high blood pressure, a borderline diabetic, I felt a sense of glee that he is not faring well in a cage. I know intellectually that this is not healthy for me, but it doesn't stop me from doing it. I hope one day it simply won't matter, but I am not there yet.

I keep track on the prison website and through confidential informants.

Kaila

I have not kept tabs on the prisoner; I became afraid of letting the parole hearing people know my address and phone numbers after I started having children. I didn't want to be tracked. I don't ever want to see him again, unless he is dead. This has impacted my life because I hope that he is never released, yet I can't bring myself to face him again. I have looked him up online just to make sure that he is still a prisoner; that's how I keep track of him.

I'm still afraid.

Halia

We have not attended any parole hearings; however, we have maintained contact with the criminal justice system and have learned that there were three different ways that the convict could apply to get out of prison. The only way to determine if an application for early release had been started was to call every month or wait for an early-release hearing notification to arrive days before the hearing.

Long-Term Life Changes

Grieving the loss of a loved one is a natural and predictable part of life. Grieving the violent death of a loved one requires far greater emotional, intellectual and social resources.
—Charles Figley, PhD

Long-term changes can include both symptoms and resiliencies discussed in Chapter 2 and includes survivor missions. Some of the Survivor Writers weigh in here with more helpful tips for you to consider.

Do not twist yourself into a pretzel *trying to extract something positive out of something that is truly bad. Sometimes things are just plain awful.* (Marina)

Post-traumatic stress disorder —symptoms may include:

- You experienced a life-threatening event.

- Your response was intense fear, horror or helplessness.

- You relive experiences of the event with distressing images, memories, upsetting dreams, or flashbacks.

- You feel frozen, emotionally numb at times.

- You are on guard or alert for signs of danger.

- These symptoms last longer than a month.

- The symptoms interfere with your ability to go about your normal daily tasks.

Adapted from the
Mayo Clinic website

Lives have been on hold and consumed with the "whodunit" part of the story. Survivors hold off on their own needs in order to participate, for one of the very last times that they can, on behalf of their loved one to see justice done. It is only when this busy-ness has quieted that survivors take time to see what their playing field looks like.

When I think of long-term changes, I am thinking of the stories that survivors have told me about the lasting impact of this horrific event of murder in their world. The range covers the worst to the best outcomes of the human experience.

Some of you have told me that you know your grandparent died early due to a broken heart and the strain of murder. Many survivors have gotten counseling years after this loss, finally realizing that the failures and illnesses in their lives related to that horrific loss. Like in the movie Titantic, retelling the story that has been buried triggers intense emotions again.

Some have talked about their inability to work or have made new career choices. These changes may include volunteer work that supports crime victims after homicide. Changes can be both positive or negative, and are usually a combination of the two.

Traumatic Grief

Traumatic grief will show itself in a variety of ways unique for each person. It is not about individual weakness; it is about experiencing an event that is beyond everyday experiences. **It is a normal reaction to an abnormal event**, a devastating experience for all who lose someone to murder. My research shows that depression, post-traumatic stress disorder (PTSD) and/or substance abuse were found most frequently as long-term difficulties experienced by survivors. (Saindon, 2012)

Survivors may reach out for help from counselors for the first time many months or years after the death of their loved one. This may cause problems in being able to qualify for funding (Crime Victims' Compensation) that each state provides to help pay for counseling services.

For example, California has required that a victim apply for coverage within three years after the crime was committed. Your state will have its own rules and your victim advocate can answer that question for your circumstances. When many cases take four years or more, a three-year time limit is well past. Co-victims' choices become more limited or unavailable—like our soldiers who do not report their needs until services are less available to them. This may contribute to the explanation as to why more soldiers have died from suicide than in war in Afghanistan. Like all those exposed to violence, we need to work together for better solutions. Check with your Key Contacts for the resources available in your state.

We have learned another lesson from the work with soldiers. Different than soldiers who are trained to kill or be killed and suffer greatly from being a part and witnessing such losses, our victims were living their everyday lives. They were not expecting, nor trained to anticipate, the killing or being killed.

Studies show that early treatment, in the first three months, can prevent a lifelong diagnosis of post-traumatic stress disorder.

Many co-victims do not get the care they need early enough. Rose tells us this when her doctor says she will have this all her life. Marina mentions panic attacks that she has periodically.

Larry Edwards addresses this subject in his book *Dare I Call It Murder?: A Memoir of Violent Loss* (2013). He writes of self-medication with alcohol and about his inability to tell his story without tears. He did not seek help through professional counseling services for several decades, but when he did, he says it helped him reduce stress and focus on his loved ones' lives rather than their deaths.

He also discovered that his story proved beneficial to others. Many readers sent him emails and cards thanking him for

Depression—symptoms may include:

- Depressed mood, feeling sad, empty or tearful most of the time.

- Feeling little or no pleasure.

- Significant weight loss or gain, little appetite.

- Sleep too much or too little.

- Tired with little energy.

- Feelings of worthlessness or guilt.

- Trouble thinking or making decisions.

Adapted from DSM IV

Substance-abuse symptoms

A maladaptive pattern of substance use leading to impairment or distress, as manifested by one (or more) of the following, occurring within a 12-month period:

- Recurrent substance use results in a failure to fulfill major role obligations at work, school, or home.

- Recurrent substance use in situations in which it is hazardous (e.g., driving an automobile).

- Recurrent substance-related legal problems (e.g., arrests).

- Continued substance use despite having recurrent relationship problems caused by the use of the substances (e.g., arguments with spouse).

Adapted from DSM IV

writing the book. They said they realized that they were not alone and for the first time could speak openly about their loss and the trauma they endured.

This is the area I think is so missed in adequately responding to co-victims of homicide, whose focus is on the criminal case, where they have little say. There is no gatekeeper who emphasizes the seriousness of these consequences early enough to refer folks to care. It is years later that survivors realize that their health, well being, or roadblocks in life started when their loved one was murdered.

The management of overwhelming symptoms after a violent death is helped by utilizing existing resiliencies and remembering lives of loved ones.
—**Edward Rynearson, MD**

Health Risks of Traumatic Grief and PTSD

More comprehensive information is also widely available online. Contact a licensed mental health professional to confirm a diagnosis and get recommendations for services. They are all qualified to diagnose mental disorders. While there are an increased number of professionals trained in providing treatment in the aftermath of homicide, this list is still small or unavailable in many communities. It isn't always necessary for someone to be experienced in violent death bereavement to be a good fit for you, but it is a good place to start and ask for. The potential for developing a working relationship can usually be achieved after a few visits.

Survivor couple JJ and Mary continued seeing a therapist they had been working with and felt comfortable with before their son was murdered. If you do not feel well-matched, look for other referrals to better meet your needs. This is a serious and critical time—be selective.

Restorative Retelling

The model I have worked with and recommend is *Restorative Retelling* (Rynearson, 2001). This approach has fit well with other existing therapies I have been trained in. My own research with Restorative Retelling, working mostly with homicide survivors, has shown a significant decrease in symptoms. It is adaptable for many cultures, groups, individuals, and families. The management of overwhelming symptoms after a violent death is helped by utilizing existing resiliencies and remembering lives of loved ones.

My earlier book, *The Journey: Ten Steps to Learning to Live with Violent Death* (2008), is based on this restorative retelling model. While using this model is not a substitute for therapy, the book is a self-help or facilitator's guide based on this evidence-based model. It includes calming exercises, words of inspiration, and Survivor Writers going through each step. You will find information about this book and restorative retelling in the resource section of this chapter.

Medications

Medications work well for depression and may help you function better as you deal with the times that are most difficult. Research is solid in medications being able to help with depression, but is still unclear as to which medications are helpful with post-traumatic stress disorder. Don't hesitate to ask for what you can do in support of recommendations for medications. Ask your therapists to tell you what signs indicate that you no longer need medication.

Faith

Faith issues can have long lasting results. The range of survivors' experiences is vast. It goes from "I got much closer to my faith community," and "I couldn't have done this without my church family," to "Where was God? There can't be a God. God would not have let this happen." Co-victims may stay connected to their faith community and be available when others face tragic events as well.

The range of survivors' experiences . . . goes from "I got much closer to my faith community," . . . to "Where was God? There can't be a God." (Anonymous)

Rose tells us: "My father lost all faith in God" in her Victim Impact Statement. Changes in one's faith community can be both a blessing or a curse in the way survivors move their lives forward.

Forgiveness

Pressure may be put on you to forgive the person who killed your loved one. The rationale is that you will never be okay until you do. While this may be well intentioned, I know of no evidence to support this idea. I know of very few survivors who are willing to do this. One very religious survivor said it this way: "I am not going to do the work on forgiving him; I am going to leave that up to God." Kim Goldman expresses similar sentiments in her book, *Can't Forgive* (2014). (See Resources at the end of this chapter.)

Restorative Justice

There are also many Restorative Justice programs that work with perpetrators and victims to enable a conversation between the two. Very strict and lengthy preparations go into this so as to not cause any unnecessary harm to victims and be assured of the inmates' intentions. I have no experience of anyone I knew or worked with that did this, but it may be something you want to check out. I understand the goal is not forgiveness, but a conversation that may answer some questions you have. Resources show many links for Restorative Justice to ministries or programs that also work with adolescents.

Survivor Questions: *What life changes have there been for you, for family members? Have you or members in your family been treated for distress? Do these reactions still occur?*

Write your answers in your notebook.

Rose

My father had four strokes, one of them major, from the time of the murders till the arrest was made. Without a doubt this contributed to his death, which came much sooner than anyone would have expected. No one says it out loud to me, but I feel like some of them blame me in some way.

My husband has often been the forgotten one in all of this. He was expected to be the strong one, the one to keep everything together; frankly, to keep me alive. He had no actual say in any of the decisions because from the very beginning he was deemed the "stepfather" although he was Victoria's father in her eyes, and those are the only eyes that should have mattered. Actually, people thought he should "get it together, get over it, move on, etc." because it wasn't like she was his blood. She didn't have to be; she was his daughter 100%, and he was her father 100%. I cannot tell you how hurtful and wrong that was to do to him. He struggles more today than he did in the beginning because he was so busy then trying to hold everything together. He said just the other day, with tears streaming down his face, that his soul/spirit broke and he hasn't found a way to put it together.

We lost everything when Victoria and Louis died: first and foremost them, the people we once were, our home, our jobs, our life savings, everything, except each other. We lost the simple things one takes for granted. We don't laugh as easily as we once did, don't socialize or go out, we don't see the world as we once did, I wouldn't call us happy by any means. We pretty much just struggle getting through one day to the next. Some days are easier than others, and some even have meaning if I am doing something to help someone else, but no days are like they used to be. Our lives consist of "before and after," and those two worlds are completely different.

As for PTSD, yes, I was diagnosed with that as well as complicated grief, depression, and anxiety disorder. I will probably always be on some medications. Fortunately, I had been in recovery for alcoholism for over five years when this happened, and it was something my daughter was so proud of that she had my sobriety date tattooed on her arm. Having a drink wasn't even an option for me; it would dishonor her in such a way that I would never be able to live with myself. I have been blessed not to have had any craving, which has helped me honor that part of our lives.

Marina

My father's younger brother died of a broken heart; his body simply lingered on for fourteen more years. He idolized my father. I still remember how happy he was when Dad threw him a retirement party approximately one year before the murder. He was looking

206

forward to spending more time with his beloved wife. The murder devastated him. Every time I saw him between the murder and the trial, he had a stunned, agonized look. Tears always rimmed his eyes. Seeing Dad's killer go free after the mistrial pretty much finished him off. He carried his fathomless grief and rage to his grave.

I did forge a relationship with Dad's older sister. That continues to this day. I also stay in touch with one of Dad's old girlfriends. She spent years with him, and shared many stories with me. After the murder, we spent a lot of time reminiscing. She told me things I never knew about Dad. What a precious gift.

I continued on with my boyfriend for some years. I would not have gotten through the entire ordeal without him, but the murder undoubtedly extended a relationship that carried with it some crucial incompatibilities. We ultimately broke up, but parted as friends.

My mother and I had been estranged ever since she subjected me to a brutal verbal attack some nine years before the murder. After the murder, she never contacted me to ask if I was OK. After four years, she called. Let's just say that I appreciate that she was a great mother at times, especially given the fact that she struggled with a retarded child virtually on her own, as well as a messy divorce, and money problems. I carry the good parts of her with me, but the bad outweighs the good, and I keep my distance in order to preserve my emotional health.

My sister and I were estranged at the time of the murder. Some six months before, she accused me of hating my father. Flabbergasted, I nearly crashed my car that night while driving home in a violent rainstorm. Tormented, I called Dad the next day. He assured me that he had never felt any such thing. He told me that he loved me, and that he was proud of the woman I had become. We ended the call by expressing our love for one another.

My sister did us both a huge favor. I visited Dad even more often in the six months that preceded his death. I let my guard down, even though his drinking, depression, and distracted moods made it difficult. We had some special moments, and I treasure that time.

The biggest change is that now I have a family of friends, and I am far more social and outgoing than I was before. My life can be as full of activity or peaceful solitude as I choose.

Best of all, I have met the man I shall marry—and I will be marrying for the first time in my life. We are wondrously compatible, something I have never before experienced. Our life together is a joy.

You see, murder can tear you down, destroy all of your notions of life, and leave you bereft of all hope and contentment. Directed healing is hard work, but it can lead to a healthier, less fearful existence.

My depression was situational and very normal. Why wouldn't I experience depression over such a horrific event? I assure you that anybody ignorant enough to tell me to "get over it," "move on," "don't feel anger toward your dad's murderer," or even, "don't be sad," got an earful. I guess **murder enhanced my "clear the decks" modus operandi.**

I mean, really, what stupid things to say!

I hated experiencing traumatic grief symptoms at the time, but I needed to feel them in order to process grief. I did experience PTSD about four years after the murder, when a friend's son got into serious legal trouble.

She planned to do nothing to help him. He was an adult, and she felt it was time for him to suffer the consequences of his actions. Three weeks later she did a complete flip-flop, and I came to the realization that as a crime survivor, I

and worked very hard to use the calming techniques I read about on the website.

I still have one occasionally, but eventually I find a way to short-circuit it.

Anxiety stays with me, but that is something I have lived with all of my life. I find the best way to alleviate it is to perform a task I have put off. Doing something pleasurable

---

The sensation of imminent doom was overwhelming. (Marina)

---

could endure the friendship no longer. Many of the primal fears I felt after the murder came cascading back. I felt panicked, so I called my most trusted friends. I was definitely losing my grip. I am a pretty calm, reasoned individual, so this was profoundly alarming to me.

All three of my friends said I sounded just as I had immediately after the murder: out of breath, and frightened. My thoughts bounced about like pinballs —logic went right out the window. I wasn't making sense.

The sensation of imminent doom was overwhelming. I was frustrated because I had just come back from a trek in the Himalaya, and I felt truly powerful and full of joy for the first time in four years. I was furious that this friend had once again brought her son's troubles into my life. That was a very healthy reaction, and it led me to curtail the friendship, even as I appreciated all the support she had given me through the years. I suffered panic attacks as well. Not very many, as I am largely placid, but they definitely happened. Luckily, a friend recognized what I was going through, as he too had experienced them. I looked up "panic attack" on WebMD

and/or creative helps. Exercise is helpful as well. Sometimes getting a hug, or scratching my parrot's head calms me.

The most pervasive manifestation I call the "ghosts"; i.e., emotions, thought processes, and physical reactions not unlike those I experienced after the homicide. I have endured several deeply traumatic life events since the murder. Maybe they weren't as bad as the murder, but they were still very bad. One was a head-on collision, one was a serious financial betrayal by family members, and one was my brother's violent attack. Any dealings with my mother today can bring on the ghosts, too. At any rate, I experience anxiety, self-loathing, fear, and depression. Insomnia, forgetfulness, and various physical symptoms may also be present. Indigestion and odd-feeling heart actions come to mind.

I must tell you that **I use the word "ghosts" because these triggers usually arise at unexpected moments.** They can also plague me in the middle of the night, or follow me around in the daytime. Sometimes they don't have to even reflect any current reality. I can usually use techniques I learned to deal with the lesser phantoms. With guidance, those techniques work pretty well on the major ones as well.

When the ghosts get really bad, I seek support from my friends, or obtain therapeutic help. It's crucial not to let the ghosts go unaddressed. They can really affect one's health and well-being on a long-term basis.

Survivors will be tempted to downplay or ignore negative events. After all, most of them aren't ever going to be as bad as the murder, right? Wrong, wrong, wrong.

Pay attention to your emotions, your body, and your thought processes. Sometimes you can deal with ghosts by yourself; sometimes you will need to ask the help of a friend, or even a therapist. Just don't try to numb yourself to what you are experiencing. It can really affect your life.

Harrier

My parents' deaths ripped my family apart, at the time of the deaths and again 30 years later after a true-crime book hit the street with an inaccurate account of their deaths. The FBI named my brother as their prime suspect in the murder investigation, but he was never prosecuted. That divided my family into feuding factions.

My youngest sister, a key witness in the case, vowed to lie in court, effectively protecting our brother and undermining the prosecution. I and other family members had little contact with either of them afterward, and that continues to this day. It left a big gap in my life, and I found a "family of friends" to fill that gap. In addition, my mom's sister and I forged a stronger relationship.

I did not seek professional counseling at the time. But after 30 years of denying the effect the deaths had had on my relationships with others, especially my marriage, I entered the Survivors of Violent Loss Program.

Then the true-crime book came out, and I went into a tailspin. All of the bottled-up emotions boiled to the surface: anger, depression, guilt, anxiety. I could not work effectively, took a medical leave from my job, and ultimately had to quit. I contemplated suicide. I went into individual counseling through SVLP and was diagnosed with PTSD. That counseling saved my life and saved my marriage.

Kaila

My mother blamed me for the murder of my sister; she then became real bitter and cold. Due to the rejection of my mother's attention, my other sister was severely depressed. I believe that she committed suicide. She left four kids behind.

No one in my family got help; there is too much pride in our family. I received help when I saw what was happening to my family; I couldn't take it anymore; I knew I needed help and that's when I met the Survivors of Violent Loss Program. My sister that committed suicide didn't want help.

Yvonne

By coincidence I located a copy of a poem I'd written many years ago.

A Mother Gone

Life was so unfair
Why? There are no answers
Though I try desperately
You are not nameless, forgotten
A best friend, my hero,

Time goes by, the ache is still there
I look for your smile, a laugh,
   anything to erase a last memory
I fight for you though the past
   cannot be changed
Anger at a man who doesn't care

Halia

Several family members have suffered from and have been treated for substance abuse, anxiety, and PTSD.

I will not dare go hiking alone or to a stranded beach area by myself. Parking lots at night are always a very scary place to be.

Survivor Questions: Are there places or things that you do not do? What are the rules regarding safety, assessment of people that have changed for you, your family? How are you different that you attribute to the murder of your loved one(s)?

Write your answers in your notebook.

Rose

I don't put much emphasis on holidays anymore. I feel out of place even around family. Everyone wants to celebrate the holiday, and all I am thinking is Victoria and Louis aren't here, so what is there to celebrate? I also hate that feeling of thinking everyone wished I would get over it, or at least pretend for the time being so they would be more comfortable. I do honor Victoria and Louis on their birthdays, Mother's Day, but I have had to change how I even do that over the years because we used to have balloon releases at the cemetery, but that is no longer a place I find any peace due to the vandalism that has occurred over the years there.

I cannot go into a mall in my town because Victoria loved the mall and we spent many endless hours at every one of them. When Louis was born, we took him along and we considered that our exercise for the day; walking the mall. I am not a big fan of shopping anyway, but it is just another thing that was taken from me.

Ironically, I don't have a problem going into malls in other cities or states, but that is because they hold no memories for me; I do, however, stay out of Victoria's favorite stores.

Certain restaurants are off limits *as well; if we ate there often I can't go. One exception is the restaurant where we had the last meal that we shared as a family, three days before the murders. I for some reason can go there because I feel close to them there. It was a great day, and I want that memory to live on inside me forever.*

I cannot go on a certain section of the freeway because it overlooks where they were murdered. My husband and I avoid it at all costs and will go miles out of our way not to have to think of where they were murdered. You can actually see her apartment from the freeway and on the few occasions I have forgotten and been stuck passing it, my knuckles turn white, my teeth are clenched, and I feel like I will either faint or throw up. I am working on some of these things though, because I am trying to take my power of the situation back rather than feel powerless.

Marina

I asked my fiancé this question. He has known me for a comparatively brief time in comparison to other important folks in my life. I wanted to know if anything struck him about how I operate. He said, "If someone does anything that really hurts or upsets you, you don't want to be around them anymore. You ignore them. You cut them out of your life."

True. This goes beyond the day-to-day upsets or conflicts of any relationship.

The behavior doesn't even have to be directed at me personally. Basically, if a person hurts me badly or makes me feel unsafe due to unstable behavior, then that person is out. New acquaintances that do this are swiftly eliminated, before the relationship progresses any further. Period. Life is too short to be spent around bullies, manipulators, drama addicts, or crazy people. Additionally, I steer clear of folks who indulge in unending pity parties for no good reason, other than that they crave attention. People who complain or constantly feel sorry for themselves can bring me down pretty quickly, so I avoid them.

I don't really like to be in restaurants that are too noisy, or places that blare music so loudly that it inhibits relaxation. Don't really like crowds, but I wasn't crazy about them before. Crowds are annoying, and if something goes wrong, they can turn into a mob scene. I am very uncomfortable sitting with my back to windows or doors. I like to see who's coming and going in case a threat arises.

My friends are my family now. They have my best interests at heart, and they love and accept me for who I am. They don't try to change me, and they don't criticize me unless it's warranted. They are all gen-erous, affectionate folks without malice or cruelty in their hearts.

I would say I fear travel a little more than before, but that really started with the head-on collision in 2011. A friend who was driving broke her neck in two places. She had to be confined to her home for seven months to avoid paralysis.

She is also a murder survivor (she lost her sister to a hit-and-run driver who got off on a technicality). She was not at fault in the head-on collision. A young guy who was driving like a bat out of hell crossed over the double yellow line on a hairpin curve and crashed into us.

I escaped with a few bruises, thanks to my air bag. My friend and I both agree that the crash brought back the trauma of murder, both physiologically and psychologically. We don't drive as much as we used to, and we avoid driving on two-lane country roads, something we both used to enjoy. We acknowledge depression and a preoccupation with violent dying. Our feelings have settled down somewhat, thank goodness. But the fear is there, lurking. We do our best to manage it. Most people go through relatively frictionless lives and don't know they can die at any moment. Unfortunately, we do. At least we can compare notes.

I also have cut back on traveling alone at night. I used to drive at night all the time. I still drive up to L.A. occasionally to visit my best friend. The odd fundraiser or dinner gets me out alone, but otherwise I avoid it.

I'm not the Good Samaritan I once was. I will still jump to help people if I feel safe doing so, but I try not to put my life on the line in any way if there are other folks around to help. I have heard too many stories from survivors whose loved ones died trying to save someone else.

There is a strength and resilience to the depths of my soul that I developed out of sheer survival after the loss of my sister.

(Halia)

Harrier

I cannot tolerate loud noise, loud music, or loud people. Physically, it causes me pain and I want to lash out. I try to put on a polite or even smiling public face, but my feelings can create awkward familial and social situations when I must separate myself from others, or I refuse to go into a public place that has loud, obnoxious music playing.

I cannot be in stores for any length of time. All shopping excursions are short and quick. If there are long lines at the checkout, I either don't shop, or I may leave the cart in an aisle and simply walk out without buying anything.

I cannot tolerate rude or clueless drivers, and I must consciously curb my desire to act out "road rage."

Even though my parents died aboard a boat, I still enjoy being on the water; listening to the wind and water relaxes me. *However, I cannot go aboard my parents' boat.*

Kaila

I have become very picky when it comes to picking friends. *They have to prove worthy of being in my circle. I speak openly with my children about people and situations, yet allowing them to live a healthy life.*

Halia

When writing the Victim Impact Statements for the Sentencing Hearing and talking with family/friends, the one consistent theme I heard was that their worldview had been shattered by my sister's death, and that each in one way or another had come to see the world as an unsafe place.

There is a strength and resilience to the depths of my soul that I developed out of sheer survival after the loss of my sister. After the wounds cut so deep, and the tears begin to dry, like the master potter, a new shape, a new capacity, the ability to withstand not only my grief but that of others too is now possible.

Survivor Writers' Tips

Here Survivor Writers give you more ideas about how to manage for the long-term issues. You will also find a list of things you can do for sleep issues following the survivors' responses.

Survivor Question: What are your tips/lessons regarding the questions asked earlier in this chapter?

Suggestion for readers: If you become overwhelmed at a certain question or section, walk away, get some fresh air, put the book down for awhile, or go on to a different section. This book isn't intended to be finished in any certain amount of time. It is a guidebook, and you may feel one way about a question today, and a month from now answer it completely differently; that is part of the evolving grief process.

When you're ready, write your answers in your notebook.

Rose
Don't put so much emphasis on getting justice. *I am not saying don't fight for it, because you have to; you are their voice. I am saying don't think that if you do get to court, and you do get a conviction, that everything will be right with the world again. Your loved one will still be dead, and there is no real justice in that.*

Be gentle with yourself. *Don't let anyone tell you how you should be feeling or acting, that you should get over it by now, how you should walk through the darkness; you have your own journey, and you are the one who will have to find your way. Let go of people that are not supportive, at least for the time being. This will take every ounce of strength you can muster and even that won't be enough sometimes.*

This is a lifelong process; the hole in your heart does not go away; *the pain can be as intense at any given time as it was on day one. It may knock you down when you least expect it, but you will stand again. Find ways to honor your loved ones' lives, and when you are ready, focus on that and not on how they died. Their lives were so much bigger than that moment in time when someone murdered them.*

Take everything with a grain of salt. *What works for one may not work for you. There is no right or wrong way to grieve; it is as individual as the relationship that you had with your loved one. Take it easy on yourself; this isn't a race; there is no finish line; go at your own pace and do what works for you! Not what the outside world is telling you. Often times not even what those closest to you are telling you to do. Don't be discouraged if what worked for you yesterday doesn't work for you today. Your grief is ever evolving and often times your strategies to address your grief have to evolve also.*

If you can, ***try to get to a place where your focus isn't on just the murders,*** *the justice system, etc., but on honoring the life of your loved one and doing things that reflect that honoring; some of the noise and chaos of the rest of the stuff is less loud and intrusive all the time. It doesn't make it go away, but there* can be moments where you catch your breath and **remember your loved one with a smile, and not always with such pain in your heart.**

Marina

A negative event can result in a positive outcome, but it may take years to see it.

Do not twist yourself into a pretzel *trying to extract something positive out of something that is truly bad. Sometimes things are just plain awful. Be prepared to step out of the way and let the*

one else, for that matter—to exploit you for their own self-aggrandizement or personal gain.

Just as homicide shows you who you really are (*if you are honest and self-aware*), **it shows you the true nature of those around you.** *Murder brings out the best and the worst in people. When a family member says or does something that feels like a true betrayal, pay attention. Do not waste the rest of your life in the service of someone else's flawed perspective. Be courageous. Be prepared to break free and start all*

Protect yourself. You'll add years to your life and enjoy more of the life you have left. (Marina)

---

bad things be what they are. Avoid remaining static for too long, though. Prolonged inertia can breed anxiety and depression.

Remember that most things aren't fatal. *When they are, and it's your time or someone else's time, there is little you can do. Sometimes things can be reframed and viewed from a different angle; sometimes they can't. Try to work on knowing the difference.*

Your assumptions about family may be turned upside down. Maybe you will become closer to some family members and estranged from others. Try to be flexible and understanding, because all of us are capable of saying or doing deplorable things under the influence of homicide. But don't be so flexible that you allow family to rob you of your self-respect. Don't be a patsy. Don't submit to emotional cruelty or allow relatives—or any-

over again. There are many good people out there who only wish you well. Put yourself out in the world. Go and find them. You can create your own family, as I have.

Don't let anyone make you feel guilty because you don't want to do something they want you to do. **Don't let anyone tell you how you should think, feel, or act.** *Don't let anyone make you responsible for his or her happiness. You aren't.*

Your feelings are yours, and your journey is unique. Always try to keep a civil tongue, *but listen to your inner voice when it tells you someone or something is just plain bad for you. Deep down inside, you know the difference.*

Protect yourself. *You'll add years to your life and enjoy more of the life you have left. And there is so much more. I am living proof.*

Can't Sleep? Here Are Fifteen Tips You Can Try

By Connie Saindon, MA, MFT

Sleep problems are a common symptom for people recovering from traumatic events. Your usual methods for falling asleep may no longer work. Disturbing thoughts of reenactment, rescue, or reunion may interfere with your sleep cycle. Nightmares and sleep terrors occur in response to adjusting to shattered realties.

Practice "Good Sleep Hygiene." Here are some tips for you to try:

1. No reading or watching TV in bed. These are waking activities. If your insomnia is chronic, it is not a good thing to do, says Dr. Alex Clerk, head of the Stanford Sleep Disorder Clinic in Palo Alto.

2. Go to bed when you're sleepy-tired, not when it's time to go to bed by habit.

3. Wind down during the second half of the evening before bedtime; 90 minutes before bed, don't get involved in any kind of anxiety-provoking activities or thoughts.

4. Do some breathing exercises or try to relax major muscle groups, starting with the toes and ending with your forehead.

5. Your bed is for sleeping; if you can't sleep after 15-20 minutes, get up and do something relaxing.

6. Have your room cool rather than warm.

7. Don't count sheep; counting is stimulating.

8. Exercise in the afternoon or early evening, but no later than 3 hours before bedtime.

9. Don't over-eat or eat within 2-3 hours before bedtime.

10. Don't nap during the day.

11. If you awake in the middle of the night and can't get back to sleep within 30 minutes, get up and do something else.

12. Have no coffee, alcohol or cigarettes 2-3 hours before bedtime.

13. When you have disturbing dreams or nightmares, add an ending that you want.

14. Schedule a half-hour for writing or drawing your concerns and hopes in a journal every night to free up your sleep from processing your dilemmas.

15. Listen to calming music or a self-hypnosis tape for sleep.

If sleep problems persist, contact your physician or mental health professional.

I'll Cry Again . . .

I cry again, this time for the Boston Marathon;

Time before it was the removal of memorabilia from the grave site of a murdered mother and infant;

Before that, I cried again and again and again for Sandy Hook;

I cry again for the first conversations between Dad and Yvonne about her mother who was murdered when she was just ten.

I'll cry again, and again and again . . .

I cry when I read about the lives of homicide detectives, and how their lives are impacted. The horrors they attempt to objectify to pursue the who-dun-its. The disappointments and blame they take on when justice isn't served.

I'll cry again when being safe is an illusion and being free is thwarted . . .

Can't run a marathon, can't go to first grade, can't leave objects of love at a gravesite, can't go to class, can't drive home from work, can't go to work, can't say no to going to the Prom, can't say no when asked for a cigarette, can't ride a bike in one's neighborhood . . . can't play at the park, can't help a friend or sister out with her abusive boyfriend . . . can't open your door at home . . .

I'll cry again, again and again . . .

I will continue to cry . . . and not go to Murder Mystery Cafés, watch made up murder stories, nor support guns. It is now my nature to live life seriously.

As I know I will cry again, and again and again.

The tears won't stop. There are too many stories in addition to the new ones that pile on.

Nor will it end for me not to buffer my tears with roses, irises, gardens, quiet, photography, cooking adventures, walks along the ocean, cups of tea, turning off the TV and more . . .

I know I will cry again . . . it is the nature of murder . . . and I will fight back with reciprocal intensity at what is beautiful in this world.

I know that I grow and increase my convictions with the strengths I see in each survivor I know.

I know we will cry . . .

—Connie Saindon, 4-15-13

Resources

Criminal

California Inmate Locater Website: Check Key Contacts in your state for your resource. They will need the inmate number to help you. http://inmatelocator.cdcr.ca.gov.

Crime Victims Action Alliance: The CVAA was created to give victims a stronger legislative voice. http://www.cvactionalliance.com.

The Journal of the American Probation and Parole Association: Free Publications & Reports. http://www.appa-net.org.

Murder Victim Families for Human Rights: organization of murder victim families formed to oppose the death penalty. http://www.mvfhr.org.

Pro Death Penalty Advocates; http://www.prodeathpenalty.com.

The National Victims Constitution Amendment Project http://www.nvcap.org.

The United States Bill of Rights found at: http://www.ushistory.org/documents/amendments.htm.

A Victim's Guide to the California Parole Hearing Process: iCAN/Crime Victim Assistance Network Foundation, Sacramento, CA. The iCAN Foundation provides services, free of charge, to victims of crime throughout the state of California and across the country; the services include counseling, advocacy, accompaniment to court and parole hearings, resources and referrals, and general information. http://www.ican-foundation.org.

VINE (Victim Information and Notification Everyday), an online national network that allows you to obtain timely and reliable information on prisoners. https://www.vinelink.com/vinelink/initMap.do.

Victim Support

Anti-Violence Partnership of Philadelphia, founded by Crime Victim Advocate Deborah Spungen. http://avpphila.org.

Balanced and Restorative Justice: The focus is on work with adolescents. https://www.ncjrs.gov/pdffiles/bal.pdf.

Homicide Survivors website, Tucson, Arizona; https://www.azhomicidesurvivors.org.

Mayo Clinic; http://www.mayoclinic.com.

National Center for PTSD, Dept. for Veterans Affairs; http://www.ptsd.va.gov.

Separation and Loss Services, Virginia Mason Medical Center, Seattle, Washington, affiliated with **Homicide Support Project**, founded by Edward Rynearson, MD; provides services for adults and children (aged 7-18) whose loved one has died as the result of a sudden, violent death. https://www.virginiamason.org/grief-services.

Substance Abuse Diagnosis; http://www.behavenet.com.

Survivors of Violent Loss: Founded by Connie Saindon; provides Restorative Retelling services for survivors of violent death. http://www.svlp.org.

Safe Horizons: a victim assistance agency that provides support, prevents violence, and promotes justice for victims of crime and abuse. http://www.safehorizon.org.

Books

And I Don't Want to Live This Life: A Mother's Story of Her Daughter's Murder, Deborah Spungen, Ballantine Books, 1996.

Can't Forgive: My 20-Year Battle with O.J. Simpson, Kim Goldman, BenBella Books, 2014.

Dare I Call It Murder?: A Memoir of Violent Loss, Larry M. Edwards, Wigeon Publishing, 2013.

Forgive for Good, Fred Luskin, HarperOne, 2001.

Homicide: Hidden Victims, A Resource for Professionals, Deborah Spungen, SAGE Publications, 1997.

No Time For Goodbyes: Coping with Sorrow, Anger, and Injustice After a Tragic Death, Janice Harris Lord, Compassion Press, 2006.

Retelling Violent Death, Edward Rynearson, MD, Brunner/Routledge, 2001.

The Journey: An Adult Self-Help Workbook Kit, Ten Steps to Learning to Live With Violent Death, Connie Saindon, Survivors of Violent Loss, 2008.

Trauma and Recovery: The Aftermath of Violence, Judith Lewis Herman, MD, Basic Books, 1992.

Online

Alaska Department of Corrections Vine Link https://doc.alaska.gov/probation-parole/victim-notification.

California Department of Corrections and Rehabilitation: Search for Victims' Services; http://www.cdcr.ca.gov.

Two California Examples of forms for victims to be notified http://www.courts.ca.gov/documents/cr110.pdf. http://www.cdcr.ca.gov/Victim_Services/application.html.

The Law Dictionary, featuring Black's Law Dictionary Free Online Legal Dictionary 2nd Ed. https://thelawdictionary.org.

USLEGAL.com; http://definitions.uslegal.com/p/post-conviction-relief-proceeding/.

* Some Web addresses may have changed since publication.

10

Remembering and Missions

Lives are like rivers, eventually they go where they must, not where we want them to.
—Richard Russo, *Empire Falls*

Remembering

It is understandable that people remember how someone was murdered. Everyone remembers how a loved one died. It shakes us all to the core of our lives and community. The horrific and traumatic nature of a violent death is deeply experienced. Each layer of complexity adds to that memory as well as how the story unfolds over time. We are hard wired to remember the most intense moments of our lives.

They say memories are golden.
Well, maybe that is true:
I never wanted memories;
I only wanted you.

—Author Unknown

Murder is beyond words; therefore, it has not been surprising when survivors express what has happened to them in many art forms. Art talks in ways that help us say and see something in different ways. **The Pongo Teen Writing Project**, founded by Richard Gold, invites young people to heal themselves through writing poetry. He asks them to write from the heart about who they are and what they've experienced. This writing allows the many troubled youth he has worked with to put their pain on paper. Pongo has writing activities that can help survivors after a death, and these activities are available for free, along with other resources, on the Pongo website. (See Resources at the end of this chapter.) This award-winning program also has produced several publications.

A major component in the work that I and my team have done is to encourage the memory of the lives of loved ones, which aids in the management of the overwhelming pain of this horrific event and accompanying memories. I say it simply: We want to foster resiliency (people's existing strengths and abilities) in the service of reducing symptoms and rebuilding lives.

Survivors worry that they will forget who their loved ones were, that their loved ones' lives stood for nothing. One of my brothers apologetically admits he knows how our sister died, but he doesn't remember her.

Consider these words from Rose, one of our survivor writers:

> *. . . it is one of my greatest fears that my Daughter and Grandson will be forgotten; my second fear is that they will always be remembered for how they were murdered, and I want to change that now to how they lived.*
>
> *On July 26, my daughter and grandson became Angels. From this day forward, this will no longer be referred to as the day they were murdered.*
>
> ***July 26 will now be their Angelversary!***
>
> *In no way does this excuse or negate what happened to them that evening, but it has nothing to do with who they were or how beautiful their lives were.*
>
> *What I want people to remember is that my daughter was a beautiful, funny, sweet, caring woman who was loved by so many. I want Victoria to be remembered for the funny sarcastic sweet girl that she was. She was strong in her beliefs and didn't fall into cliques at school because she thought they were dumb, and she didn't like people to be ignored or classified as a geek. She was one of the first people to introduce herself to a new student. She had the best of friends that loved and adored her, and when Louis came along, he was special to all them as well. Victoria wanted to be the best mom there was, and she questioned her ability. But if you ask anyone, she was a great mom. She was smart book-wise, not real good with common sense. But that made her Victoria.*
>
> *She was also a mother who was madly in love with her beautiful baby boy. He was simply an Angel on Earth, full of love, smiles, and not a care in the world. He knew how much he was loved. Louis was a ball of love that could not have brought more joy to everyone he came in contact with. His smile makes me smile because that is how I always remember him, smiling.*
>
> ***Please take a moment out today to remember my Daughter and Grandson; they are not forgettable.***

It has taken Rose much longer to begin talking about her grandson. She found a creative way to bring him to life. She wrote a letter as if he were talking to everyone on what would have been his eighth birthday. Loved ones are forever young, as it is hard to imagine them older than the age they were when they were killed. This is a great effort and example here of separating loved ones lives from their deaths.

> *Hi, it's me!*
> *Today I would be 8 years old. I would say how time flies, but I know for my grandparents, family, and friends, it hasn't been anything but a long, drawn-out, living hell. I want them and everyone else to know I am okay and happy to be home. I am with my mom and that made leaving all of you a little easier. Please don't be sad for us; we will see you all again.*

My grandma helped me write this! She wants everyone to listen to this song by Kenny Chesney called "Who You'd be Today," because it keeps playing over and over in her head. I guess it reminds her of us.
    Love you all,
    Angel Baby

The words in this song that Rose tells us about may fit many of you. The lyrics acknowledge that loved ones are gone while inviting you to imagine their future. Recalling memories like these are medicinal when they give life and meaning. Over time you may be able to separate the memories of their lives and their deaths more and more.

In Chapter Three, you were asked to describe your loved one and talk about who he or she was. Chapter One asked what symbol you might have for them which represented their lives. Of course, there can be many symbols, as each family member may come up with one that fits her or his individual memories, hopes, and relationships.

When remembering a loved one's life, it can help if you are able to substitute talking about their death with a different occasion. I created both The Holiday Memorial and the River of Remembrance (described later) to help with this. By no means is there any strict prohibition against talking about how our loved ones died; I am suggesting that you participate in these events or create your own events as a respectful movement toward remembering their lives, as well as providing a guide for your own community or personal events.

The following exercises will help you focus on remembering the life of your loved one.

When is your "angelversary"? How would your loved one(s) want to be remembered? What examples do you have of how you remember them?

Write your responses in your notebook.

Murder as Entertainment

Murder is mostly played out in newspapers or newscasts, but also books and magazines. Unfortunately, this makes it harder for survivors to focus on the life of their loved one(s). The death and loss is difficult enough for families to bear, but they may be additionally traumatized by inaccuracies and the liberties taken in published accounts or reenactments of a loved one's death.

As I mentioned in Chapter 3, Larry Edwards, in his book **Dare I Call It Murder: A Memoir of Violent Loss** (2013), describes how he learned of a true-crime book that contained an inaccurate account of his parents' deaths. (See Resources.)

Also mentioned in Chapter 3, the "60 Minutes" interview with Deborah Spungen in which she describes the movie made without any input from her or family members. Incidents like these have been the impetus for survivors to try to correct such wrongs. Deborah Spungen's work in developing the Antiviolence Partnership in Philadelphia helped address issues like this.

Parents of Murdered Children, Inc.® (POMC) initiated the Murder Is Not Entertainment (MINE)ᔆᴹ Program in 1993 to alert people to society's insensitivity toward murder and its aftermath. The organization states on its website: "'Murdertainment' continues to revictimize those who have already been affected by the murder of a loved one, ignores the aftermath of murder and sets a poor example for the nations' youth." (See Resources.)

By engaging in practices and activities that counteract these death-oriented publications and productions, survivors can strengthen their resiliancies and focus on remembering and honoring the lives of their loved ones, as Larry Edwards and Deborah Spungen have done.

Beyond Words

Words are difficult to use when it comes to describing the experience of life after murder. Rituals and ceremonies do what words cannot do. They are vehicles for respectful expression of losses. Such events can help free up overwhelming emotion, allowing its expression in a private or shared activity. The use of art, poetry, music, and dance can say what cannot be said in words. During the annual Mexican event *Día de Muertos* (Day of the Dead), altars are built of a loved one's favorite food, possessions, and objects. Sugar skulls and marigolds are traditional as well.

Such events act as an aid to strengthen bonds between individuals and their community in the aftermath of a murder when feelings of safety and trust are shattered. I invite you to continue to find ways of remembering your loved ones' lives. I have visited some places and observed ways that others have chosen to preserve memories after violent deaths. You will find photos of my visits in a gallery listed in the Resources section at the end of this chapter.

Victim Assistance Coordinating Council (VACC), is an organization in my community that sponsors a candle light vigil during National Crime Victims Week, sponsored by the Office of Victims of Crime. Many communities hold events during this week. Look locally for ones you can participate in or organize. Contact VACC to find out what they do for inspiration for your community. Members of this organization include all the crime victim agencies, nonprofit agencies and professionals that work with crime victims.

The **Oklahoma City National Memorial & Museum** is a remarkable site that is a must-see. The memorial not only tells about the bomb blast and the aftermath, but it has many ways of remembering those who were impacted that day. Among its important works is a room that holds a photo of each person who died, along with a symbol of something that was important to each of them.

The mission statement says, in part: "The Memorial must include biographies of the victims written by the families of the victims and photographic representations."

The symbols include such items as a baseball, a piano, a rattle, an American flag, cowgirl boots, Marine Corps decal, bowling ball and pins, lipstick, teddy bear, doughboy, stethoscope, Mickey Mouse, bible, stuffed dog, arrowhead, porcelain egg, crossword puzzle, and a clown.

The entrance to the museum welcomes visitors with:

We come here to remember those who were killed, those who survived and those who changed forever. . . . May all who leave here know the impact of violence. May this memorial offer comfort, strength, peace, hope, and serenity.

Similarly, in Boston, the Garden of Peace is a Memorial to Victims of Homicide located near the Boston Commons. This relatively small area makes up for its size by its big heart and density of meaning. Anyone connected to Massachusetts who has had a loved one murdered can have a spot in this garden. Rocks and walls are engraved with names of loved ones who were killed.

The River of Remembrance is now an annual event in the San Diego-area community. I initiated it after learning about the "Trail of Tears" our Native Americans suffered. I suggested to my program advisors that we have a River of Tears for folks marked by stones placed in the shape of a river for those who died of murder. My wise team suggested the River of Remembrance instead, and this event took root. It is held at the **Crime Victims Oak Garden**, which was created as a place for crime victims to plant trees in memory of their loved ones. This garden was created by the efforts of the family of Cara Knott, a murder victim who was found under the bridge at this location.

Since then, this event has been supported by local agencies that work with the families of homicide victims. Keeping with the importance of re-membering the lives of loved ones, a craft table has been added. Participants are given white T-shirts to paint a memory of their loved one; the T-shirt is then hung on a clothesline for all to see. This event is now held on or near the National Day of Remembrance of Murder Victims, recognized annually on September 25.

John Lennon's death marks a special place in Central Park in New York City: A sidewalk mosaic spells out the word **"Imagine"** in a section dedicated to Lennon. The area is called "Strawberry Fields" and is located across from Lennon's apartment, where he was shot.

Tucson, Arizona, has a special place in a public park called the **Children's Memorial Park**, with a sculpture and engraved names, that's been set aside for remem-bering children who died; it has the reminder that *"We need not walk alone."*

Friends and colleagues Vilma Torres of Safe Horizons and BethAnn Halzey, Director of the Crime Victims' Assitance Unit at the Bronx District Attorney's Office, tell me about an activity they do in December in New York called **"The Lighting of the Tree of Angels."** Participants are invited to bring an angel to put on a tree dedicated to the victims of homicide and the loving memories they leave behind. Participants are asked to imagine a tree where angels rest when they are tired of soaring, where they are never forgotten, a place where we could find them—a place they call home.

Our **Survivors of Violent Loss** program in San Diego has an annual event where survivors come together for a **Holiday Memorial** in mid-December. The survivors help create the event by bringing a symbol of their loved one to hang on the tree and food to share. They are invited to express words of inspiration for others as well. Items hung on the tree have been traditional ornaments as well as a rooster, candle, feather, cork, a yarn bow, Necco wafers, cards, Hostess cupcake, tennis ball, bookmark, peace sign, large varnished cookie, hot wheels car, oven mitt, pencil, and a Hershey's kiss. Folks can take their symbol home or leave it to be put up the following year, whether they are present or not.

Please contact Survivors of Violent Loss with your examples, no matter how small, to add to the online collection: cdsnetwork1@gmail.com.

Customize Rituals for the Holidays and Anniversaries
"To ease pain of loss and traumatic grief"

By Connie Saindon, MA, LMFT

It is well known (among both private and public professionals) that anniversary dates and holidays, especially the first one, can be difficult for those whose loved one has passed away. When this loss is an unnatural death, holidays can seem unbearable and insurmountable. Thoughts of merriment may arouse feelings of guilt and worries of being disloyal.

Rituals are necessary for the management of fears and adapting to the changes necessary in relationships after death (Goffman). Rituals serve to acknowledge change without threatening the overall social order. Ceremonies help with adapting to what has happened. Rituals allow one emotional engagement along with creating a safe distance to ease the overwhelming pain of loss. Ceremonies work to compartmentalize the review of losses amid reminders.

Symbols help replace painful intrusions and memories. An example of this is when Ann worried about what she would do with the neck and tail of the turkey at Thanksgiving. She stated that her brother, a homicide victim, always made a fuss and got the turkey parts every year. This holiday, she ate the tail in honor of her brother. She chuckled about her experience saying: "I don't know what he ever saw in them: they're all fat!" Ann moved from being frozen about what to do, into an activity that honored her brother and gave her an unexpected laugh; something she had been unable to do since his death.

Family Therapists' Evan Imber Black and Janine Roberts recommend setting up a separate activity prior to a holiday to acknowledge loved ones to free up the actual holiday. An example would be setting aside a special night and inviting friends or family to bring favorite foods for an informal gathering and memories.

This special time could also be a time when photos are gathered to begin a memory album. This album could be worked on annually with more photos and stories collected each year. For example, my family created an album to help remember our sister who was a murder victim. Many different gatherings were set up to do the album. Copies were made of photos and returned to their owner. Each family member selected photos and stories for their page. The album dedication says, "to our loving sister and daughter who lives on in all of us."

Not doing a special and separate activity tends to burden stressful holidays even more. Hoping to slip past such events without overwhelming reminders is difficult to do. A special time before the holiday can both honor the memory and mark the loss of your loved one. This frequently reduces the strain of the actual holiday.

It is important that rituals and ceremonies be customized. When one has lost an infant, doing an album may not work, as there may be few photos and stories. One father who's young son was murdered has a ritual whereby he buys his mother a new snow baby snow globe to add to her collection honoring her grandson. Another father who states "heroin murdered my son" is heard singing songs at benefits from the CD that his son helped him write.

A new and quite spontaneous evening happened after the first of our projects' support groups had ended. Realizing that the groups ended early in December, and participants had the holidays to face, we informally asked folks to gather one evening and bring a symbol of their loved one, which they could hang on a holiday tree. All were invited. We had a room full, with songs, inspirationals and ornament/symbols hung one-by-one. This has become a well received annual event.

To develop your own rituals, considers some of the following ideas and let us know what you do. Your rituals will give others ideas when their thinking is blocked due to SUGS—sudden upsurges of grief (our term based on the work of Therese Rando). SUGS usually result in temporary confusion that participants call "brain mush" when reminders flood them with pain.

Activities can include the telling of stories around a fireplace, or bonfire; going to the burial site and praying, chanting, singing; serving the needy, making charitable contributions; doing a difficult feat such as a hike, balloon ride, or a surfboard paddle-out. Items to use for rituals could be candles, rosemary (for remembrance), seeds, sand, feathers, balloons, crayons, rocks, ribbon, music, stars, or irises (for hope).

It is important to remember that although these ideas may help to ease the pain of this loss, nothing will bring the loved one back or erase all the images of how they died. There's no "getting over it," but this may be one more step in your journey.

References

- Goffman, E., 1971. *Relations in Public*. New York: Harper and Row.
- Imber-Black, E., Roberts, J., 1992. *Rituals for Our Times*. New York: Harper Collins.
- Rando, T., 1993. *Treatment of Complicated Mourning*. Champaign, IL: Research Press.
- Saindon, Connie, 2008. *The Journey: Adult Survivors Individual Workbook Kit, Ten Steps to Learning to Live with Violent Death*. svlp@svlp.org

Survivor Question: Do you have a symbol that represents your loved one? What does the symbol mean in remembering your loved one?

Write your answers in your notebook.

Connie Saindon

My symbol for my younger sister "Tiny" is the iris. This symbol was chosen because of Tiny's love for lavender. She wore a dress of this color at my wedding six days before she died. I later found out that the iris is a symbol for hope.

Rose

It was hard to pick a symbol that represented both my daughter and ten-month-old grandson. At their funeral I was given a bronze statue of an angel staring at a butterfly on her hand. It symbolized both of them. After that an artist friend of the family did this drawing of that statue; it only seemed fitting that I would choose that as my symbol. It is unique like they were.

Marina

I chose a tail feather from my late Amazon parrot, Gideon, as my symbol. Gideon was a Christmas gift from my father. It was 1969, and I was ten years old. I still remember the thrill of coming into the den that morning and seeing a cage with a big red bow on it next to the Christmas tree.

Harrier

I have two sea shells, one for each parent. They sit on the fireplace mantel in the family room of my home. My parents lived aboard a sailboat, and they were killed and buried at sea. These sea shells represent their love for and association with the sea.

Kaila

My symbol is the weeping angel. This angel represents how I felt. I had failed my sister. I had fallen into depression.

Yvonne

In this image drawn and contributed by my daughter, I'm able to visualize a message from our mother: "I never left you. Though you cannot see or touch me, I will always be near to protect you. In your deepest pain and despair if you listen with your heart, you will feel all of my love around you. Just close your eyes and you will see I never left you, I am still here."

Halia

The symbol I have for my sister is an ear of corn, as it exemplifies the spirit of generosity that my sister shared with me and others. She lived in a house in Southern California and had planted corn in the back yard. After watering and tending to the small stalk for weeks on end, it produced just one ear of sweet corn. Knowing it was my favorite, she picked that ear of corn and gave it to me! She and I were raised by our grand-

parents in our formative years, and Grandma instilled some Eastern spiritual beliefs in us from her Asian heritage, which my sister expressed through acts of kindness to friends and strangers alike.

Mary

"Ohm"—this is a symbol that was important to my son. As an adult, he always wore a necklace with the ohm symbol on it. It was part of his way to find peace within himself as he dealt with stresses of young adulthood and making ends meet. Later many of his friends had the ohm symbol tattooed on their forearms. Ohm cookies were made by my cousin and sent to them the night they all gathered together to get their tattoos.

JJ

I like bamboo, which very well represents my son. Japan was his birthplace, and he had faithfully cared for a large bamboo arrangement we had left behind when we moved to California. Bamboo's symbolism for the Japanese involves integrity, with an openness on the inside, open for new ideas. Our son was at a point in his life where he was opening up his adult life and ready for new ideas.

Valeria

The name Valeria means brave, strong, and valiant—everything our son was to us. He no longer has a voice, so we chose a name that represented the qualities he demonstrated, especially on the night he came face to face with evil. For us, the "Winged Victory" statue represents this.

Evelyn

This icon is a cameo likeness of the daughter-sister our family lost, worn by her mother.

Survivor's Mission

> *. . . not everyone can be famous, but we can all be great because greatness is defined by service . . .*
>
> —**Martin Luther King, Jr.**

Losing a loved one to violence compels many to engage in what Judith Herman (1992) describes as a "survivor's mission" to make changes as a result of their loved one being a murder victim. This mission can be quite personal and not known to the public. I would not have spearheaded the work I have done if my sister was not murdered. For example, I volunteered for three years to do crisis intervention with the police department while I researched the best of what is available to survivors in the aftermath of murder. Without that involvement, the Homicide Support Project, now called **Survivors of Violent Loss,** would not exist. I wouldn't have published clinical research of our results, nor trained and supervised many in the use of cutting-edge strategies in violent-death bereavement. Nor would I have made presentations at many conferences or authored any material in this specialty, including writing this handbook.

One of my books, *The Journey: Ten Steps to Learning to Live with Violent Death* (2008), is available as a guide for self-help or support-group facilitation. I could not *not* have done this work. This was a necessity for me to bring what I could to such a misunderstood and inadequately served group. Other "mission" examples include:

The **Marilyn Amour** study (Rynearson, 2006) found that for many families "the pursuit of what matters" comes in the latter phase of violent-death bereavement. Commitments of direct actions involving (1) declarations of truth, (2) fighting for what is right, and (3) living in ways that give purpose to the loved one's death, become active and personal.

Hope Gallery is an online photo gallery of donated images created as a place where Survivors can go to view for a moment a beautiful image or to help them recalibrate their thoughts and images for a moment or two. The images that have been donated for this purpose came from places in the United States, as well as other countries: New Zealand, Germany, Croatia, England, France, Montenegro, Antarctica, and more. Hope Gallery, in its Events Gallery, also shows photos of different events across the nation that remember loved ones who died from violence. (See Resources.)

Antiviolence Partnership of Philadelphia (AVP) was founded 30 years ago by Deborah Spungen as a support group for families following the murder of her daughter Nancy by a member of the Sex Pistols rock group. She is now a nationally recognized author, advocate, and trainer. (See Resources.)

Parents of Murdered Children, Inc.®, was started by parents in Cincinnati, Ohio, in 1978 after the murder of their 19-year-old daughter Lisa by her former boyfriend. (See Resources, Chapter 2.)

Candy Lightner founded **Mothers Against Drunk Drivers** (MADD) in 1980 after her 13-year-old daughter, Cari, was killed by a repeat drunk-driving offender. Cindy Lamb—whose daughter, Laura, became the nation's youngest quadriplegic at the hands of a drunk driver—soon joined Candy in the crusade to save lives. (See Resources, Chapter 8.)

Martha Cooper's Memorial Walls in New York City shows a form of public expression that arose because of the many tragic deaths. Graffiti artists began accepting commissions to create murals commemorating the lives of victims of violence. It is not unusual to find paintings of favorite cars, motorcycles, articles of brand-name clothing, or even beer bottles mixed with doves, angels, and religious symbols. Most New York cemeteries are located far from the city, so the memorial walls offer a place closer to home to gather and grieve for lost relatives and friends. These walls offer solace in the face of tragedy. (See Resources.)

United States Constitution: One stark realization that many see is the lack of support for co-victims in the criminal justice system. Mission-driven co-victims often forge campaigns to right wrongs. One such campaign is to correct the absence of protections for crime victims. While 23 protections for the accused exist in the U.S. Constitution, there are **NONE** for crime victims.

The National Center for Victims of Crime (NCVC) was created in 1985 by Ala Isham and Alexander Auersperg in memory of their mother, Sunny Von Bulow. They were motivated by their mother's victimization and their family's traumatic experience with the criminal justice system. The founders believed it was fundamentally wrong that crime victims were often shut out of and "re-victimized" by the very system that was supposed to help them. They wanted to redefine what justice for crime victims means by giving the victims a voice in the criminal justice system. (See Resources.)

The Crime Victims Action Alliance (CVAA) began as the Doris Tate Crime Victims Bureau, formed in 1992 and based in Sacramento, California. The organization was named in honor of Doris Tate, the mother of Sharon Tate, a victim in the Charles Manson murder spree. It was Doris's wish that crime victims have a regular voice in the California legislature. (See Resources.)

Amber Alert: AMBER is officially an acronym for **America's Missing: Broadcast Emergency Response**, but it was named for Amber Hagerman, a nine-year-old who was abducted and murdered in Texas in 1996. (See Resources.)

Marsy's Law, the California Victims' Bill of Rights Act of 2008, was initiated in 1983 after Marsy Nicholas, then a senior at **UC Santa Barbara**, was stalked and murdered by her ex-boyfriend. Her murderer was tried and sentenced to life in prison *with the possibility of parole*. Although he died in prison one year before Marsy's Law passed, the Nicholas family attended numerous parole hearings, which haunted them for years. (See Chapter 4.)

Survivor Questions: Are you involved in a what Judith Herman describes as a "Survivor's Mission"? How do you help other survivors, your community or your family? Do you have ideas about what you might do some day?

Write your answer in your notebook.

Rose

I became involved in many areas of crime victim advocacy; it was all I really knew at that point, and I wanted to help others in a way that so many had helped us.

None of us know how to go through this, and the criminal investigation phase is one many of us don't understand. It's easy to think the investigators don't care, and it's where we often make the most mistakes without even knowing it. These families trust me because I am "one of them." I have found that their questions are much like the ones I had, so being able to put my horrific experience into a different framework and use it to help them navigate the unknown makes me feel like I am doing something that has a purpose.

I do court accompaniment and go over the "criminal justice system" with the survivors. Knowledge is power; it is also peace of mind.

I also facilitate a violent loss support group where I work with families that are starving for someone to understand them. It gives them the opportunity to speak with others who are walking in the same shoes. For me, a support group was vitally important because as hard as others tried, they couldn't feel what I was feeling, nor would I want them to. To be in a group of people like me made me feel less crazy, less alone in the world, because the people in the group "got it."

I learned coping skills that I still use today, and I share them with my group. I take great pride in a family as I see them find their own way through the darkness and learn to stand again. I take great pride in the families in my group who reach out to a new person or family and offer their own insights. I see them give back what they have learned, and I see the way it helps others in return.

I get more from reaching out and supporting a family than I could ever give them; they teach me so much as we walk this journey together.

***I also host events** that were already in place long before I entered this arena. I only do so for the ones **that honor the lives of our loved ones**, and do not focus on the deaths. These events always leave me feeling like I got to know others' loved ones, and they got to know mine. They are not forgotten, at least not by us.*

Marina

My primary mission is to help survivors of violent loss in various ways. I attend outreach events, and underwrite various survivor activities and programs. In my day-to-day life I often come across survivors by pure happenstance. If they are interested, I tell them my story, and encourage them to seek therapeutic help if they are truly struggling with the fallout of traumatic loss.

My secondary mission is no less important. Two months after the murder I received a VHS tape in the mail. In it, the governor of our state explained the justice system process for murder. I guess it was generated when Dad's case was filed by the DA's office. The presentation was short, and almost clinical—like a film documenting the medical effects of some exotic disease. It ended with general assurances regarding the efficacy of the justice system in our state.

It was woefully inadequate. I felt like I had been promised a sumptuous meal, and received a packet of stale saltines in its stead.

There was no help at the local library. Barnes and Noble had nothing but a book called, "Losing a Parent." It had one chapter on violent loss. It was a very short chapter, and I read it over and over. It was of minimal help.

I dreamed of a book that would help people like me. I was too wounded and weak at the time to contemplate actually writing such a book. I never really thought it would ever happen. With the publishing of this book, my dream has come true. It is my fervent hope that survivors will finally have what I did not—a source of hope, inspiration, and education to guide them through their own journey through this harrowing thing we call violent loss.

Harrier

I have become an advocate for survivors of violent loss through my writings and activities. I work with and attend events sponsored by the Survivors of Violent Loss Program. This has helped me become more empathetic of others' losses, rather than resentful. Before my involvement, I found it easy to believe that no one could know or understand my pain, but I no longer feel that way. By interacting with others, I have come to realize how much they suffer, too, even if it's not immediately apparent.

By contributing to this "club that no one wanted to join," I feel better about myself and others who have endured a violent loss in their lives, and if my support helps them find a little peace within, then that is an apt reward.

Kaila

Currently, I'm not involved in any support group, but I have shared my story and I know I have inspired some people. My mission would be to help others through the feelings that I experienced from this horrific tragedy. These questions have helped me; the more I talk about my experiences, I know that someone can relate to a feeling and see that it does get better without forgetting our loved one.

Halia

Providing support to survivors in online communities and twelve-step support groups has been a cathartic form of healing. I am also about to complete graduate school in the counseling field with plans to work in trauma and violent loss.

Resources

Books

And I Don't Want to Live this Life, Deborah Spungen. Ballantine Books, 1996.

Dare I Call It Murder?: A Memoir of Violent Loss, Larry M. Edwards. Wigeon Publishing, 2013.

Meaning-Making for Survivors of Violent Death, Marilyn Armour. *Violent Death: Resilience and Intervention Beyond the Crisis*, Edward K. Rynearson, editor, 2006.

R.I.P. Memorial Wall Art, Joseph Sciorra & Martha Cooper, Thames & Hudson, 2002.

Online

Amber Alert; https://www.amberalert.com.

Antiviolence Partnership of Philadelphia; http://avpphila.org.

Children's Memorial Garden, Tuscon, AZ http://tucsoncleanandbeautiful.org/other-programs/childrens-memorial-parks/.

Garden of Peace, A Memorial to Victims of Homicide, Boston, MA http://gardenofpeacememorial.org.

MADD (Mothers against Drunk Driving); http://www.madd.org.

Marsy's Law; http://www.marsyslawforall.org.

National Victims Constitution Amendment Project; http://www.nvcap.org.

Oklahoma City National Memorial and Museum http://www.oklahomacitynationalmemorial.org.

Parents of Murdered Children, Inc.® (POMC); http://www.pomc.org.

Photos of the Boston Peace Garden, Oklahoma City Memorial and Museum, Tucson's Children's Memorial Park and New Orleans Sculpture Garden at http://hopegallery.smugmug.com/events.

Pongo Publishing; http://www.pongoteenwriting.org.

Survivors of Violent Loss Holiday Memorial, River of Remembrance http://hopegallery.smugmug.com/Events/.

Victim Assistance Coordinating Council; http://sdvacc.com.

* Some Web addresses may have changed since publication.

Epilogue

Lament to Survivors

I had my turn,
>to do what I could;
>to learn and serve:

Members
>of the "forever club,"
>loved ones of murder victims.

Branded so deeply,
>with permanent stains
>and horrific memories.

I had my turn,
>to do what I could;
>to learn and serve.

The living dead of
>unfinished souls,
>their forever young.

I had my turn,
>to do what I could;
>to learn and serve,

As I step aside
>my heart still cries,
>for those who moan;

I had my turn,
>to do what I could;
>to learn and serve.

As I make room,
>while others try
>to strengthen and succeed.

I had my turn,
>to do what I could,
>to learn and serve.

I had my turn.

—Connie Saindon, 2013

References

American Probation and Parole Association (APPA). (2012). *Perspectives: The Journal of the American Probation and Parole Association.* Voice of the Victim: A Perspectives Spotlight Issue. Retrieved 2013 from http://www.appa-net.org/eweb/docs/appa/pubs/Perspectives_2012_Spotlight.pdf.

Arthurson, Wayne. (2011). *Fall from Grace.* New York, NY: Tom Doherty Associates: Forge Books.

Black's Law Dictionary: Free Online Legal Dictionary, 2nd Ed. Retrieved 2013 from http://thelawdictionary.org/discovery/

Bonnie & John. *Courthouse Survival Advice.* Retrieved 2013 from http://svlp.org/copingcourthousesurv.html.

Bucholz, Judie A. (2002). *Homicide Survivors: Misunderstood Grievers.* Amityville, NY: Baywood Publishing Co.

California Commission on Peace Officer Standards and Training (CalPOST). (2009). *Victims of Violence: A Guide to Help Bring Justice* [DVD].

Castro accepts plea deal to avoid death penalty; prosecutors recommend sentence of life without parole [Web]. CBS. Retrieved 2013 from http://www.cbsnews.com/news/ariel-castro-update-castro-accepts-plea-deal-to-avoid-death-penalty-prosecutors-recommend-sentence-of-life-without-parole/.

Cervantes, Gene. (2012, May). *For the Most Part.* Citizens Against Homicide newsletter.

Citizens Against Homicide newsletter. (2012, May). Retrieved 2013 from http://www.citizensagainsthomicide.org/may-2012-newsletter/.

Cold Case Investigations and Forensic DNA (CODIS). National Institute of Justice. Retrieved 2013 from http://www.dna.gov/solving-crimes/cold-cases/howdatabasesaid/codis/.

Corwin, Miles. (2004). *Homicide Special.* New York, NY: Henry Holt and Co.

Crime Clock. (2010). U.S. Department of Justice, Office of Justice Programs, Office for Victims of Crime. Retrieved 2014 from http://www.fbi.gov/about-us/cjis/ucr/crime-in-the-u.s/2010/crime-in-the-u.s.-2010/offenses-known-to-law-enforcement/crime-clock

Crime in the United States. (2010). U.S. Department of Justice, Federal Bureau of Investigation. Retrieved 2013 from http://www.fbi.gov/about-us/cjis/ucr/crime-in-the-u.s/2010/crime-in-the-u.s.-2010.

Crime Victims Action Alliance. Retrieved 2013 from http://www.cvactionalliance.com.

Criminal Law Dictionary. Retrieved 2013 from http://www.sandiegocrimedefense.com/criminal-law-dictionary.html.

Currier, Joseph M., & Holland, Jason M., & Coleman, Rachel A., & Neimeyer, Robert A. (2008). *Perspectives on Violence and Violent Death: Bereavement Following Violent Death: An Assault on Life and Meaning.* Amityville, NY: Baywood Publishing Co., pp. 177-202.

Diagnostic and Statistical Manual of Mental Disorders, 4th Edition, Text Revision (DSM-IV-TR). (2000). Arlington, VA: American Psychiatric Association.

DNA: Critical Issues for Those Who Work with Victims: President's DNA Initiative. (2007). U.S. Department of Justice, Office of Justice Programs, Office for Victims of Crime. This 24-minute DVD raises awareness for victim advocates, criminal justice practitioners, and others who work with crime victims on the issues involved for those whose cases involve DNA evidence.

Doka, Kenneth. (Ed.). (1995). *Children Mourning, Mourning Children.* New York, NY: Taylor and Francis.

Doka, Kenneth. (1996). *Living With Grief After Sudden Loss: Suicide, Homicide, Accident, Heart Attack, Stroke.* New York, NY: Taylor & Francis. [Produced as a companion to the DVD of the Hospice Foundation of America's third annual teleconference.]

Edwards, Larry M. (2012, August 18). *PTSD & Survivors of Violent Loss* [Weblog]. Retrieved 2013 from http://polishingyourprose.wordpress.com/2012/08/18/ptsd-survivors-of-violent-loss/.

Edwards, Larry M. (2013). *Dare I Call It Murder: A Memoir of Violent Loss.* San Diego, CA: Wigeon Publishing. http://www.dareicallitmurder.com.

Freitgag, Carrie. (2003). *Aftermath: In the Wake of Murder.* Elliott City, MD: Chevron Publishing Co.

Geberth, Vernon J. (1983). *Practical Homicide Investigation: Tactics, Procedures, and Forensic Techniques.* Boca Raton, FL: CRC Press.

Goffman, Erving. (1971). *Relations in public.* New York, NY: Harper and Row.

Goldman, Kim. (2014). *Can't Forgive: My 20-Year Battle with O.J. Simpson.* Dallas, TX: BenBella Books.

Gone, But Not Forgotten! New Mexico Homicide Survivors, Inc. Retrieved 2013 from http://www.nmsoh.org/scripts/memorial.asp.

Gupta, R.J. & Bhattacharya, A. (Screenwriters), & Gupta, R.K. (Director). (2011). *No One Killed Jessica* [Motion Picture]. India: UTV Spotboy.

Hendricks, James E., & Byers, Bryan D. (Eds.). (2006). *Death Notification: The Theory and Practice of Delivering Bad News* (NCJ-215593). Crisis Intervention in Criminal Justice/Social Service, Fourth Edition, pp. 341-373.

Herman, Judith. (1992). *Trauma and Recovery.* New York, NY: Harper Collins Publishers.

Herman, Susan. (2010). *Parallel Justice for Victims of Crime.* Washington, DC: National Center for Victims of Crime.

Hickey, Eric. (2003). *Encyclopedia of Murder & Violent Crime.* Thousand Oaks, CA: Sage Publications.

Homicide Resource Paper. (2012). U.S. Department of Justice, Office of Justice Programs, Office for Victims of Crime. Retrieved 2013 from https://www.ovcttac.gov.

iCAN Foundation. Retrieved 2013 from http://www.ican-foundation.org.

Imber-Black, E., & Roberts, J. (1992). Rituals for Our Times: Celebrating, Healing, and Changing Our Lives and Our Relationships. New York, NY: HarperCollins.

Janoff-Bulman, Ronnie. (1992). *Shattered Assumptions*. New York, NY: The Free Press.

King, Martin Luther Jr. (2013, August 28). One Historic March, Countless Striking Moments. NPR [radio broadcast].

Macquarrie, Brian. (2009). *The Ride: A Shocking Murder and a Bereaved Father's Journey from Rage to Redemption*. Boston, MA: Da Capo Press.

Martinez, Joselyn. (2013, June 11). 'How I caught my father's killer': Actress tracks down 'murderer' 26 years later after finding him on the internet. Retrieved 2013 from http://www.dailymail.co.uk/news/article-2339384/Actress-tracks-fathers-killer-26-years-using-70-search-website.html.

Matsakis, Aphrodite. (1992). *I Can't Get Over It: A Handbook for Trauma Survivors*. Oakland, CA: New Harbinger Publications, Inc.

Mayo Clinic [Website]. Retrieved 2013 from http://www.mayoclinic.org.

McCollister, Kathryn E., Michael T. French, and Hai Fang. (2010). The Cost of Crime to Society: New Crime-Specific Estimates for Policy and Program Evaluation, *Drug and Alcohol Dependence* 108(1). Retrieved 2014 from http://www.ncbi.nlm.nih.gov/pmc/articles/PMC2835847/.

Miller, Ted, & Cohen, Mark, & Wiersema, Brian. (1996). The Extent and Costs of Crime Victimization: A New National Institute of Justice (NCJ #184372). U.S. Department of Justice, Office of Justice Programs, National Institute of Justice. Retrieved 2013 from https://www.ncjrs.gov/pdffiles/costcrim.pdf.

Moore, Steve. (2014, January 6). Investigations and the Families of Victims [Blog]. Retrieved 2014 from http://www.gmancasefile.com/1/archives/01-2014/1.html.

National Sheriffs' Association (NSAJD, producer). (2008). *First Response to Victims of Crime* [DVD]. Washington, DC: U.S. Department of Justice, Office of Justice Programs, Office for Victims of Crime.

Neimeyer, R.A. (1998). *Lessons of Loss: A Guide to Coping*. New York, NY: McGraw-Hill/Primis Custom Publishing.

New Directions Bulletin. (1998, August). U.S. Department of Justice, Office of Justice Programs, Office for Victims of Crime. Retrieved 2013 from https://www.ncjrs.gov/ovc_archives/directions/pdftxt/bulletins/bltn1.pdf.

Newtown residents plead for privacy on Sandy Hook shooting anniversary [Web]. CNN. Retrieved 2013 from http://www.cnn.com/2013/12/09/us/connecticut-newtown-anniversary-privacy/.

Norris, F. H. (1992). Epidemiology of trauma: frequency and impact of different potentially traumatic events on different demographic groups. Journal of Consulting and Clinical Psychology, 60, 409–418.

Parents of Murdered Children, Inc.® Retrieved 2014 from http://www.pomc.org.

Porch, Dorris D., & Easley, Rebecca. (1997). *Murder in Memphis: the True Story of a Family's Quest for Justice*. Far Hills, NJ: New Horizon Press.

Post-conviction Relief Proceeding Law & Legal Definition. USLEGAL.com. Retrieved 2013 from http://definitions.uslegal.com/p/post-conviction-relief-proceeding/.

Rand, Hannah. (2012, June 25). Actor Dylan McDermott solves mystery of mother's tragic murder 45 years later. Daily Mail Online. Retrieved 2013 from http://www.dailymail.co.uk/news/article-2164445/.

Rando, Therese A. (in press). *Coping With the Sudden Death of Your Loved One: A Self-Help Handbook for Traumatic Bereavement.* Indianapolis, IN: Dog Ear Publishing.

Rhodes, Richard. (1999). *Why They Kill: Discoveries of a Maverick Criminologist.* New York, NY: Alfred A. Knopf, Inc.

Roberts, Robin. (2012, November 20). *Good Morning America* [television broadcast]. New York, NY: ABC News.

Rynearson, Edward K. (2001). *Retelling Violent Death.* New York, NY: Routledge: Taylor Francis Group.

Rynearson, Edward K., (Ed.). (2006). *Violent Death: Resilience and Intervention Beyond the Crises.* New York, NY: Taylor Francis Group.

Saindon, Connie, et al. (2013). Restorative Retelling for Violent Loss: An Open Clinical Trial. In *Death Studies Journal, 2013.* New York, NY: Taylor Francis Group.

Saindon, Connie, (2008). *The Journey: Adult Survivors Individual Workbook Kit, Ten Steps to Learning to Live with Violent Death.* San Diego, CA: Survivors of Violent Loss.

Saindon, Connie. (2012). Murder, Homicide and Trauma. In Charles Figley (Ed.), *Encyclopedia of Trauma.* Thousand Oaks, CA: Sage Publications.

Salloum, Alison, (1998). *Reactions: A Workbook to Help Young People Who Are Experiencing Trauma and Grief.* Omaha, NE: Centering Corporation.

Scott, Ridley, & McDougall, Charles, & Zucker, David W. (Executive Producers). (2012, November 18). *The Good Wife,* season 4, episode 8 [TV]. Retrieved 2014 from http://en.wikiquote.org/wiki/The_Good_Wife_(TV_series).

Smith, Harold I. (2012). *Borrowed Narratives: Using Biographical and Historical Grief Narratives with the Bereaving.* New York, NY: Routledge: Taylor Francis Group.

Spungen, Deborah. (1983). *And I Don't Want to Live This Life,* Ballentine Books.

Stowers, Carlton. (2003). *Scream at the Sky: Five Texas Murders and One Man's Crusade for Justice.* New York, NY: St. Martin's True Crime Library, St. Martin's Press.

Survivors of Violent Loss. Retrieved 2013 from http://www.svlp.org/support.html.

Williams, Mary Beth, and Poijula, Soili. (2002). *The PTSD Workbook: Simple, Effective Techniques for Overcoming Traumatic Symptoms.* Oakland, CA: New Harbinger Publications, Inc.

Wolin, Steven, and Wolin, Sybil. (1993). *The Resilient Self: How Survivors of Troubled Families Rise Above Adversity.* New York, NY: Villard.

Wolterstorff, Nicholas. (1987). *Lament for a Son.* Grand Rapids, MI: Eerdmans Publishing Co.

Zuckerman, Amy, & Nystedt, Karen. (1998). *Point of Fracture: Voices of Heinous Crime Survivors.* Tuscon, AZ: A. Zuckerman.

* Some Web addresses may have changed since publication.

About the Author

Connie Saindon is a licensed Marriage and Family Therapist and among the few specialists in the field of violent death bereavement. She is the founder of the nonprofit Survivors of Violent Loss Program in San Diego, which began in 1998. Her commitment to violent loss bereavement is related to the loss of her sister, aged 17, to homicide in 1961.

Ms. Saindon's training includes the Restorative Retelling Model developed by Edward Rynearson, MD. She co-authored a preliminary study that showed significant decreases in symptoms using this model.

She has provided program development, clinical services, training, and supervision of medical residents, interns, and clinicians. Subsequent research resulted in two more studies published in *Death Studies Journal, Fall 2013*, of which she has been a primary and contributing author. These studies cover 14 years worth of work, with results showing significant decrease in client symptoms related to traumatic grief, complicated bereavement, and post-traumatic stress. She is a frequent presenter at national conferences on this specialized topic.

Ms. Saindon's training programs have included online courses and two-day training for mental health professionals, universities, and crime victim advocates with the Office of Victims of Crime. Course titles include: The Restorative Retelling Model, Violent Death and PTSD, and Violent Death: Fostering Resilience While Healing Wounds.

She is author of *The Journey: Ten Steps to Learning to Live with Violent Death*, an adaption of the Restorative Retelling Model for adult self-help and paraprofessionals. She also is a contributing author of *Violent Death, Resilience and Intervention Beyond the Crises*. She has written articles on murder as well as homicide for the *Encyclopedia of Trauma*. She has worked as a consultant for the Department of Defense, augmenting the mental health services for active-duty military and their families during war.

Ms. Saindon has received citizen awards from community groups such as the Psychiatric Society and Victim Assistance Coordinating Council.

When not pursuing her professional interests she may be found kayaking in the Atlantic or Pacific oceans, skiing, walking her dog, or taking photographs.

About the Artists

The cover photo, *War & Peace*, is courtesy of **Nicole Toesca**, a fellow survivor/co-victim of violent loss. The photograph, taken in 2008 at Ventimiglia Harbor in Italy, contrasts the peaceful beach scene with the eroded battlements erected to fend off an attack from the sea during World War II—fitting symbolism for survivors of violent loss. More of Nicole's work may be seen at: www.photoartscapes.com.

The back cover illustration, *The Iris*, is courtesy of **Margaret Steven**, who completed the painting in 2011. A gift to Connie Saindon, the iris is a symbol of hope for Connie's sister "Tiny."

Made in the USA
Las Vegas, NV
31 December 2021